Business Confronts Terrorism

Business Confronts Terrorism

Risks and Responses

Dean C. Alexander

THE UNIVERSITY OF WISCONSIN PRESS
TERRACE BOOKS

The University of Wisconsin Press
1930 Monroe Street
Madison, Wisconsin 53711

www.wisc.edu/wisconsinpress/

3 Henrietta Street
London WC2E 8LU, England

1   3   5   4   2

Printed in the United States of America

Library of Congress Cataloging-in-Publication Data
Alexander, Dean C., 1965–
Business confronts terrorism : risks and responses / Dean C. Alexander.
p.   cm.
Includes bibliographical references and index.
ISBN 0-299-18930-9 (hardcover : alk. paper)
1. Terrorism—Economic aspects.   2. Business—Effect of terrorism on.
3. Terrorism—United States—Prevention.
4. Industries—Security measures—United States.
5. Business enterprises—Security measures—United States.
I. Title.
HV6432.A433   2004
363.32—dc22   2004012635

Terrace Books, a division of the University of Wisconsin Press,
takes its name from the Memorial Union Terrace, located at
the University of Wisconsin–Madison. Since its inception in 1907,
the Wisconsin Union has provided a venue for students, faculty, staff,
and alumni to debate art, music, politics, and the issues of the day.
It is a place where theater, music, drama, dance, outdoor activities, and
major speakers are made available to the campus and the community.
To learn more about the Union, visit www.union.wisc.edu

Contents

Disclaimer

The author expended extensive time and energy in preparing this book. He relied upon information, derived content, and incorporated materials that were perceived to be correct at the time. Nevertheless, the author cannot guarantee the completeness and accuracy of all the contents of this publication.

It is critical to underscore that the inclusion or omission of any companies or industries herein does not imply any endorsement nor judgment whatsoever as to the products, services, capabilities, and financial attributes of any firm; or in the case of an industry, the sector's viability or importance in the economy.

Moreover, the author does not intend the reader to undertake (or refrain from undertaking) any business, security, safety, health, nor any other decisions, actions, or activities based on any information contained in this book. Any matter discussed in this book should not be relied upon in substitution for the exercise of independent judgment by the reader or in consultation with an adviser.

Against this backdrop, the author cannot accept liability for any decisions, actions, or activities that may be taken by any person or entity based on anything contained in this publication.

Business Confronts Terrorism

Introduction

Central banks and stock exchanges are bombed. Suicide bombers ravage cinemas, nightclubs, and theaters. Planes crash into skyscrapers and government buildings. Multiple bombs explode on commuter trains. Thousands of people are killed and injured while millions more are terrorized by these attacks.

These scenarios could be part of a future Hollywood movie. Sadly, they are representative of previous terror attacks against industry and government interests worldwide. Moreover, they are harbingers of global terror threats.

In 1996, a suicide truck bomber rammed into the front of the Sri Lanka Central Bank in Colombo, killing 88 people and injuring 1,400. Four years later, a car bomb in the parking deck of the Jakarta Stock Exchange triggered subsequent explosions, leading to over 15 deaths and dozens of injuries.

Entertainment venues have been prime targets of terrorists during the past few years. In Bangladesh, 17 people were killed and nearly 300 people were wounded in bombings at four cinemas in 2002. That same year, several bombs exploded at two nightclubs in Bali, Indonesia, resulting in 202 deaths and hundreds of injuries. Nearly 120 theatergoers died during an attempted rescue at a Moscow theater sieged by terrorists in 2002.

On September 11, 2001, 19 hijackers commandeered four aircraft into the World Trade Center in New York, the Pentagon, and a field in Pennsylvania—not the intended target—leading to nearly 3,000 deaths, thousands of injuries, and hundreds of billions of dollars in direct and indirect damage. Widely referred to as 9/11, the attacks spurred numerous political, military, intelligence, legal, social, and economic consequences.

From contributing to U.S. and allied military operations in Afghanistan and Iraq, sweeping legislation in matters of homeland security and law enforcement, to broad social and political transformation—such as the integration of nearly two dozen U.S. government agencies into the Department of Homeland Security (DHS)—the multi-dimensional implications of this horrific terrorist incident were profound.

Europe's own 9/11-like tragedy took place on March 11, 2004. More specifically, Spain's 3/11 occurred when ten bombs exploded on four commuter trains in Madrid. The well-coordinated attacks resulted in the deaths of 190 individuals and about 1,500 injuries. The incidents injected an uncomfortable sense of vulnerability within Western society. The 3/11 incidents also gave pause that future, large-scale terror tragedies could unfold both regionally and globally; and that, perhaps, the worst was yet to come.

While terror's effects span political, military, intelligence, legal, social, and economic realms, another paradigm—terrorism's implications on business—merits closer scrutiny given its relation to economic security. Terror metamorphoses business, causing firms to deal with current threats and craft plans to reduce future challenges. Terrorists weaken industry and society through their manipulation of economic system components—companies, nonprofits, labor, capital, and technology— against their targets.

Industry responses to such developments run the gamut from strengthening security measures and increasing public-private partnerships in combating terror, to redesigning labor-management interactions in light of the post-9/11 era. Other business reactions to terror include the expanded activities of homeland security firms as well as a reconsideration of customer relations, logistics, and other integral segments of business. Subsumed within this dynamic are issues such as counterterror costs, potential damage from political violence, risk mitigation, and reasonable responses within existing legal systems and political frameworks.

This book focuses on three key issues in the relationship between terrorism and business: (1) terror threats and the role that terrorists and their sympathizers play in the economic system; (2) business responses and public-private efforts to reduce such threats; and (3) terror's impact on business. In addressing these issues, this volume hopes to contribute to a better understanding of the complex and ever-evolving tensions of industry's confrontations with terrorism.

Threats

Whatever definitional approach to terrorism one takes, specialists on terrorism seem to be in agreement about key components of the activity: the *act* (e.g., unlawful), *perpetrators* (e.g., individuals, groups, states), *objectives* (e.g., political), *intended outcomes and motivations* (e.g., fear and frustrations), *targets* (e.g., individuals, business, government, and nongovernment), and *modus operandi* (e.g., hijackings).

By its very nature, the terrorist is victorious even when he causes no physical casualties. The threat of force, and its psychological impact, suffices. Also, minimal casualties resulting from an incident can aid the terrorist group in meeting its propaganda objectives. The 9/11 and 3/11 attacks instilled fear in millions of global citizenry.

The multifaceted and nefarious threats that terrorist groups represent worldwide encompass traditional challenges (e.g., bombings, hijackings, kidnappings, hostage-taking, and assassinations) and modern threats such as superterrorism (e.g., biological, chemical, radiological, and nuclear) and cyberterrorism.

Terrorist threats can be categorized in two principal ways: The first relates to threats based on the type of target that is involved. Terrorists have targeted: civilian and military interests; businesses and infrastructure sites; and government, religious, and civic facilities. The record demonstrates that no segment of the population has been immune from terrorism. Terrorists, unfortunately, do not view any target as off limits. Terrorists even justify killing innocent children in the name of their "higher cause."

A second type of targeting can be analyzed by studying the modus operandi used to undertake attacks. As indicated above, terrorists used traditional operations with hopes (and some limited success) of engaging in acts of superterrorism and cyberterrorism. The expanding terror trend includes resorting to suicide bombings, spectacular attacks, and simultaneous attacks. Threats are increasingly omnipresent and global. Terror attacks can occur anywhere and at anytime.

Terrorists have already carried out attacks against a multitude of targets by using several tactics simultaneously. While some modifications as to the modus operandi are inevitable—using explosives-laden boats to attack highly populated locations (e.g., passenger cruise ships)—the future trend is towards eye-catching attacks with resulting mass casualties and mayhem. The relative ease and potential frequency of uncomplicated attacks (e.g., suicide bombers) may actually instill greater fear than larger-scale incidents.

The motivation of terrorist attacks is obviously relevant in planning what targets to attack. While the roots and objectives of terror are manifold, the emphasis of this book is to illustrate the vast array of business and nonbusiness sectors that have been victimized. This will contribute to a better understanding of how to protect future targets, both in the United States and overseas.

It is critical to view the use of terrorism in a strategic context rather than merely as an irritant or nuisance. The consequences to a nation of inadequately comprehending this distinction can lead to terrorism becoming a component of everyday life. In turn, basic government and business functions are undermined, with potential—at the extreme—to lead to near anarchy.

Terrorist sympathizers and abettors, individual terrorists, stand-alone groups, international terrorist networks, and state-sponsors of terrorism carry out political violence. Domestic and international groups have attacked national and foreign targets. The broader the cooperation among terrorist groups and their supporters worldwide, the more lethality they can inflict. In turn, the greater the difficulty faced by the potential victims of terrorism to prevent such threats. Collaboration between organized crime and terrorists further complicates the dynamic.

As the emphasis of this book relates to the ramifications of terrorism on business, a discussion of specific terrorist group "grievances and goals" is beyond the scope of the publication. Nevertheless, the underlying nature of these "grievances and goals" ranges from a variety of political, social, economic, religious, and/or single-subject issues.

Terrorists' fascination with attacking business interests provides a premonition for future attacks. This is especially so in the transportation and tourism industries.

Principal targets of Palestinian suicide bombers have been buses. This mode of transportation is often attacked because: the targets are plentiful and often minimally protected; many targets exist in a small area; only one perpetrator is needed to undertake the attack (excluding the bomb-maker and other logistics operations); relatively inexpensive components are required; suicide bomb belts and vests are fairly easy to hide, particularly during winter months; public transportation is easily accessible and inexpensive to enter; and a compact, combustible setting allows for maximum carnage.

Terrorists adjust their modus operandi in carrying out such attacks. For example, suicide bombers have sneaked (or pushed) onto buses and detonated themselves. When several security measures were established at the bus entrance, some attackers shifted to exploding themselves outside the bus, including at bus stops.

An alternative recently used by terrorists is to drive an explosives-laden car alongside of a bus and detonating the explosives. Such was the case in an October 2002 car bombing near a bus in Hadera, Israel. That incident resulted in 10 deaths and 40 injuries. Other means of attack against buses include a February 1990 incident during which a tourist bus near Ismailia, Egypt, was boarded by terrorists. There, the perpetrators opened fire with automatic weapons and grenades, killing 11 and injuring over 20 others.

Closer to home, in February 2003, Federal Bureau of Investigation (FBI) Director Robert Mueller spoke of other prospective threats, including poisoning food and water supplies. Even more ominous would be the widespread use of biological, chemical, or radiological terrorist tools against the populace. In March 2004, Director Mueller projected about terror attacks during the Republican and Democratic conventions in summer 2004 and during the fall 2004 elections.

The 9/11 incidents show that terrorists also choose some targets for their symbolic value, as was the case with the World Trade Center in New York (economic power) and the Pentagon (military power). Therefore, it was not surprising when in March 2003, the U.S. Park Service designated six sites—the White House, Washington Monument, Statute of Liberty, Liberty Bell Pavilion, St. Louis Gateway Arch, and Mount Rushmore—as likely terrorist targets because they symbolize American democracy. As terror groups, such as al Qaeda, have a tendency to return to sites previously targeted, future attempts to hit the White House, Capitol, and Central Intelligence Agency headquarters are expected.

Government, business, and individuals have taken numerous steps to be more cognizant of threats and garnered many successes at home and abroad in combating terrorism. However, challenges still exist. Also troubling is the fact that each terrorist operation—successful or otherwise—provides a terror group with additional information with which to refine its deadly craft.

Although society often improves its defenses, terrorists need to be "successful," only once, while prevention and security needs to be at its peak at all times. As such, threats will continue to exist, and a determined terrorist organization may—at times—be able to undertake an operation to completion.

In Chapter 1, terrorist threats are addressed as follows: previous terrorist threats against U.S. and non-U.S. targets, and recent attacks against business and nonbusiness interests. Chapter 2 focuses on contemporary and future terrorist threats.

Terrorists in the Economic System

Terrorists and their supporters take advantage of opportunities and loopholes within the economic system to further their murderous goals. Leveraging the fruits of the economic system enables terrorists to obtain financial, organizational, and operational assistance (e.g., arms, training, intelligence, and information).

Terrorists and their abettors utilize existing traditional frameworks—such as companies and nonprofit entities—to raise funds, receive support, and integrate themselves into the community. Traditional and nontraditional financial systems present in the economic systems are used as well.

Perpetrators of political violence also undertake a variety of criminal activities (e.g., counterfeiting currency, credit cards, and ATM cards; misappropriating and using credit card information; forging documents; identity theft; money laundering; drug trafficking; corruption; commercial espionage; and general criminal activities) in violation of permissible norms in an economic framework.

Prior to the 9/11 attacks, intelligence and law enforcement services had some difficulty recognizing characteristics and behavior of terrorists affiliated with distinct terrorist groups. Post–September 11, U.S. government analysts have generally tended, in relation to al Qaeda, to closely scrutinize young men from Islamic and Muslim countries who try to enter (or already reside in) the United States.

As a result, al Qaeda introduced some changes to their recruitment and operational tactics in the United States and abroad. Terror groups are recruiting individuals who may not—at first glance—trigger greater scrutiny by government officials. Also, al Qaeda has recruited converts to Islam in American and foreign jails.

Al Qaeda is using citizens from non-Arab countries (e.g., European countries) for their operations. This was the case with British citizen

Richard Reid, who tried to ignite a shoe bomb on a Paris-Miami flight in 2001. Palestinian-based terrorist groups also recruited two British citizens to undertake a suicide bombing in Tel Aviv in 2003.

By 2003, U.S. government officials publicly disclosed their apprehension that al Qaeda may use "Western-looking" individuals to undertake terrorist attacks. There has also been an increase in the use of women participating in terrorist incidents, particularly in suicide bombings, as exemplified by recent cases of Palestinian and Chechnyan women involvement in attacks.

It should be remembered that the use of proxies outside a particular terrorist group's "ethnic" affiliation to undertake terrorist attacks in other parts of the world, as well as the participation of women, has occurred in the Irish Republican Army, Baader-Meinhof, and Asian organizations (e.g., Japanese Red Army). In the past, various women have carried out significant leadership and operational roles in terrorist groups, including: Baader-Meinhof (e.g., the co-founder was a women), Symbionese Liberation Organization (e.g., Patty Hearst was involved in a bank robbery), and Tamil Tigers (e.g., a woman suicide bomber killed Indian Prime Minister Rajeev Gandhi).

The recruitment of children by terror groups worldwide is particularly reprehensible. This trend is expanding as well. In March 2004, Israeli forces stopped a 14-year-old boy wearing a suicide bomb vest and an 11-year-old boy carrying explosives. From September 2000 through March 2004, Palestinian youths carried out nearly 30 suicide bombings.

These developments—among others—clearly demonstrate the moral bankruptcy of terror and the urgent need to explore non-violent means to pursue political goals. In fact, non-violent political efforts engender more concessions, faster from those in power than does terrorism—as long as such discourse is grounded within reasonable and achievable parameters.

Chapter 3 chronicles the various means by which governments, companies, nonprofits, and individuals assist terrorists—by omission or commission—to achieve their goals. This discussion will show that, at times, different segments of society directly and indirectly contribute to the proliferation of global terrorism.

Financing Terror

Terrorist groups use a variety of means—from simple to complex—to secure funds for their activities. Terror funds are derived from both legal (e.g., personal savings and legitimate business revenue) and illegal (e.g., criminal acts such as drug-trafficking and financial fraud) sources. Funds raised are distributed to various factions of terrorist groups through a number of methodologies.

The different tools that terrorist organizations employ to fund their deadly activities include: the use of traditional and alternative financial services entities (e.g., banks and hawalas [informal money transfer systems firmly established in Asia and the Middle East]); charities; trading in commodities (e.g., "conflict" diamonds and gold); bogus financial instruments; currency smuggling and wire transfers; drug-trafficking; extortion, money laundering; smuggling products; securities fraud; and scams.

In 2002, the U.S. Department of Treasury provided a number of examples of transactions and situations that might be indicative of terrorist financing. For instance, rogue firms might make significant cash withdrawals from business accounts that are out of the ordinary. Alternatively, a terror-linked company may use multiple bank accounts that forward money to several overseas beneficiaries.

State-sponsors of terrorism have always provided funds and other assistance to terrorists groups. The Soviet Union provided financial, training, and operational assistance to terrorist groups worldwide. North Korea was involved in undertaking a number of terrorist operations, including attacks against a South Korean delegation in Burma.

Syria and Libya provided the Popular Front for the Liberation of Palestine (PFLP) significant financial assistance. In 1993, Iran reportedly allocated $15 million to Hamas to undertake attacks that would interfere with the peace treaty between Israel and the Palestinian Authority. Iran also provided substantial financial support to several Palestinian groups.

Former Iraqi President Saddam Hussein awarded up to $30,000 to each family of a Palestinian suicide bomber. In March 2003, a Palestinian-based affiliate of the Iraqi Baath Party, the Arab Liberation Front, awarded $10,000 to the family of a Hamas suicide bomber.

Terrorists with their own financial resources, such as Osama bin Laden, can fund newly organized groups as well as bankroll existing terrorist cells. Bin Laden's wealth was estimated to be nearly $300 million. A Paraguayan trading company, run by Assad Muhammad Barakat, is believed to have funneled about $50 million to Hizballah during the past decade. Individuals with ample means can serve as pseudo "lenders-of-last resort," should other funding sources run dry.

The costs of undertaking terrorist attacks range from virtually a few dollars to hundreds of thousands of dollars. In that sense, terrorism is sometimes referred to as "warfare on the cheap." Obviously, depending on the size, sophistication of weaponry, training, and complexity of the operation, the costs can vary dramatically. The 9/11 attacks are estimated to have cost $500,000 to put together. But, they resulted in direct and indirect economic damage in the hundreds of billions of dollars.

Some terrorist attacks can be relatively simple and inexpensive to initiate: a stabbing requires only a knife or sharp object as the weapon; an attack with a rock is cost-free. Along those lines, a Palestinian, who attempted to hijack an Israeli plane bound for Turkey, said that he chose the flight because it was inexpensive. Contrast that with Mohammed Haydar Zammar, suspected of belonging to an Islamic terrorist group in Europe, who had adequate funding to pay for 40 trips from Europe to Pakistan.

The costs of operating terrorist groups range from thousands of dollars to tens of millions of dollars if one includes funds for training, housing and general support, weaponry, human capital, and operational support. For instance, the annual operating expenses of terror group Basque Fatherland and Liberty (ETA) was estimated to be about $10 million. Some intelligence agencies have estimated that al Qaeda's annual budget runs in the tens of millions of dollars.

Money is the life-blood of terrorism. Companies, foundations, and individuals who knowingly and directly assist both subnational and state actor terrorists in carrying out their criminal actions are a component of the problem of terrorism, rather than, part of the solution.

All steps to prevent terrorists from obtaining funds are essential in coping with the challenge. By undermining their funding capabilities, terrorist organizations are harmed. Thereby, it is less likely that their deadly operations occur, or if they do, they will be less effectual than otherwise.

Chapter 4 delves into the numerous ways terrorist groups raise funds to finance their carnage. Various governmental and nongovernmental responses to terror finance are also addressed.

Security

As highlighted above, terrorist threats against business are manifold. Terrorism is relatively easy and inexpensive to activate yet very difficult and extremely costly to counter. Business, too, is cognizant that it has limited financial resources with which to reduce terrorist threats. In turn, the tension between providing sufficient security without expending excessive resources has gained greater resonance.

Corporate America's greater recognition of terror dangers has led to huge resources being allocated to security. The time, manpower, and funding allocated to security measures vary greatly depending on the company's industry, size, geography, international activities, symbolic value, and the probability and ease of being targeted.

Whether industry has the products and services available to undertake preventive or corrective steps, coupled with the costs involved in carrying out such actions, are also relevant issues (e.g., the costs and implementation of anti-missile technology on commercial jets in light of terrorists' use of shoulder-fired missiles against such targets).

Industry's security efforts are also influenced by whether government and/or industry security mandates exist. If so, what types of accompanying sanctions, if any, attach should a company fail to abide by government and/or industry security guidelines. A complicating security issue is that many employees do not obey company-posted security measures and thereby contribute to weaker defenses.

The financial implications of improved security measures are worth keeping in mind. For example, the matter of who carries the costs of such measures—companies, industry, government, and/or consumers—is a significant factor in whether anything is actually done. Analogously, should costs be formally designated as "security charges" (e.g., airline security fees) or subsumed within rising prices for products and services without attribution. Businesses deemed soft terror targets—restaurants and movie theaters—may impose security charges.

Due to these and other reasons, at times, industry is apprehensive to implement adequate security responses. Yet, companies must comprehend, as Sen. Jon Corzine (D-NJ) suggested, that in the post-9/11 era security is a component of corporate citizenship. Indeed, the advantages of establishing a corporate security program are manifold: protecting assets (human, physical, technological, and financial), ensuring business continuity, reducing litigation risks, lowering insurance costs, and reducing dangers to customers and employees.

Chapter 5 discusses general themes related to corporate security, including its costs. It presents an overview of security service providers and describes some useful antiterrorism measures. A discussion of information security, risk and vulnerability assessments, risk management, and business continuity/disaster planning is presented. Last, some security responses in a number of industry sectors—real estate, transportation, maritime, aviation, chemicals, and sports—are discussed.

Public-Private Partnership in Combating Terrorism

Another manifestation of how terror transforms business can be witnessed within the context of the public-private partnership in the war on terrorism. This ever-evolving relationship between two spheres—industry and government—is convoluted. Generally, though, it can be delineated as follows: government supporting business, industry aiding government, and impediments to further cooperation between the two players. Chapter 6 discusses the trilateral spheres of public-private sector interactions.

During the next decade, government expenditures on homeland security products and services are expected to reach the hundreds of billions of dollars. Antiterrorism efforts of government aviation and health officials will lead to the acquisition of hundreds of millions of dollars of explosive detection equipment and pharmaceuticals. The public sector provides funding and elementary research to homeland security firms, such as in the pathogen antidote space.

The growing public-private partnership in aviation security involves the federalization of airport screeners and allocating government funds—direct and indirect—to airlines and homeland security products and services. Greater government interaction with industry relative to aviation security included: reinforcing cockpit doors; airlines receiving funding for security purposes; security training for flight crews was overhauled; and approval of arming pilots with firearms and stun guns.

Industry-government cooperation in aviation security also includes: recruiting, investigating, and training federal baggage screeners; analyzing passenger movements and baggage reconciliation; assessing airport architectural and structural designs in light of greater use of large bomb-detection devices; improving access control systems and more secure identification forms for airline and airport employees; and further integrating airline and airport security systems with law enforcement and intelligence data sources.

The government's terror threat system has been raised some six times during the past two years. Such pronouncements remind industry and society of terror threats. Diverse businesses, including chemical companies, oil refineries, and nuclear power plants, heightened security measures due to self-assessments and/or government warnings.

Yet, the benefits of disclosing possible threats must be couched by the risks that excessive, unfounded warnings may create hysteria and stymie sales. Ultimately, "crying wolf" can lead the public to ignore future credible warnings of terror attacks. But, even more harmful would be if government fails to disclose known risks and a terror incident occurs.

At the same time, industry provides information about potential terrorist threats. In fall 2001, for example, a Minnesota flight school notified law enforcement officials about the suspicious behavior of Zacarias Moussaoui, an al Qaeda operative initially presumed to be the 20th hijacker on 9/11. In other instances, financial institutions cooperate in freezing alleged terrorist funds.

Government may place restrictions and oversight on business so that terrorist threats are reduced. For instance, new regulations place additional obligations on businesses to provide information on employees and customers that may be connected to terrorism. In the case of a national crisis, government may put pressure on companies to provide critical goods, such as pharmaceuticals, at low prices.

In order to cover the costs associated with improved maritime security—more government agents monitoring crews and cargo—government considers whether to impose user fees on sectors and businesses. Airline passengers are subject to a security fee that partly covers the outlays associated with increased aviation security.

Rising costs associated with new government rules precipitated companies to pass on such outlays onto customers. For instance, "Knowing Your Customer," precepts (e.g., investigation of clients to ensure that firm is not doing business with terrorists) has led banks to pass on security expenditures in the form of greater fees.

Another post-9/11 creation, the DHS essentially coalesces some two-dozen government institutions with some 170,000 personnel under one roof. The massive shift of government staff and duties associated in the creation of DHS impacts the public-private dynamic in many ways, including government procurement.

Even when industry can produce goods helpful in reducing the impact of terrorism (e.g., vaccines) government obstacles may arise. For instance, a lengthy regulatory approval process may undermine the speedy market entry of a product (e.g., Bioport's anthrax vaccine). Indeed, the developing public-private partnership in homeland security is complex.

Terror's Effects on Labor and Management

Any future terrorist attacks in the United States will undoubtedly victimize workers in this country. As such, there is a need to highlight terrorism's impact on labor-management relations so that we can better assess how to respond to this challenge should it occur.

Labor is a potential victim of terror as well as an important partner in combating this menace. Due to terrorism, management faces new responsibilities and more lawsuits as it deals with its workforce. Labor segments are experiencing risks and opportunities because of terror. Multiple shifts and changes in the labor market are spurred by the war on terrorism.

Terrorist incidents can harm both workers and managers: a terrorist bomb does not distinguish between labor and management. A catastrophic terrorist incident can result in the deaths of thousands of employees from one industry, such as was the case with finance sector employees during September 11. Suicide bombers targeting mass transit or restaurants have already killed or injured hundreds within these sectors. In the future, a possible attack on a nuclear facility or port could severely victimize another segment of workers.

In some circumstances, employees are able to survive terror attacks by not being at work on the day of an attack due to sickness, a meeting outside the office, or travel plans. Others are not so fortunate—including workers who survived the initial World Trade Center attack in 1993 but not 9/11. As such, fate or chance, also play in role in the potential victimization of labor.

Parts of the labor market may be less susceptible to certain types of terrorist attacks: executives flying on corporate jets encounter reduced risk of hijacking. Concurrently, senior personnel—whether in the United States or abroad—are more vulnerable to kidnappings or assassinations by terrorist groups than entry-level employees.

Workers with unique security and business continuity expertise are integral parts of a management team should a serious attack undermine corporate assets, particularly information technology. Therefore, any incapacity or death to this segment of the workforce would further undermine company efforts to continue operations.

Positions that at this time may seem higher risk—postal workers and flight attendants—previously were characterized as less so. Frontline employees in today's war on terrorism—firefighters, police officers, emergency medical technicians, bomb disposal personnel, security guards, and the military—faced varying degrees of dangers prior to September 11. Today, their burdens are magnified as workload and risks have escalated. In some cases, their roles have added new dimensions from being principally reactive (e.g., responding to a fire) to also defensive in nature (e.g., protecting themselves against and in the aftermath of terror attacks). Despite these challenges, some individuals actually embrace homeland security roles.

National Guard and military reserves have been called up for operational work in various locations, including Iraq, Afghanistan, and the Philippines. To varying degrees, U.S. activity in those countries is spurred by terrorist activities and/or threats thereof.

As we have seen, many public sector employees—police, firefighters, and emergency medical technicians—play critical roles as first responders during, and in the aftermath, of a terrorist attack. So too, private sector employees can be viewed as part of the solution as they manufacture gas masks, germ detection devices, and pharmaceuticals. Defense contractors and their employees offer the government diverse products and services instrumental in combating terrorism.

Unfortunately, the labor market also includes persons that collaborate with, or support, terrorists by: supplying funds (e.g., arising from legitimate and illegal businesses), conducting business with front organizations, or providing products and services used by terrorists. Terrorists, particularly "sleepers," may become employed in disparate sectors targeted for a future terrorist attack (e.g., chemical or water-treatment plants) or in a position that will not attract too much attention (e.g., "students" working at a university library or restaurant).

In this post–September 11 era, labor expects employers to play new security-related roles in addition to providing a job and a wage. Labor envisions that employers should play a semi-paternalistic/quasi-governmental function: provide physical security, emotional assistance, and guidance in times of turmoil. For its part, management must balance the need to protect its workforce while conducting business under increasingly complex market conditions (e.g., rising direct and indirect costs due to terrorism).

It is incumbent on management to adduce how to continue operations without the contributions of key employees for extended periods. Business suffers when military reserves are called up for active service. Also, firms are harmed should an employee become incapacitated following a terrorist attack at work, on the way to the office, or in some other circumstance (e.g., eating at a targeted hotel restaurant or fast-food establishment).

Given the specter of terrorism, more employers are taking into greater consideration diverse skill sets and attributes (e.g., foreign languages, overseas experience, military and security background, government security clearances, and business continuity expertise) that prior to 9/11 were less relevant to many employers. Companies and government are challenged by demands to hire more persons with unique capabilities (e.g., native Arabic speakers) while concurrently ensuring that such persons do not trigger security concerns (e.g., several native Arabic-speaking translators in Guantanomo Bay were suspected of aiding foreign interests, including al Qaeda).

Employers may find themselves the objects of litigation initiated by injured employees and families of employees who were hurt or perished during a terrorist attack. The claimants may argue that the employer failed: to provide adequate security (e.g., bullet-proof limousines), offer alternative means of travel (e.g., corporate jet), or have in place appropriate evacuation measures in case of an attack. Excessive investigation of prospective employee backgrounds or monitoring workers in the name of corporate security may lead to lawsuits against management.

Chapter 7 addresses terror's victimization of labor, including physical and emotional effects. Employer and governmental support during crises, terror's effects on military personnel, workforce challenges and opportunities, and post-9/11 employer issues are also discussed.

Terror Impacts Trends in Business

The daily barrage of predictions of terrorist attacks against numerous business targets—chemical plants, shopping malls, aviation, mass transit, and financial institutions—has accelerated the need to highlight additional lessons learned thus far on the impact of terrorism on business. While various chapters illustrate some of the magnitude of terror's impact on business, additional perspectives are delineated in Chapter 8. In particular, Chapter 8 addresses these matters accordingly: initial impact of large-scale terror attacks on business, subsequent industry responses, and long-term structural issues affecting business.

Chapter 8 covers the initial impact of catastrophic terrorism in terms of economic and sector consequences, including ramifications on financial markets and effects on business activity. Industry responses crafted thereafter include: shifts and flexibility within and among business sectors; nurturing and expansion of homeland security companies; funding such entities; and mergers and acquisitions in the homeland security space. Transcending consequences of terror on business are then addressed: terror costs in terms of outlays and rising transaction costs; security at a business location; interactions with customers; ramifications on sourcing, inventory, and logistics; and legal issues.

With that in mind, an elementary base from which to assess the preliminary effects of terrorism on business is worth highlighting here. Significant terrorist attacks may negatively impact several sectors simultaneously—commercial aviation, insurance, hospitality and tourism—during an initial period (e.g., 9/11 and 3/11 attacks). At the same time, opportunities might be created and expanded in other industries—such as corporate security, defense, biometrics, and explosives detection. Product lines may be removed from the market or limited, depending on the severity of the attack (for example, terrorism insurance becomes scarce and expensive after 9/11).

A terrorist incident on one portion of an industry, such as commercial airlines, can have positive ramifications on other segments of the same industry, such as corporate jets. A terrorist's use of one business service (e.g., postal system) can lead to opportunities in unrelated business sectors (e.g., pharmaceuticals), as demonstrated during the anthrax attacks in fall 2001.

Business tends to focus substantial attention on the most recent threat while often ignoring future challenges. Following the 9/11 attacks, commercial aviation implemented wide-ranging changes in its security framework. Unfortunately, security in other transportation modes (e.g., passenger trains, buses, and subways) has yet to receive adequate attention. Sadly, only major attacks on disparate settings will initiate greater focus on other risks. The 3/11 attacks on commuter trains appear to have (finally) spurred more interest in ground transportation security in the United States and abroad.

Another consequence of a terrorist attack on a business is that a company can become a plaintiff (e.g., a corporate tenant sues a landlord) or defendant (e.g., an employee's estate sues a corporate tenant). Lawsuits may arise directly from a terrorist incident (a patron in a restaurant or shopper at a store) or indirectly (a doctor misdiagnoses anthrax exposure). Lawsuits against terrorist groups and their state-sponsors are other avenues. Government funding of victims' compensation programs ease some financial burdens.

The proliferation of companies offering numerous products and services under the guise of homeland security or counterterrorism is noteworthy. Such goods and services have a large variance as to their usefulness in responding to or reducing the threats of terrorism. This development may be designated as the Homeland Security Business Age—the successor to the Internet boom and bust. Investment in homeland security firms and extensive media coverage of terrorism has hastened its development.

The Internet boom was short-lived due to unreasonable expectations of growth in the Net and the inability to easily make money from this new medium of commerce. Unfortunately, the Homeland Security Business Age will likely endure as the threats of terrorism are real, numerous, and global. Illustrative of this menacing trend include terrorist attacks in Baghdad, Bali, Istanbul, Jerusalem, Madrid, and Moscow during 2002–2004, which resulted in hundreds of deaths and thousands of injuries.

The post–September 11, 2001, record of homeland security companies can be delineated as follows: companies directly or tangentially helpful in the war on terrorism; and those exploiting the fears of the U.S. population to extract profits. The defense industry plays an important role in fighting terrorism by supplying critical weaponry and related goods and services to the military and law enforcement agencies.

Some of the weapons used in the war on terrorism—as carried out in Afghanistan and Iraq—include jet fighters, unmanned aerial vehicles, submarines, and missiles. American forces also have at their disposal other products (e.g., night-vision gear and hand-held computers) when they engage on the battlefield.

The 9/11 attacks brought to the forefront security products and services that enable government and businesses to monitor and safeguard sensitive locations, spot terrorists through biometric systems, authenticate documents, detect explosives, provide physical security and protection to vulnerable facilities and personnel, and investigate the background of customers and prospective employees. Additional businesses instrumental in countering terrorist threats and ensuring business continuity include computer security software, emergency management software, data storage and recovery services.

Manufacturers of medicines (e.g., Cipro and iodine pills) and vaccines (e.g., anthrax and smallpox) experienced additional sales following rising fears of superterrorism (biological, chemical, and nuclear).

This phenomenon also led to a further demand for germ detection products and remediation services. Forensics investigative services were called upon to assist medical and investigative teams following the terrorist attacks.

Declining commercial airline use due to the risk of hijackings enabled companies providing videoconferencing, teleconferencing, and Internet-based collaboration tools to expand market share. Mild disruption to mail distribution due to the fall 2001 anthrax attacks led to heightened use of e-mail and the consequent rise in demand for e-mail management software.

Special equipment (e.g., biohazard suits and gas masks) made available to first-responders of terrorism (e.g., police officers, firefighters, and rescue workers) demonstrated the critical role of homeland security firms in the war on terrorism. Consumer interest in "survivalist" products (e.g., electric generators and water purification systems) developed in anticipation of possible superterrorism attacks.

Clearly less agreeable are firms marketing various contraptions, such as: untested emergency parachutes for employees in skyscrapers; bogus bomb detection and germ detection machines; unproven aquarium-like apparatuses purported to be helpful when opening anthrax-laden mail; and placebos marketed as genuine pharmaceuticals and vaccines. Furthermore, some online and brick and mortar stores offer counterterrorism products of dubious utility. Such "merchants of fear" may jeopardize the credibility of the mainstream homeland security industry. More importantly, they can undermine national security and endanger society.

Investment in homeland security stocks spurred after 9/11 may lead to the development of formal, professional investment vehicles for this sector (e.g., stock indices, mutual funds, and unit investment trusts). More venture capital firms are investing in homeland security firms than before the September 11 attacks. Extensive mergers and acquisitions in the homeland security space have also taken place.

The proceeding chapters will elucidate the broad challenges that terror inflicts on business, industry responses to such threats, and the transformation of business due to such circumstances. It is important to underscore that the book's emphasis is on terrorism's challenges to and ramifications on American business. Nevertheless, global terror and business dynamics are cited for additional perspectives. Global experiences are addressed so that American industry's struggle with terrorism should not be viewed as unique.

1

Overview of Terrorist Threats

An explosives-laden truck crashes into a hotel. A suicide bomber carries out an attack at a shopping mall. Electricity grids and railroad tracks are sabotaged. Terrorists attack a housing complex with gunfire and bombs. Sarin gas is released in a crowded subway.

Such terror incidents have occurred globally during the past decade. The United States is a principal target of terrorism. Not only do domestic extremist groups commit acts of terrorism at home, but also, international groups carry out attacks against American targets abroad. Attacks by foreign terrorists on U.S. soil occurred less frequently than attacks on Americans abroad, although the 9/11 incidents are an obvious dramatic exception. It is expected that more terror attacks by foreign groups will occur in the United States.

The United States has been the most popular single target of international terrorism. Also, global citizenry—officials, diplomats, military officers, businessmen, and children—have been victimized by both state-sponsored terrorism (e.g., Libya, Iran, Sudan, and Syria) and substate groups, including Marxist-oriented (e.g., Germany's Red Army Faction), nationalists (e.g., Abu Nidal Organization), Islamic fundamentalism (e.g., al Qaeda), and ideological mercenaries (e.g., Japanese Red Army).

This chapter addresses various terrorist threats, including: previous terrorist threats against U.S. and non-U.S. targets and recent attacks against business and non-business interests worldwide. In doing so, we will gain a better understanding of broad private and public targets that have been attacked by terrorists worldwide. This exposure will enable us to have a better grasp of the vast challenges society faces as terrorists view all persons and entities as "worthy of punishment."

Selected Attacks by Foreign Terrorists against U.S. Targets

The most spectacular and deadliest terrorist incidents in U.S. history were the September 11, 2001, attacks. In this twenty-first century "Pearl Harbor," 19 al Qaeda terrorists, wielding knives and box-cutters, hijacked 4 U.S. aircraft, which they used to crash into the Twin Towers of the World Trade Center in New York City, the Pentagon, and a third location, not the intended target, a field in Shanksville, Pennsylvania.

Nearly 3,000 people died and thousands others were injured. The 110-floor World Trade Center twin building, the symbol of American financial prowess, collapsed. Other buildings in the World Trade Center complex and surrounding area fell, partially collapsed, or were severely damaged. Portions of the Pentagon sustained serious damage but were completely rebuilt within a year. The hundreds of billions of dollars in direct and indirect costs arising from the 9/11 attacks, coupled with broad post-9/11 legal enforcement, legal, political, social, and military responses to terrorism, demonstrate the momentous impact of the incidents.

Prior to 9/11, the al Qaeda network carried out other attacks in the Untied States including: the February 1993, bombing of the World Trade Center in New York, killing 6 people and injuring over 1,000; and the June 1993, a Pakistani terrorist opened fire outside the headquarters of the Central Intelligence Agency (CIA), killing 2 and wounding 3 CIA employees. Also that month, the FBI caught a group planning to attack New York City landmarks and various political figures.

Major al Qaeda operations against U.S. interests abroad include:

- November 1995: A car bomb explosion outside the American-operated Saudi National Guard training center in Riyadh, Saudi Arabia, killed five Americans and two Indians.
- June 1996: A car bombing attack at Khobar Towers, a U.S. Air Force housing complex in Dhahran, Saudi Arabia, killed 19 soldiers and wounded hundreds more.
- August 1998: Two truck bombings outside the U.S. embassies

in Nairobi, Kenya, and Dar-es-Salaam, Tanzania, killed 234 people, 12 of them American, and wounded over 5,000 others.
- October 2000: The suicide bombing of the USS *Cole* killed 17 and wounded 39 American sailors in Aden harbor, Yemen.

An analysis of American business victimization by domestic and international terrorist attacks abroad illustrates that nearly every type of business sector engaged in by U.S. companies overseas has been targeted. A wide range of U.S. industries that were affected by terrorism overseas were: financial and banking; energy; aviation; automobile and tires; technology, industrial, and defense; mining and engineering; tourism and hospitality; franchises and beverages; pharmaceutical and consumer products; retail; service firms; and other business categories.

These U.S. business targets were singled out because of their symbolism such as the "American way of life" visibility as well as for other practical reasons, including vulnerability of target considerations. The U.S. enterprises attacked overseas ran the gamut from Fortune 500 companies to small firms. The following is a partial list of U.S. companies, from different sectors, that were victimized by terrorism overseas during the past forty years:

- Automotive and Tires: Chevrolet (Mexico), Chrysler (Argentina), and Goodrich (Philippines).
- Aviation: Bell Helicopter International (Iran), Pan American Airlines (United Kingdom), and Trans World Airlines (Lebanon).
- Energy: Mobil (South Africa), Standard Oil (Lebanon), and Texas Petroleum (Colombia)
- Financial and Banking: Bank of Boston (Argentina), Citibank (Greece), Diners Club (Colombia).
- Franchises and Beverages: Coca-Cola (France), Kentucky Fried Chicken (Peru), and McDonald's (Turkey).
- Mining and Engineering: Bolivian-U.S. Mining (Bolivia), Fisher Engineering (Iran), and Minnesota Mining and Manufacturing (Spain)
- Pharmaceutical and Consumer Products: Colgate-Palmolive (Mexico); Johnson & Johnson (Mexico), and Squibb (Argentina)
- Retail: Sears, Roebuck & Co. (Brazil), and Woolworth (Germany)

- Service Firms: Mail (DHL Worldwide Express, Chile), Advertising (McCann-Erickson, Turkey), and Insurance (American Life Insurance, Turkey)
- Technology, Industry, and Defense: Bechtel (Indonesia), Rockwell International (Iran), Union Carbide (Mexico), and Xerox (Argentina)
- Hospitality: Intercontinental (Jordan), Marriott (Sri Lanka), and Sheraton (Argentina).

Selected Attacks by Domestic Terrorists against U.S. Targets

During the 1990s domestic terrorist groups in the United States, which include right-wing, left-wing, and single-issue groups (e.g., Animal Liberation Front, Earth Liberation Front, and radical anti-abortion groups), have generally caused less damage than international terror groups here.

An exception to that was the April 1995 attack by a cadre of domestic terrorists. During the deadliest terrorist attack on U.S. soil up to that time, a bomb blast destroyed the 9-story Alfred P. Murrah federal building in Oklahoma City. This devastating attack, perpetrated by two American terrorists, claimed 168 lives, including 19 children, and wounded 674 people. The explosion, emanating from the detonation of a truck-based, 4,800-pound ammonium nitrate fuel oil bomb, destroyed the federal building while severely damaging or destroying other buildings.

Several radical domestic groups—the Earth Liberation Front (ELF) and Animal Liberation Front (ALF)—have attacked business interests as they view Corporate America as harming the environment and animals, respectively. Other single-issue terror groups—including White supremacists, splinter militia, and radical anti-abortionists—have also undertaken diverse terrorist attacks in order to further their goals, though generally against nonbusiness interests.

U.S. extremist environmental groups include the ELF and the ALF. The FBI estimates that between 1996–2002, the groups undertook about 600 criminal acts in the United States resulting in over $42 million in damages.

In fall 1998, the ELF admitted to setting fires at a Vail, Colorado, ski resort, resulting in over $12 million in damages. In August 2003, over 100 sport utility vehicles were set on fire and vandalized in California. In March 2004, William Jensen Cottrell, a member of the ELF, was charged with arson and conspiracy in vandalizing the vehicles. The chosen targets symbolized—for the terrorist groups—exploitation of nature (e.g., cutting trees and damaging the ecosystem) and waste of limited natural resources (e.g., through the negative environmental consequences of gas-guzzling cars).

In October 2002 in Boston, the government indicted a dozen animal rights activists associated with Stop Huntingdon Animal Cruelty (SHAC) for stalking and threatening to burn down the house of an executive of Marsh Inc., a leading insurance broker. The harassment stemmed from the company's alleged business activities with Huntingdon Life Sciences, a British drug testing firm that has used animals in its operations. The SHAC is accused of trying to drive Huntingdon out of business by threatening its clients and business partners.

In December 1999, federal agents arrested two antigovernment militia members in Elk Grove, California, in connection with a planned attack against a facility where 24 million gallons of liquid propane were stored. In May 2002, two men were charged with planning to bomb electrical power substations and a National Guard armory in South Florida (Miami-Dade County). In June 2002, the leader of the Pennsylvania Citizens Militia was arrested for planning to bomb an FBI office in State College, Pennsylvania.

For several weeks during fall 2002, the Washington, D.C., area was paralyzed by sniper killings of nearly a dozen people. As the attacks occurred while the victims were engaging in a typical daily activity—buying gas, shopping for food, going to school—it raised the specter of the vulnerability of society to indiscriminate violent attacks. Although the two perpetrators of the Washington, D.C., area attacks were not connected to any terrorist organization, there was intense speculation that al Qaeda members carried out the attacks.

The sniper attacks caused some people to adjust their daily activities—from exercising outside to forbidding children to use outdoor playgrounds. In fact, a *Washington Post* poll found that many people felt more personally threatened by the sniper attacks (44%) than during the September 11 incidents (29%) or anthrax attacks (13%). Such findings seem to confirm the premise that repetitive, small-scale terrorist attacks may instill greater fear than large-scale terrorist incidents as they reinforce individual vulnerability.

Selected Terror Attacks against Business Worldwide

On numerous occasions, terrorist groups have indicated their desire to undermine economic interests. Terrorist groups worldwide have made good on such threats, attacking key business and economic symbols, including stock markets, central banks, business districts, and critical infrastructure (e.g., electricity grids and oil pipelines).

By undermining a country's financial interests and capabilities through small- and large-scale attacks, countries are harmed in several ways. For instance, a severe terrorist attack can cause significant physical destruction in terms of human life, national infrastructure, and company assets. Also, the costs of rebuilding after a large-scale terrorist incident as well as responding to terrorist threats take away resources from other societal needs. The costs of rebuilding the World Trade Center in New York (renamed Freedom Tower) are estimated at $12 billion.

As noted earlier, a number of financial centers, including stock exchanges and central banks, have been targeted by terrorist groups in the past as they represent economic power and wealth. For instance, terrorists attacked the Bombay Stock Exchange and Jakarta Stock Exchange in 1993 and 2000, respectively.

In 1996, the Tamil Tigers undertook a suicide terrorist attack against the Sri Lankan Central Bank building in Colombo, resulting in 88 deaths and 1,400 injuries. The incident destroyed or damaged a number of buildings, including hotels. The attack caused significant economic and psychological damage, particularly as it occurred in the center of the Colombo's business district. In the following year, a truck bomb and subsequent gunfight near Colombo's tallest building—which houses the Colombo Stock Exchange—led to 15 deaths and over 100 injuries.

In Israel, terrorist attacks against business interests with many civilian customers have been widespread. Since 2000, there have been hundreds suicide bombing and other attacks against Israeli restaurants, discos, pedestrian malls, hotels, gas stations, bus stops, buses, and casinos. Economic interests have also been attacked in Egypt, Indonesia, and Spain (e.g., tourism); Colombia (e.g., oil); Japan (e.g., transportation); and Greece (e.g., banks).

Following the conviction of Kurdistan Workers' Party (PKK) leader Abdullah Ocalan in summer 1999 in Turkey, there were multiple attacks against Turkish-owned businesses in Germany by suspected Kurdish terrorists, including: Molotov cocktails were thrown at a Turkish shop in Stuttgart and in a Turkish café in Berlin; and Turkish cafes and a grocery store were firebombed near Bonn and Dusseldorf, respectively.

Selected Attacks against Business Targets Globally (2001–2003)

The examples below are illustrative of the breadth of terrorist attacks against diverse business targets globally, including: energy, entertainment and leisure, financial services, hotels, media, real estate, restaurants, retail, and transportation sectors.

ENERGY

Colombia: Six bombs exploded along the Cano Limon–Covenas pipeline, perpetrated by the Revolutionary Armed Forces of Colombia (FARC) (2001).

Israel: A Palestinian suicide bomber killed three people at a gas station in Ariel (2002).

Pakistan: The Muslim United Army group bombed nearly two dozen foreign-owned gas stations in Karachi (2003).

Yemen: A speedboat packed with explosives rammed and damaged a French oil tanker, the *Limburg* (2002).

ENTERTAINMENT AND LEISURE

Bangladesh: Bombings at four cinemas in Mymenshingh resulted in 17 deaths and nearly 300 injuries. Additional attacks against Bengali entertainment events included: a circus, wounding 30 people; and a bombing at an open-air concert, killing nine and wounding 50 (2002).

Colombia: A car bomb killed 36 and wounded 160 at a sports and social club in Bogota (2003).

Indonesia: Several bombs exploded at two nightclubs in Bali resulting in 202 deaths and hundreds of injuries (2002).

Israel: A Palestinian suicide bomber carried out an attack outside the Dolphinarium disco in Tel Aviv, killing 21 and wounding 120 (2001).

Russia: Fifty Chechen terrorists took over a Moscow theater with 700 civilian hostages. After a nearly three-day siege, Russian Special Forces pumped gas into the theater in order to subdue the attackers. The gas was a bit too effective, leading to the deaths of nearly 120 hostages. The Chechens were killed either by the gas or Russian Special Forces, who later stormed the theater (2002).

FINANCIAL SERVICES

Greece: In Kholargos, two foreign bank branches were set on fire by the Anarchic Attack Group (2001).

Turkey: A truck bomb exploded near a building housing British-based bank HSBC in Istanbul. Another truck bombing that same November day against the British Consulate in Istanbul also caused significant damage. The two incidents resulted in nearly 30 deaths and some 450 injuries (2003).

HOTELS

Indonesia: A car bomb outside the J.W. Marriott Hotel in Jakarta resulted in 14 deaths and over 150 injuries (2003).

Iraq: A suicide terrorist detonated a car bomb alongside the Baghdad Hotel, killing seven and injuring over 40 others. The hotel housed U.S. contractors and Iraqi government officials (2003).

Israel: A Palestinian suicide bomber blew himself up during a Passover Seder held at the Park Hotel in Netanya, killing 29 and injuring 140 (2002).

Kenya: A vehicle packed with explosives crashed into the Paradise Hotel lobby in Mombasa, causing 13 deaths and injuring scores of others (2002).

Spain: A car bomb exploded at a hotel in Roasas. The resulting toll at that tourist resort was one death and three injuries. In Salou, a car bomb exploded at a hotel, killing 13 people (2001).

MEDIA

Great Britain: A car bomb exploded at the BBC's main television production facilities in London (2001).

Greece: The Revolutionary Cells bombed the offices of two newspapers, *Efta Imeres* and *Athlitiki Gnomi,* in Ioannina (2002).

Pakistan: A *Wall Street Journal* reporter, Daniel Pearl, was abducted and killed by al Qaeda-linked terrorists (2002).

REAL ESTATE

India: A grenade was thrown at a conference center in Srinagar, where peace talks between the Indian government and Kashmiri separatists took place (2001).

Indonesia: In Lombok, a bomb exploded outside an office of the U.S. firm Newmont Mining Corporation (2001).

Saudi Arabia: A British executive at the Saudi French Bank was killed by a car bomb that exploded in an expatriate compound in Riyadh (2002). Al Qaeda members attacked a gated residential community in Riyadh, killing 17 and injuring scores of others (2003). A similar assault against several housing complexes in the capital took place, killing 35 people, including eight Americans (2003).

RESTAURANTS

Indonesia: A bomb exploded at a McDonald's restaurant in Makassar, killing three people (2002).

Israel: A Palestinian suicide bomber carried out an attack at a Sbarro pizzeria outlet in Jerusalem, killing 15 and injuring 130 (2001). A suicide attack at a restaurant in a gas station in Haifa killed 15 and injured 40 (2002). A suicide bomber at a Jerusalem café caused 11 deaths and 54 injuries (2002).

Lebanon: Two American fast-food franchises, KFC and Hardees, were bombed in Beirut (2002).

RETAIL

Algeria: Several bombs exploded at an outdoor market in Ouled Yaich, causing two deaths and 18 injuries (2002).

Israel: A Palestinian suicide bomber conducted an attack at a pedestrian mall in Jerusalem, killing 11 and injuring 180 (2001).

Philippines: A bomb blast outside a department store in General Santos killed 14 people and wounded 69 others (2002).

Spain: Two suspected members of the Basque Fatherland and Liberty (ETA), who transported nearly 300 pounds of explosives, planned a deadly New Year's Eve bombing spree at shopping centers in Madrid (2002).

TRANSPORTATION

India: A bomb exploded on a commuter train in Bombay, killing nearly a dozen people and injuring over 60. A number of bombings in Bombay taxis resulted in over 50 deaths (2003). A bomb exploded at a bus stop in Kupwara, killing 2 and injuring 32 others (2001).

Israel: Between 2001-2003, Palestinian terrorists attacked Israeli public transportation—buses, bus stops, trains and stations—over 100 times with bombs or guns. In those attacks, nearly 200 people were killed and over 1,000 were wounded. A suicide bomber boarded a commuter bus in Haifa, killing fourteen people and wounding over forty others (2003). A suicide bomber detonated himself abroad a children-filled Israeli bus in Jerusalem, killing over 20 and injuring more than 100 (2003).

Kenya: Two shoulder-fired surface-to-air missiles narrowly missed a Boeing 757 as it took off from Mombasa's airport bound for Israel (2002).

Nepal: Five people were killed and another 17 were injured after a passenger bus exploded after hitting a landmine placed by Maoist terrorists in Sindhuli. Among the dead were a teacher and a businessman (2002).

Pakistan: A suicide bomber destroyed a shuttle bus parked outside a Karachi hotel in Pakistan, killing 11 (including 10 French engineers) and wounding 34 others (2002).

Philippines: A bomb was detonated on a commuter bus in Manila, killing 3 people and injuring 24 (2002). A bomb attack at the Davao International Aiport resulted in over 20 deaths and 150 injuries (2003).

Russia: A suicide bombing aboard a passenger train in southern Russia—the Stavropol region—killed 41 persons and injured some 150 people (2003).

United States: An Egyptian immigrant killed two people at the El Al counter in Los Angeles International Airport before El Al guards shot and killed him (2002). Richard Reid, a British citizen, attempted to ignite explosives in his sneaker while traveling on a flight from Paris to Miami. Other passengers and airline crew subdued Reid, who later admitted to conducting the failed attack on behalf of al Qaeda (2001).

Selected Terror Attacks against Nonbusiness Targets

The examples below illustrate some terror attacks that have taken place against nonbusiness targets between 2001-2003, including: educational facilities, government/nongovernment organization structures, medical buildings, and religious institutions. In doing so, we will better understand that terror risks negatively impact all segments of society, including nonindustry targets.

EDUCATIONAL FACILITIES

China: Two bombs exploded at cafeterias of leading universities in Beijing—Beijing University and Tsinghua University—wounding nearly a dozen people. It is believed that a terrorist group connected to Uighurs, a Turkic ethnic group, was responsible for the attacks (2003).

Israel: A bomb exploded in the cafeteria of the Rothenberg
   International Student Center in Hebrew University, resulting in
   eight deaths (including five Americans) and over 30 injuries
   (2002).

GOVERNMENT/NON-GOVERNMENT ORGANIZATION FACILITIES

Russia: A female suicide bomber, who intended to explode herself
   at the Russian Parliament (Duma), detonated her explosive belt
   near the National Hotel in Moscow. This incident resulted in
   six deaths and over a dozen injuries. In another attack, a suicide
   truck bomber destroyed several Russian government buildings,
   homes, and apartment buildings in Chechnya, killing over 40
   and injuring about 200 (2003).
Greece: Two bombs exploded at a judicial complex in Athens,
   injuring a policeman (2003).
India: A car bomb exploded at the State Legislative Assembly
   Building in Kashmir, killing 15 and wounding another 40 (2001).
Iraq: A suicide bomber in an explosive-laden cement truck
   destroyed part of the United Nations (UN) compound in
   Baghdad, killing the UN Special Envoy Sergio Vieira de
   Mello and injuring over 20 others. The attack also damaged
   neighboring buildings, including the National Spinal Cord
   Injury Center Hospital. Several car bombs exploded outside the
   local headquarters in Baghdad of the International Committee
   of the Red Cross, killing at least 35 people and injuring over 250
   persons. A suicide truck bomber killed 29 and injured nearly 100
   when he rammed the Italian military headquarters in Nasiriyah.
   A car bomb exploded near the Jordanian Embassy in Baghdad,
   resulting in 11 deaths and over 50 injuries. Multiple suicide
   bombers attacked Iraqi police stations killing dozens (2003).
Italy: Two bombs exploded outside the police headquarters in
   Genoa, Italy, shortly after Italian prosecutors determined that
   the killing of a protester during the Genoa G-8 Summit in July
   2001 was an act of self-defense and not murder (2002).

MEDICAL FACILITIES

Russia: Over fifty people were killed when a suicide truck bomb
   rammed a hospital in Mazdok (2003).
Saudi Arabia: A U.S. doctor at Saad Medical Center in Dhahran
   was severely injured by a letter bomb (2001).

RELIGIOUS INSTITUTIONS

India: Islamic terrorists killed at least 29 and wounded over 70 people at a Hindu temple in Gujarat (2002).

Iraq: A massive car bombing at a Shiite mosque in Najaf killed about 100, including a senior Shiite cleric (2003).

Israel: A suicide bomber struck at a Jewish religious academy (yeshiva) in Jerusalem, killing 10 and injuring 50 (2002).

Pakistan: Islamic terrorists killed seven people at a Christian charity in Karachi (2002).

Philippines: A bomb exploded at an open-air Christian shrine in Zamboanga, killing one and wounding 16 people (2002).

Tunisia: An al Qaeda operative crashed a tanker truck filled with propane outside the Ghriba Synagogue on the resort island of Djerba, killing 21 tourists, including 14 Germans (2002).

Turkey: Simultaneous suicide bombings targeting two synagogues in Istanbul—Beth Israel and Neve Shalom—resulted in 23 deaths and over 300 injuries (2003). The Abu Nidal group killed 22 worshipers in a raid on Istanbul's Neve Shalom synagogue in 1986.

Thwarted Terrorist Attacks

Since the September 11, 2001, incidents, numerous potentially significant terrorist attacks have been stymied or intercepted by U.S. and foreign government officials worldwide. In December 2002, FBI Director Robert Mueller stated that close to 100 terrorist attacks globally were thwarted since 9/11. More recently, in March 2003, Attorney General John Ashcroft noted that terrorist conspiracies were uncovered and stopped in many countries, including in the United States, Gibraltar, Singapore, Saudi Arabia, Yemen, and the Straits of Hormuz.

The capacity of governments to prevent attacks is due to many factors: better intelligence, greater cooperation with industry and the public, infiltration of terrorist groups and better monitoring of their activities, and weaker opponents. That being said, it is impossible—even under the most stringent security measures—to prevent all attacks. This is particularly so when dealing with suicide bombers and perpetrators who are not concerned about surviving an attack.

The challenges of thwarting terror attacks are particularly evident in Israel. There, police and military personnel routinely prevent suicide bombings through: interception of attackers prior to undertaking an operation, other intelligence and operational activities, and surrender by prospective suicide bombers, including some children. Still, Palestinian terrorists undertook numerous successful terror incidents, including a multitude of suicide attacks.

Governments have prevented or interfered with many terrorist attacks during 2002–2003 including:

- In 2002, in Great Britain, police arrested three North African men in connection with an alleged plot to release cyanide gas on the London Underground, which has three million travelers a day.
- In 2002, a Palestinian hijacker who tried to hijack an El Al flight told Turkish interrogators that he wanted to divert the plane back to Tel Aviv and crash it into a building in a September 11-like attack.
- In summer 2002, al Qaeda operatives planned to use truck bombs and an explosives-filled airplane to crash into the U.S. embassy in Kenya. Fortunately, Kenyan police prevented the plot.
- During December 2002, Pakistani police foiled a suicide bomb plot in Karachi in which Islamic terrorists planned to ram a car—with 250 sacks of ammonium nitrate, a fertilizer that can be used as an explosive—into a car carrying U.S. diplomats.
- In January 2003, British antiterrorism officers arrested seven North Africans in connection with possession of ricin. Ricin is a potential bioterrorist agent and 6,000 times more poisonous than cyanide. To be lethal, ricin must be ingested, inhaled, or injected. Subsequent investigations suggest that a ricin-linked operation was planned in the United Kingdom or France. According to some reports, instructions on how to produce ricin—from castor bean seeds—was found at an al Qaeda training facility in Kabul, Afghanistan.
- In May 2003, two Moroccans were detained in Saudi Arabia, allegedly involved in a plot to hijack a commercial plane and crash it into a high-rise building in Jeddah.
- In July 2003, U.S. government authorities uncovered evidence that al Qaeda planned to hijack a plane in London and crash it into a major building in the city.
- In September 2003, three teenage girls, including twin sisters,

were detained in relation to a prospective suicide attack at a supermarket in Rabat, Morocco. The attack was planned to take place in the alcohol section of the supermarket; traditional Islam prohibits the use of alcohol.

- In fall 2003, Yemeni authorities undermined a multi-pronged plan using explosives-filled cars to attack the American, British, and German embassies in Sanaa.
- During winter 2003, the United States, France, Mexico, and Great Britain canceled or delayed some two dozen flights, spurred by intelligence that al Qaeda terrorists planned to carry out hijackings and undertake 9/11-type attacks (e.g., ramming the plane into a building or exploding it over a large city). There was also speculation that terrorists might sneak onboard biological, chemical, or radiological agents that would disperse during an explosion.
- In December 2003, Pakistani President Pervez Musharraf survived a number of assassination attempts, including two major incidents involving remote-control bombs and suicide truck bombs.

Conclusion

Domestic and international terror groups pose significant threats worldwide. The breadth of terrorist incidents from 9/11 through March 2004 demonstrates the vast challenges ahead. With respect to attacks against business interests, no sector was immune. Nonbusiness interests were under attack as well, including government and nongovernment facilities. Among business and nonbusiness targets, terrorists did not spare their fascination with lethality and brutality, as evidenced by scores of diverse attacks and extensive carnage. Some victories in deterring and stopping terrorist onslaughts prior to their initiation or completion took place during the past few years. While it is hoped that the future will be more sanguine, the contemporary and future threats discussed in Chapter 2 suggest otherwise.

2

Contemporary and Future Terror Threats

Chemical agents are released into the ventilation system of a train station. Simultaneous cyberterrorism attacks cripple electricity grids. A "dirty bomb" explodes at a financial center. Deadly pathogens are introduced into the food supply. An explosives–laden cargo plane crashes into an open-air stadium.

These scenarios illustrate some contemporary and future terror threats. This chapter builds upon the earlier perspectives by examining contemporary and future terrorist threats, including terrorist tactics and targets. Additionally, U.S. government terror warnings and advisories will be discussed.

Government Terror Warnings and Advisories

From 9/11 to February 2003, the FBI issued over 100 terror warnings to state and local law enforcement and investigated over 3,000 terrorist threats on American soil. In March 2002, the U.S. government established the Homeland Security Advisory System (HSAS). The HSAS provides notice of possible terror threats as well as guidance thereto. Five threat conditions were identified, each with a corresponding color and terrorist risk level attached: low risk of a terror incident (green), guarded risk (blue), elevated risk (yellow), high risk (orange), and severe risk (red).

The greatest probability and severity of a terrorist attack attaches with the red threat level (severe risk). The HSAS commenced at elevated risk (yellow) but was elevated to high risk (orange) — and subsequently returned to elevated risk—on about half a dozen occasions since inception through 2003.

The public has been exposed to the changes in the HSAS levels through government press conferences and extensive media coverage of the topic. HSAS is binding on the government's executive branch but has resulted in corresponding responses by state and local government agencies and some businesses.

The HSAS was intended to focus on specific regions of the country and certain sectors of the economy. But thus far, there have been inadequate findings—in the main—as to specificity of potential threats. Analogously, Rep. Christopher Cox (R-CA) has proposed modifying implementation of the HSAS system to allow for regional warnings and not national premonitions.

Initially, the public and industry paid close attention to the HSAS and how it would impact—if in any way—their daily lives or businesses. As HSAS warnings accelerated in frequency, interest waned. Some have asserted that the pronouncements were more of an irritant than a productive resource. Perhaps it was the nature of several warnings—but no actual attack—that engendered fatigue among the population. There is also speculation that terrorists have observed government and business responses to HSAS changes and adjusted their modus operandi for future operations. This is not to suggest that the HSAS does not provide an important function.

The government has also exposed the public to information regarding preferred responses in case of a terrorist-initiated emergency. Citizens were urged to put together an emergency supply kit and establish a family communications plan. It was recommended that an emergency supply kit include: flashlights, battery-powered radio, extra batteries, blankets, first aid kit and medicines, manual can opener, three days of non-perishable food and water, duct tape, and plastic sheeting. Also encouraged is a safe room to guard against airborne contaminants. On the matter of a family communication plan, the government suggested establishing a plan to be able to communicate with each other in the event of disparate types of attacks.

Likewise, the Transportation Security Administration, an agency of the Department of Homeland Security, set out a list of items that are not permitted as carry-on items on airplanes. Among items on the prohibited list are: ammunition, automatic weapons, dynamite, hand grenades, knives, meat cleavers, numchucks, pepper spray, pistols, razor blades, revolvers, rifles, screwdrivers, shot guns, spear guns, and swords. Despite these admonitions, thousands of airline passengers—including some with malevolent intent—tried to bring some of the contraband items onto planes.

Terrorists' Modus Operandi

Terrorist groups undertake various tactics to achieve their goals based upon, among other things, their capabilities and motivation. For our purposes, we will review the following types of operations: bombings, suicide attacks, cyberterrorism, and superterrorism (biological, chemical, radiological, and nuclear).

Bombings

There are a number of explosives and bomb threats that face government and industry. The FBI National Capital Response Squad/Joint Terrorism Task Force has described some types of bombs and their explosive-capacity characteristics. The various types of bombs include: pipe (5 lbs. of TNT), briefcase/suitcase (50 lbs. of TNT), compact sedan (500 lbs. of TNT), sedan (1,000 lbs. of TNT), passenger/cargo van (4,000 lbs. of TNT), small moving van/delivery truck (10,000 lbs. of TNT), moving van/water truck (30,000 lbs. of TNT), and semi-trailer (60,000 lbs. of TNT). Obviously, disparate bombs require different evacuation distances should they be encountered.

The aforementioned discussion of bomb threats is not an academic exercise. For example, terrorist-crafted bombs were used during the 1993 World Trade Center attack in New York and Oklahoma City attack in 1995. There are other alarming dangers. In September 2002, Israeli government officials intercepted a vehicle carrying a mega-bomb: 1,300 pounds of explosives, two barrels containing gasoline and metal shards, and a cell phone rigged as the detonator.

In a May 2002 incident, a bomb attached to the underside of a tank truck exploded inside Israel's biggest fuel depot. The site is located near a densely populated residential area and near an interchange of three major highways. The bomb was detonated by a cell phone but resulted in limited damage because the terrorists targeted a truck carrying diesel fuel, rather than the much more flammable gasoline tanker.

In the most dramatic terror attack on European soil since 9/11, ten remote-control bombs exploded on four commuter trains in Madrid, killing over 190 and injuring some 1,500 people on March 11, 2004. This incident was quickly viewed as Spain's 9/11—known as 3/11. It demonstrated the vast carnage that bombs can generate.

Suicide Attacks

One of the expanding tactics terrorist groups use worldwide are suicide attacks. In May 2002, FBI Director Mueller surmised that it is inevitable that suicide bombers will conduct attacks in the United States. That same month, Vice President Richard Cheney predicted that it is likely that suicide attacks will take place in this country. U.S. counterterrorism officials have acknowledged that it is difficult to prevent suicide bombers attacking anywhere, let alone against soft targets, such as hotels, restaurants, malls, and social clubs.

As noted in Chapter 1, suicide attacks have taken place worldwide against business (e.g., transportation, restaurants, entertainment) and nonbusiness sectors (government and nongovernmental sites). Suicide attacks have included small-scale attacks (e.g., assassination of Rajeev Gandhi) to large-scale attacks (e.g., suicide bombers against U.S. targets in Beirut in 1983 as well as attacks against Italian and UN interests in Iraq in 2003).

An al Qaeda affiliate group undertook a series of suicide bombings in May 2003, killing 42 persons and injuring over 100 in Casablanca, Morocco. In November 2003, several suicide bombings against religious, business, and (foreign) government facilities took place in Istanbul, Turkey. Those attacks resulted in dozens of deaths and hundreds of injuries.

Both isolated suicide attacks and simultaneous, multiple operations have occurred. Men and women have been employed to undertake such attacks. The latter have been recruited because they tend to reduce attention of law enforcement authorities that generally suspect men. Yet, more frequent use of women in operations makes it likely that more women will be scrutinized as well.

An example of the use of women in suicide attacks includes the July 2003 incident when two Chechen women conducted suicide bombings at a concert in Moscow, killing a dozen civilians. Several Palestinian groups have used women—including girls and mothers—to conduct suicide operations. Also, in May 2003, a female suicide bomber from the far-left Revolutionary People's Liberation Party-Front detonated herself in a café in Ankara, Turkey.

Cyberterrorism

The Internet Security Alliance, an industry association, reports that cyber attacks have spawned from simple attacks with low levels of intruder knowledge (e.g., password cracking, disabling audits, and backdoors) to more advanced attacks (e.g., packet spoofing, denial of service, and "stealth"/advanced scanning techniques).

Cyberterrorism includes the use of paralyzing and destructive electronic keyboard attacks on civilian and military critical infrastructure nerve centers in furtherance of political goals. Were cyber attacks to coincide with an incident of 9/11 proportions (or worse)—such as during a bioterrorist attack—then this type of electronic warfare could cripple health information and emergency response systems.

Suffice it to mention several catastrophic scenarios of cyberterrorism, such as: altering formulas for medication at pharmaceutical plants; "crashing" telephone systems; misrouting passenger trains; changing pressure in gas pipelines to cause valve failure; disrupting operations of air traffic control; triggering oil refinery explosions and fires; scrambling the software used by emergency services; "turning off" power grids; and detonating simultaneously numerous computerized bombs around the world. Cyberterrorists' access to the resources of state-sponsors of terrorism would exacerbate any potential damage inflicted on government and industry assets.

Superterrorism

Superterrorism is generally defined as unconventional terrorism, such as biological, chemical, radiological, and nuclear terrorism. These types of terrorism are capable of producing massive death and destruction: possibly from hundreds to several million casualties in a single incident. Such attacks could also cause disruptions of major proportions, including adverse economic implications and widespread public panic.

In March 2003, Homeland Security Secretary Tom Ridge forewarned that al Qaeda intends to use chemical, biological, and/or radiological materials against Western targets. President Bush, in February 2003, expressed similar sentiment in noting that al Qaeda would have no hesitation to use various types of superterrorism against the United States.

In May 2003, the Department of Homeland Security organized mock terrorist drills in Seattle and Chicago, involving a fictional "dirty bomb," and pneumonic plague, respectively. These scenarios, which involved thousands of participants from various branches of the government, cost $16 million to undertake. These terror scenarios and others like them nationwide illustrate the prospective threats that U.S. government and industry experts envision might occur.

Bioterrorism

There is a growing concern of a worst-case scenario involving bioterrorism. For instance, an aerosolized release of 100 kilograms of anthrax spores in an enclosed setting is projected to cause over 100,000 deaths. The potential threat of smallpox, another form of biological weapon, has also attracted public attention. Extremely infectious and associated with a high mortality rate, a possible outbreak of smallpox would be much more devastating than the fall 2001 anthrax attacks, when five people died.

An ominous future was provided in a summer 2001 government-sponsored, simulated smallpox attack (called "Dark Winter") in Oklahoma City. The drill demonstrated that a smallpox incident could result, for example, in the exposure of millions of people in 25 states to that disease. The simulation projected some 1,000 deaths within three weeks of the initial attack and up to 300,000 victims within six weeks.

During fall 2001, anthrax-tainted letters were sent within the United States. The source of these biological weapons and the perpetrator(s) are still unknown although government authorities identified a "person of interest." The March 2003 discovery of ricin in London and presence of that biological agent in a U.S. Senate office building in February 2004 lend credence to the projection that biological agents will be used with greater frequency by terrorists.

In November 2003, Dr. Thomas Butler, a Texas Tech University Professor, went on trial, facing 69 federal felony counts, including illegally importing and transporting plague bacteria samples. Among other things, Dr. Butler transported various pathogens into the United States. This incident raised several issues, including: the broad use of pathogens at research facilities and capacity of individuals to sneak such agents into the United States undetected. Furthermore, the possible exploitation (or theft) by terrorists of such dangerous items also comes to mind.

In December 2003, the revelation of a cow infected with mad cow disease found on U.S. soil caused significant fear among government officials, industry authorities, analysts, and consumers. The infected cow was later deemed to have originated in Canada and had eaten tainted feed. Extensive beef recalls took place, and dozens of countries banned the importation of U.S. beef, including principal markets, such as Japan and Korea. The ban was similar to the nearly worldwide ban on British beef following the discovery of mad cow disease more than a decade before. The incident raised the specter of significant economic damage and widespread panic were a terrorist group able to taint a portion of the food supply.

The mad cow scare also negatively impacted the stock price of beef producers and restaurants that principally serve beef. In contrast, chicken, turkey, and egg producers companies that test for mad cow disease, and firms that allow for easy tracking of such animals saw increased demand for their products and services. Additional interest in organic food—beef and milk products in particular—was another consequence of the mad cow scare.

In February 2004, avian (bird) flu developed in parts of Southeast Asia (e.g., Thailand and Vietnam). Shortly thereafter, the avian virus reached U.S. shores. In turn, panic among U.S. poultry producers set in with precipitous declines in some poultry industry stocks.

The mad cow and avian flu incidents exemplify the broad negative implications that can result should a terror group attack the agriculture sector. It is worthy to note that terror groups have already undertaken attacks against food supplies actions in the past: Tamil Tigers attacking the Sri Lankan tea crop; and Palestinian terror groups injecting mercury into Israeli citrus products. In the United States, a terrorist group infected a salad bar with salmonella.

Chemical Terrorism

Chemical weapons include VX gas, mustard gas, and sarin. State-sponsors of terrorism have developed various types of chemical weapons. They may make them available for use by substate terrorist groups. In recent years, the only major use of chemical weapons by a terrorist group (nonstate) against a civilian population was by the Aum Shinrikyo group. This Japanese-based cult released sarin nerve gas on two occasions in Japan's subways: in June 1994 in Matsumoto City, when an attack killed seven and injured almost 150; and in Tokyo, in March 1995, when 12 were killed and some 5,000 were injured.

Al Qaeda operatives expressed interest in crop-dusting planes in relation to possible chemical or biological agent attacks against a U.S. city. The FBI has also warned about the possible release of chemical weapons into the ventilation systems of office buildings.

Radiological and Nuclear Terrorism

Radiological and nuclear terrorism dangers include: a crude explosive device designed to spew radioactive material, a massive truck bomb crashing into a plant containing stockpiles of nuclear waste; and an explosive-laden jetliner crashing into an active nuclear power plant. In March 2003, director-general of the International Atomic Energy Agency, Mohamed El Baradi, warned of the possibility of terrorists using a dirty bomb (surrounding radioactive material with explosives).

The development of a radiological device for use by terrorists is a real and grave threat. After all, radioactive materials are relatively easily found on the black market and somewhat limited expertise is necessary to craft a dirty bomb. There have been some 300 confirmed cases of illegal trafficking of radioactive materials from various countries during the past decades. In May 2003, for example, cesium 137 and stronium—potential ingredients in a "dirty bomb"—were discovered in a taxi in Tblisi, Georgia. In an elaborate sting operation the following month, Thai government authorities arrested a man who tried to sell cesium-137. In Poland, in fall 2003, government authorities arrested a group of people involved in a plot to sell radioactive cesium for about $150,000.

Attorney General Ashcroft stated that terrorist groups, such as al Qaeda, have shown significant interest in radiological devices. In 1999, al Qaeda is believed to have commenced worked on a dirty bomb at a location in Herat, Afghanistan. Captured al Qaeda operatives Khalid Sheik Mohammed and Ramzi bin al Shibh are reported to have stated that al Qaeda considered striking at U.S. nuclear facilities in September 2001.

Prospective Terror Targets

While elsewhere we delved into selected terrorist tactics and targets, this section of the book will address some prospective targets threatening individuals, businesses, sites, and the country at large. Prior to that, it is instructive to get some insight as to the mindset of terrorist targets as set out in the following extraction from an al Qaeda manual. The document details potential victims and activities that terror operatives may pursue, such as: blasting and destroying bridges, embassies, and vital economic centers.

Aviation

For over forty years terrorists have attacked airplanes by several means, including hijackings, bombings, and missile attacks. Terrorists have not lost their fascination and interest in undertaking aviation attacks. As Homeland Security Secretary Ridge remarked in July 2003, new aviation security threats are mentioned weekly.

The possible use of a jet as a missile (e.g., terrorists planned to crash a plane into the Eiffel Tower prior to 9/11) has gained more appeal by terrorists after they witnessed the momentous damage of the September 11 attacks. The November 2002 firing of two SA-7 missiles at an Israeli airline during takeoff from Kenya raised attention once again to the vulnerability of commercial aircraft of terrorist missile attacks. In February 2003, U.S. government authorities acknowledged that a number of terrorist groups already possess shoulder-fire missiles.

During a portion of December 2003, the Department of Homeland Security restricted private flights over Las Vegas, Times Square, downtown Chicago, and the Hoover Dam. This decision was made due to possible terrorist attacks using planes against buildings and structures in the United States. Times Square was a particularly sensitive potential terrorist target on New Year's Eve 2003 as over 300,000 people were anticipated to be there. Also that month, a number of European and Mexican flights to the United States were canceled due to suspicion that terrorists were planning on hijacking the flights.

In light of such threats, the U.S. government proposed requiring foreign carriers to use air marshals on flights designated by U.S. authorities as necessitating additional security. The business ramifications of such steps and adjustments to corporate security are discussed in subsequent chapters of this book.

In November 2003, U.S. government authorities disclosed possible al Qaeda attacks against U.S. critical infrastructure targets—nuclear plants, bridges, and dams—through the use of hijacked cargo planes. The targeting of cargo aviation may accelerate in the future as security in commercial passenger aviation has strengthened.

During July 2003, a Transportation Security Administration memo warned about a five-person terrorist team that might hijack a commercial aircraft with the aid of common items (e.g., cameras) modified as weapons. Authorities predicted that the terrorists would try to travel via an international flight with a U.S.-based layover. These types of passengers do not require a visa.

Other modifications to traditional aviation terrorism may include the shipping of terrorists as cargo. The "packaged" terrorist would subsequently be placed on a commercial passenger or cargo jet for ultimate delivery or explosion on board. These developments are reminiscent of a nonterror-related case. In 2003, a shipping clerk, Charles McKinley, shipped himself in a box from New York to Texas. The "packaged" McKinley slipped by several airport security checkpoints but was subsequently prosecuted.

A January 2003 General Accounting Office report on aviation security found that the majority of the estimated $12 billion of air cargo shipped annually is not screened for explosives. Other troubling revelations include the fact that about 22% of total air cargo is flown on passenger aircraft.

Other incidents demonstrate that aviation security still has some room for improvement. In September 2002, New York *Daily News* reporters were able to carry contraband (e.g., box cutters, razor knives, and pepper spray) on a U.S. flight. In October 2003, Nathaniel Heatwole, a U.S.-based university student, was charged with concealing box cutters and other dangerous items (e.g., bleach and simulated explosives) on several U.S. domestic flights from Raleigh-Durham International and Baltimore-Washington International Airports. Heatwole left these items on selected planes and subsequently informed U.S. government authorities of his actions, explaining that he wanted to show that aviation security was inadequate.

Soft Targets

Soft targets include locations where potential victims are largely unprotected, including: supermarkets, shopping malls, restaurants, theaters, buses, schools, and religious institutions. Soft targets are attractive to terrorists as they: generally have limited or no security; access is free or of limited costs; it is easy to "blend in;" the populace is often unsuspecting (though numerous suicide bombers on Israeli buses are an obvious exception); locations have many unarmed and innocent people; and sites are accentuated as to inflict extreme damage (e.g., tight quarters and extensive glass in subways and buses).

With increased security at selected government institutions, critical infrastructure sites, and some businesses, terrorist groups may well shift their operations on soft targets. The U.S. government has forewarned of possible threats against soft targets on U.S. soil. For instance, in February 2003, FBI Director Robert Mueller projected that small-scale attacks against soft targets would be easier to effectuate than large-scale attacks.

In February 2003, a man ignited a flammable liquid in a subway fire in Daegu, South Korea, which resulted in nearly 120 deaths. Subsequently, U.S. subway systems accelerated their security efforts. This incident illustrated the relative ease and expansive lethality that may arise should a terrorist perpetrate a similar incident against a soft target.

Attacks at locations with mass gatherings of people (e.g., arenas and stadiums hosting high school, college, and professional sports teams) are likewise possible targets. As security levels—if any—are extremely diverse, attention should be paid to strengthen such potential soft targets because possible harm would be significant.

With limited resources and a need to distinguish between high and low probabilities targets, thousands of such potential targets could—to their potential hazard—be left relatively unprotected. In contrast, high-profile sports events, such as the Winter 2002 Olympics in Utah and Super Bowls, received extensive security embodied by significant funding and personnel. Security at the Salt Lake City games included some 10,000 federal, state, and local personnel costing over $300 million. The upcoming Summer 2004 Olympics in Athens will be a large-scale, multinational security operation costing hundreds of millions of dollars as well.

Transportation

The transportation sector has been a prime target of terrorist groups for many reasons, including their accessibility and exposure to many potential victims. The Mineta Transportation Institute reports that between 1997 and 2002 over 195 terrorist attacks occurred worldwide on surface transportation systems, including: buses (41% of all attacks), subways and trains (22%), subway and train stations (10%), bus terminals (8%), tracks (8%), tourist buses (5%), others (5%), and bridges and tunnels (1%). These finding show that buses, bus terminals, and tourist buses comprised 54% of all attacks against mass transit.

The U.S. mass transit systems employed approximately 350,000 people and tallied more than 9 billion passenger trips in 2000. Mass transit systems, which include buses, trolley buses, commuter rails, vanpools, ferry boats, and light rail services, are valued at hundreds of billions of dollars. Ridership by transit modes in 2000 consisted of: buses (61%), heavy rail (28%), commuter rail (4%), light rail (3%), trolley bus (1%), and others (ferryboat, vanpool, and paratransit, 2%).

In October 2002, the FBI issued a warning that terrorist operatives are considering various transportation-related strategies. Among these potential threats are: destroying key rail bridges, removing sections of track to cause derailments, and targeting hazardous material containers.

A December 2003 incident involving the threat of possible placement of hazardous chemical devices near a Washington, D.C., metro station resulted in major disruptions to about 40% of the system. After several hours of delays, the alleged devices were discovered and deemed innocuous. This situation demonstrates how bomb threats on mass transit systems can have huge negative ramifications to an important commuter route. If a threat is ignored and an attack occurs, the credibility of mass transit system will have been severely damaged. Yet, frequent hoaxes and baseless threats reduce the seriousness with which industry and government may respond to a provocation.

The trucking industry, as well, faces many challenges. It is believed that tanker-truck businesses are prime terror targets, as they haul substances that include combustible and hazardous materials. U.S. gasoline tankers make about 50,000 trips every day, with limited—in some cases, nonexistent—security at fuel depots. Terrorists have used fuel-laden trucks in previous terrorist attacks, including crashing a truck carrying liquefied natural gas against a Tunisian synagogue, killing 21 people.

Over 800,000 shipments of hazardous materials take place in the United States each day. In 1997, 74.4 billion ton-miles (a ton-mile is one ton moving one mile) of hazardous materials traversed U.S. roadways. Terror concerns were heightened following the revelation that nearly 100 drums of sodium cyanide were stolen in Mexico City in 2002. The fear that the drums would be used by terrorists and smuggled into the United States showed the possible threat. Other risks include the hijacking of trucks containing chlorine cyanide.

Risks against commercial and leisure shipping interests are also noteworthy as terrorists have targeted oil tankers and cruise lines in the past. The possibility that boats or shipping lines will transport individuals and/or weaponry (e.g., arms; and biological, chemical, radiological, or nuclear materials) into the United States is not out of the question.

Energy

On August 14, 2003, there was an extensive power blackout in the Northeast. Although no links have been made to a terrorist attack, it demonstrated the reliance of American business, consumer, and government functions on steady electrical power. As such, this incident rekindled concern about the threat of terrorists attacking electrical grids and severely disrupting American commerce and safety for days, weeks, or even months. A bright side of the power blackout was the subsequent prominence of some emergency and backup power supply generators and systems that aided government, businesses, and individuals during the blackout.

During 2003–2004 Iraqi guerrillas and terrorists attacked energy infrastructure sites, including oil wells and pipelines, in their country. Similar terror attacks might be replicated on U.S. soil. Already, a plot was uncovered to bomb a large oil pipeline in Alaska. There have been many attacks against such targets elsewhere, particularly against oil pipelines in Colombia.

In recent years, al Qaeda operatives have undertaken plans to attack Saudi Arabian government facilities and assets, including a leading oil terminal complex, Ras Tanura. The economic ramifications of such an attack would be significant. The price of oil would rise dramatically, as probably would gold, while Western currencies and stock markets would likely decline.

At U.S. energy facilities (e.g., nuclear, oil, and gas) increased security measures—including fortifying physical barriers, restricting access, and supplying additional guards and training—are in place. Still, there are various government and media reports that expose weaknesses in the security sphere at energy facilities, particularly at nuclear power plants.

Financial

In the future, potential U.S. business interests targeted by terrorists may include financial markets through a combination of bombings and cyberterror attacks. For instance, the Clearing House Interbank Payment Systems (CHIPS), a computer network that links 59 of the world's largest banks operated by the New York Clearing House, could be on a terrorist target list. Approximately $292 trillion passed through the CHIPS system in 2000. Although no attacks were reported at CHIPS on September 11, a number of banks connected to the system lost service for several hours.

Simultaneous terrorist attacks against multiple U.S. commodity and stock exchanges could significantly undermine American economic strength and severely weaken the U.S. dollar, at least in the short-term. Terror attacks against the Treasury Department and Federal Reserve—whether by bombings, cyberterrorism, or otherwise—are not beyond the pale of the imagination. As witnessed overseas, terrorists have attacked central banks, financial institutions, and securities markets in Sri Lanka, India, and Indonesia. In Brazil, a criminal gang planned to bomb Sao Paulo's stock market.

Food

Vulnerabilities to U.S. food sources are critical to note. Failure to adequately safeguard such assets could lead to significant deaths, public mayhem, and severe economic damage. A May 2002 National Academy of Sciences report projected that terrorists could introduce pathogens to the food and agriculture sectors of the United States, and in doing so, cause billions of dollars in damage.

Individuals, companies, and governments are quick to respond to potential damage arising from diseased or infected food source. This was demonstrated most recently in the mad cow and avian flu scares hitting the United States and Asia, respectively, during December 2003–February 2004. The ramifications of these outbreaks led to immediate stoppage of importation of beef and chickens from "infected countries," with subsequent declines in stock price and reduced revenues from firms that operated in that realm (e.g., U.S. beef producers and Asian chicken producers).

The mad cow disease and avian flu incidents were not associated with terrorism. Yet, they demonstrate the severe, negative consequences to agriculture were terrorists to unleash a biological agent or otherwise tamper with a food staple in the United States. With those concerns in mind, in January 2002, the Food and Drug Administration (FDA) published voluntary guidelines to protect America's food supply against terrorist contamination. The suggestions, aimed at food producers, processors, transporters, and retailers, include: investigating the criminal backgrounds and immigration status of all employees; and improving the physical security of ingredients and products.

In Tangashan, eastern China, in September 2002, a man jealous of a business rival confessed to tainting his competitor's breakfast snacks (fried dough sticks, sesame cakes and sticky rice balls). While this incident was not an act of political violence, it does demonstrate the relative ease and lethality of potential terrorist attacks in the food and restaurant sectors. An American terror group poisoned a restaurant's salad bar with salmonella. These examples provide possible justification for expanding the use of background checks in the food and restaurant sectors— despite their costs to industry.

Real Estate

Terrorists are likely to continue to target residential housing, office buildings, retail sites (e.g., stores and malls), industrial locations (e.g., factories), hospitals, schools, and places of worship. These targets are of probable interest as attacks there would result in: significant casualties, destruction of property and economic value, interference with daily activities, and considerable apprehension in the public, government, and business circles.

In May 2002, the FBI warned that al Qaeda operatives in the United States might rent apartments in the United States and rig them with explosives. This announcement led to property owners undertaking measures to improve security and warn tenants of possible terrorist risks.

The specter that terrorists may contaminate building ventilation systems with chemical, biological, or radiological agents is also relevant. In May 2002, the Department of Health and Human Services released new guidelines for the protection of ventilation systems in commercial and government buildings. Among recommendations addressed were: physical security of ventilation systems, airflow and filtration, systems maintenance, program administration and maintenance staff training.

Conclusion

There are several specific reasons why the frequency and severity of terrorism will increase during the twenty-first century. First, terrorism has proved very successful in attracting publicity, disrupting the activities of government and business, and causing significant death and destruction. Second, arms, explosives, supplies, financing, and communications are readily available to terrorists. Third, an international support network of groups and states exists that greatly facilitates the undertaking of terrorist activities. Fourth, certain conditions, such as religious extremism or perceptions that the "cause" is lost, could provide terrorists with an incentive to escalate their attacks dramatically by resorting to weapons of mass destruction.

Despite the aforementioned discussion of threats it is important to underscore that a significant dent has been made against the power of terrorist groups and their state-sponsors worldwide through U.S. and allied military actions, intelligence and clandestine operations, expansive financial allocations to government entities combating terrorism, greater business cooperation in the war on terrorism, as well as public support and assistance in fighting the scourge of terrorism.

A number of principal leaders of terrorist groups, such as al Qaeda and their affiliates in a number of countries, have been captured or killed. Among these are: a September 11th mastermind, Khalid Sheik Mohammed; an al Qaeda principal Mohammed Atef; and Riduan Isamuddin (a.k.a. Hambali), leader of Jemaah Islamiyah.

Nevertheless, Osama bin Laden and Ayman al Zawahiri remain at large, as of March 15, 2004. Even if bin Laden or al Zawahiri were captured or killed, terror threats would unlikely diminish significantly as the al Qaeda has metastasizes into some eighty countries. Yet, their capture or death may actually encourage terror attacks during an initial period.

3

Terrorists and Their Supporters Participate in the Economic System

Terrorists and their abettors exploit the assets available in the economic system to their advantage. In doing so, they are able to acquire financial, organizational, and operational resources (e.g., arms, training, intelligence, and information) from governments, companies, nonprofits, and individuals.

Terrorists complement their manipulation of traditional economic resources through the commission of crimes as diverse as: counterfeiting currency, credit cards, and ATM cards; misappropriating and using credit card information; forging documents; identity theft; money laundering; drug trafficking; corruption; commercial espionage; and other unlawful activities. This chapter discusses these actors and their multi-pronged legal and illegal pursuits—all in the furtherance of terror.

Companies and Individuals Aid Terrorists

There are several means by which companies assist terrorist groups and their members. Companies do so directly and indirectly. Sometimes, they help terrorists purposely. More often, however, they do so unwittingly.

Corporations can provide: funding and launder money; employment for terrorists; accessibility to equipment and personnel; generic tools (e.g., trucks); instrumentalities of terror (e.g., dynamite or explosives); information about the local landmarks and prospective targets (e.g., highlighting vulnerabilities and access to targets); training (e.g., flight schools for 9/11 hijackers); communications, resources, and contacts; work permits (e.g., immigration); and sponsorship (e.g., employment and resources). Terrorist groups also use front companies (which combine legitimate and illegal revenue) and shell companies (opaque firms used to hide legitimate owners' interests) to finance terrorist operation.

Osama bin Laden had an international network of companies that were used to generate funds for terrorist operations as well as employ terrorists. The Islamic Resistance Movement (Hamas) earned funds from ownership of textile businesses and cattle raising. The Popular Front for the Liberation of Palestine (PFLP) owned and operated metal works facilities in Lebanon during the 1980s. Sokoa, a furniture store in Hendaya, France, served as a base for the Basque Fatherland and Liberation terror group (ETA) in the 1980s.

The Iranian government has used front companies, such as Tehran-based Kala Electric, to obtain materials and equipment for a fuel fabrication plant or enriched uranium facility. Pakistani scientists involved in the transfer of nuclear technology to Libya, Iran, and North Korea are believed to have used various companies, including Malaysian firms, to carry out their activities.

Thousands of companies provide products and services to civilian and military segments of the government. As a result, the possibility exists that some firms are either terrorist sympathizers or unknowingly employ terrorist sleeper cell members. Also, it is not unlikely that an unscrupulous company (or employee) may provide tainted products (e.g., faulty gas masks or poison foodstuffs) or harmful services (e.g., poorly trained, bomb-sniffing dogs).

Products and services are acquired for two purposes: traditional use by the law-abiding citizens or nontraditional use by terrorists (or other criminals). There are many suppliers of easily accessible basic products and services that terrorists may use to carry out their operations.

Terrorist groups may obtain: wires, switches, and timers for bombs; fertilizers and chemicals for bombs; guns and rifles for assassinations and assaults; dynamite for explosive devices; knives for stabbings; cars and trucks for vehicle bombs; use of cell phones and pay phones with prepaid phone cards, and Internet cafes to communicate with other operatives; video-cameras and cameras to scope-out a site; airline, bus, subway, and movie tickets for access to a target; access to malls, stores, and restaurants to conduct an attack or sabotage; and uniforms to impersonate a guard or hospital employee, allowing for access to targets.

An example of the results of easy access to particular products by terrorists was demonstrated by ETA's purchase of ammonium nitrate, aluminum, and sodium chloride to produce explosive materials in ETA's own factories. ETA is also alleged to have produced rifles, submachine guns, and grenade launchers in secret workshops in France. An al Qaeda-linked terror group based in Turkey chose ammonia and fertilizer as principal ingredients in a bomb that was used against several Istanbul targets in November 2003. An Isuzu pickup truck carried one of the bombs to a target during that operation.

Products Used in Furtherance of Terrorism

Law enforcement's capacity to monitor the acquisition of many products—aside from fertilizers, chemicals, guns, and dynamite—is undermined by the fact that thousands of transactions take place every day in the United States. Monitoring is further complicated if perpetrators use cash or stolen credit cards.

Limited review of cross-border trade makes it easy for terrorist groups to smuggle selected items (e.g., biological, chemical, radiological weapons) into the country. Other items, such as plastic explosives and arms, are accessible by military collaborators or unscrupulous gun storeowners.

U.S. counterterrorism officials are warned if an individual on a terror watch list attempts to purchase a weapon. Yet, an incongruity in law and policy provides that should a firearm transaction actually take place, further information about where the purchase took place and other data can generally not be disseminated to appropriate authorities.

There are several examples of individuals trying to obtain weaponry for terror groups. For instance, in May 2003, Sayed Abdul Malike was charged with making false statements in relation to his attempt to purchase C-4 explosives from an FBI agent. It is alleged that Malike also sought to purchase bulletproof vests and night goggles.

Likewise, in London in August 2003, an arms dealer, Hemant Lakhani, was charged with selling a Russian-made SA-18 missile to U.S. agents posing as terrorists. Apparently, Lakhani discussed selling additional missiles as well as tons of plastic explosives.

Also, Thailand indicted 15 individuals, including several policemen, military personnel, and gun shop owners, for illegally trading and possessing firearms as well as falsifying documents in September 2003. The group is alleged to have smuggled these weapons on behalf of Sri

Lanka's Tamil Tiger group. Also, in 2003, several Sri Lankans were arrested in Thailand in connection with smuggling pistols and 45,000 rounds of ammunitions.

Potentially troubling is the sale of genetic material (e.g., made-to-order pieces of DNA) to pharmaceutical companies and researchers. These items are also component parts of biological weapons. This threat was made all the more credible when in 2002, scientists in New York announced that they used mail order molecules to make polio viruses. This development increased attention as to whether the DNA synthesis industry deserves closer scrutiny that it has received. Additionally disquieting was the two-week manufacture of a virus from commercially-available material by a Maryland-based firm in 2003.

Another issue justifying some concern is the sale of dual use products to state-sponsors of terrorism. Relevant too is the sale of bona-fide U.S. goods in violation of the Trading With The Enemy Act (e.g., a law barring U.S. firms from doing business with "enemy" nations, such as Iran, Iraq, Libya, Syria, Sudan, Cuba, and North Korea). According to the U.S. Department of Treasury's Office of Foreign Assets Control, in 2002 nearly 90 companies conducted business with "prohibited," countries.

In January 2004, Libya admitted that it undertook extensive steps to develop and acquire biological, chemical, and nuclear weapons. Initial reports indicate that the nation took advantage of an extensive black market with respect to nuclear and other components, including relevant centrifuges, machine tools, and nuclear materials. Bogus front and shell companies, in collaboration with arms dealers and morally challenged businessmen, aided in masking Libya's activities in this realm.

Some state-sponsors of terrorism bought component parts used in producing weapons of mass destruction. German prosecutors report that Iraq acquired technology to make a long-range cannon capable of delivering radiological, biological, and chemical weapons. In May 2003, the U.S. government sanctioned China's North China Industries Corp. with a two-year importation ban stemming from the firm's sales of missile technology to Iran.

In December 2002, the U.S. Customs Service investigated whether Massachusetts-based Ptech Inc. had any financial relationship with a wealthy Saudi financier, Yasin al-Qadi. The U.S. government designated al Qadi as a terrorist financier in October 2001. Investigators also inquired whether Ptech, a computer software company with many government clients, took any actions that undermined the government. Ptech had security clearance since December 1997 and aided in constructing the Military Information Architecture Framework software used by the Pentagon to access data networks from diverse military computer systems.

Services Used in Furtherance of Terror

Terrorists have used business services to advance their operations. On 9/11 commercial airline customers took control of the planes by force—subsequent to gaining access "legitimately," in purchasing a ticket—and caused thousands of deaths. Meanwhile, postal services were the instrumentality of the commission of the anthrax attacks against media and government targets in fall 2001.

The perpetrators of the Oklahoma City attack in 1995 and the World Trade Center incident in New York in 1993 placed explosive materials in rented vehicles used in the operations. In some instances, use of a business service can actually aid in a terrorist's capture. In the 1993 World Trade Center case, a participant in the plot went to the car rental company (after the attack) to retrieve his deposit for the truck. He was arrested shortly thereafter.

Government investigations related to the 9/11 attacks and other threats (e.g., terrorist sleeper cells driving or sabotaging trucks that transport hazardous waste) gave additional perspectives on terrorists using business services providers. Some of the 9/11 attackers took flight courses at several flight schools in the United States.

Zacarias Moussaoui—at one time believed to be the 20th hijacker on September 11—took courses at a Minnesota flight school. Yet, astute thinking by personnel at the educational facility warned the FBI of some incongruity in Moussaoui's behavior. He sought to pay $8,000 in cash for his classes. Also, Moussaoui expressed an interest in taking off and landing—but not "flying"—large jets significantly above his capabilities.

On the matter of other business services, Iran hired Russian and Ukrainian scientists to assist in the production of enriched uranium or plutonium, the fissible material needed for nuclear weapons. Al Qaeda attempted to recruit Pakistani nuclear experts to craft nuclear and radiological devices for use against the West.

In fall 2003, Pakistani authorities investigated leading Pakistani nuclear scientists for allegedly providing nuclear weapons technology to Iran, Libya, and North Korea. By February 2004, the leading architect of Pakistan's nuclear program, Abdul Qadeer Khan, admitted that for over twenty years he sold nuclear weapons expertise, including blueprints and designs, to those countries. Another prominent Pakistani scientist, Mohammed Faroq, is believed to have provided nuclear material data for personal financial gain.

Mainline service providers—financiers, accountants, lawyers, and doctors—have assisted terrorists groups to carry out their objectives whether knowingly or by deception. Not only do terrorists benefit from the services of some traditional professionals, terrorists actually emerge after studying social sciences (e.g., Saddam Hussein studied law) and physical sciences (e.g., the Popular Front for the Liberation of Palestine's George Habash and al Qaeda's Ayman al Zawahiri studied medicine).

Terrorists use other services providers, such as the media, in a variety of ways. For instance, the media has served as terror targets (e.g., kidnapping and murder of *Wall Street Journal* reporter Daniel Pearl). Also, the media has been used to proliferate terrorists' demands, messages, and propaganda (e.g., national and international media outlets). The media is torn by a duty to deliver news with its moral duty not to contribute to the success of terror groups. Sometimes in doing one— propagating terror group rhetoric—the media undermines the other by aiding terrorists to relay their messages worldwide.

Terrorists from the Greek November 17 group come from diverse occupations including a painter, beekeeper, and a mechanic. Nizar Trabelsi, a former professional soccer player, admitted to be involved in planning a strike on a U.S. military site in Belgium. Imad Eddin Barakat Yarbas, an al Qaeda leader captured in Madrid in November 2001 in connection with recruiting terrorists and providing false documents, was a used cars dealer.

A fall 2002 indictment issued in Detroit alleged that two Moroccan men, Karim Koubriti and Ahmed Hannan, and an Algerian, Farouk al Haimoud, were part of a terrorist sleeper cell. The group is suspected of seeking to obtain false documents, recruit new members, and obtain weapons for future terrorist attacks in Turkey, Jordan, and the United States.

Koubriti and Hannan obtained jobs with an airline caterer near the Detroit Metropolitan Airport. Al Haimoud worked at an ice cream store inside a Detroit airport terminal. It is alleged that they sought to find weaknesses in the airport's security framework. Kourbriti and Hannan also previously worked together at a chicken processing plant in Ohio.

Prior to 9/11, U.S. authorities investigated domestic and foreign charities for allegedly supporting terrorists. For example, Texas-based

Holy Land Foundation for Relief and Development, was implicated for providing funding to Islamic-oriented terrorist groups, such as al Qaeda. The financing of terrorism is discussed in greater detail in Chapter 4.

Criminal Activities of Terrorists and Their Abettors

The criminal activities of terrorists and their abettors are pervasive in the economic system. These illegal activities are wide-reaching, such as: identity theft, drug trafficking, extortion, commercial espionage, and conspiratorial actions.

Identity Theft

The Federal Trade Commission had 162,000 consumer complaints regarding identity theft in 2002, with estimated losses to consumers and businesses at $5 billion and $48 billion, respectively. Identity theft is expected to increase in the future. The research firm, Aberdeen Group, reported that identity theft cost the world economy about $220 billion in 2003. That significant figure is projected to rise nine-fold by 2005.

Terrorist groups use identity theft to integrate their agents into society and fund their operations. Identity theft takes on various forms: fraudulently acquiring credit and bank cards as well as obtaining counterfeit, government-issued documents.

FRAUDULENT CREDIT AND BANK CARDS

Identity theft occurs through simple means (e.g., stealing a victim's mail or search through his garbage for credit card bills) or through more sophisticated methods (e.g., have an employee steal financial information or hack into a web site). Criminals have broken into commercial web sites worldwide (e.g., hacking into Egghead.com led to access of information on 3.5 million credit cards).

Terrorist groups steal credit card information to produce counterfeit credit cards. For example, al Qaeda operatives in the Midwest used skimmers (handheld magnetic readers that grab account numbers) and cc grabbers (devices allowing for the interception of credit card data sent over telephone lines).

Terrorist groups undertake identity theft activities such as obtaining Social Security numbers and financial information (e.g., bank account or credit card numbers). With such data, terrorists request new checkbooks, ATM cards, credit cards, or transfer funds out of a victim's bank account.

The Tamil Tigers terror group had operatives that produced fake credit cards and ATM cards in Canada. An al Qaeda operative based in the United States, Abdelphani Meskini, opened several bogus bank accounts in New York after receiving stolen credit card information from a customer database at a Boston gym.

Theft by computer hackers is also a threat. In February 2003 illegal access to the University of Texas computer system led to exposure of over 50,000 Social Security numbers of faculty, students, and alumni.

In 2002, the FBI received over 48,000 complaints about Internet fraud. A growing Internet scam called "phising" includes luring innocent consumers to fake websites. Once there, individuals reveal their credit card numbers and other sensitive data. It is possible that terror groups may also resort to this sort of tactic in the future—if they are not doing so already.

The growth of international outsourcing of human resources, medical, accounting, and financial services functions accelerates the possibility that extensive financial information (e.g., credit card numbers, bank accounts, brokerage records) and personal information (e.g., Social Security numbers, date of birth, and medical data) could be exploited by terrorists, "sleeper" employees, or their supporters that are based overseas. Other roles outsourced overseas, such as hardware and software development, may allow for sabotage of American company products or resources. While this appears to be a minor issue at this point, it is worth keeping track of given the potential serious harm that can arise should sabotage occur.

FRAUDULENT IDENTIFICATION CARDS

Terrorist groups counterfeit or obtain fraudulent government-issued documents such as driver's licenses, immigration documents, and passports (e.g., 9/11 hijackers paid purveyors of illegal cards). The sale of fake identification cards (e.g., licenses) and documents (e.g., passports) to terrorists makes it more difficult for law enforcement to investigate and undermine terrorist activities. False documents enable terrorists to readily acquire products and services and access to capital.

Mohamed el Atriss, an Egyptian immigrant based in New Jersey, sold fake driver's licenses to two of the 9/11 hijackers. A Minnesota company contacted law enforcement about their concern that el Atriss sought to pay cash for an expensive high-speed copier capable of embossing seals.

Another example of the relationship between some identity crimes and terrorism includes the indictment of Yong Ki Kwon, a South

Korean based in Virginia, on conspiracy to commit passport fraud. The Kwon case was connected to an FBI investigation into terrorist groups in the United States.

In October 2002, Lazahr bin Muhammad Tlilli, a Tunisian believed to be a principal in a European terrorist network, was arrested with false documents in Paris. Anil Hamdani, apprehended in April 2001 in Canada, was found with fake immigration documents from various countries. Hamdani is alleged to have provided fake documents to terrorists. An al Qaeda operative involved in the failed 1999 plot to bomb the Los Angeles International Airport is believed to have stolen the identity of over 20 persons.

Two Tunisian men involved in the assassination of Afghani leader Ahmed Shah Massoud traveled on stolen and falsified Belgian passports. Amor Sliti, a Belgian citizen of Algerian extraction, was a travel agent who provided the falsified passports and visas to individuals seeking entry to Algeria.

If access to fake identification cards is made difficult and expensive, then it will be harder for terrorists to pass themselves off as individuals with government-issued documents. As such, the government must continue to increase the complexity and multi-faceted aspects of identification cards, including greater use of biometrics (e.g., fingerprints, facial recognition, or retina scans).

Making identification documents—driver's licenses, passports, Social Security cards, and birth certificates—difficult to forge will make it more complicated for an undocumented terrorist (or sympathizer) to obtain employment at a legitimate firm. By removing this source of income (and funding) to possible perpetrators, terrorist abettors will be forced to obtain funds in other ways: from overseas sources, domestic donations, or through criminal activities individuals and organizations.

The prospects of a national identification card—undertaken within the rubric of civil liberties—is a positive development. Yet, there must be safeguards in place that information collected is not subsequently available to entities outside the government. The overseas outsourcing of government functions is also under greater scrutiny.

A complicating matter is the acceptance of foreign consulate documents, such as Mexican consulate identification cards (marticula), by U.S. state authorities as a means of identification. More than a dozen U.S. states currently recognize the cards. Yet, such documents, if forged, would enable the subsequent possible granting of legitimate U.S. documents. An updated Mexican marticula, developed in 2002, apparently has more security features that make forgery more difficult.

About 80 U.S. financial institutions accept foreign consulate documents for identification purposes when opening accounts. The acceptance is understandable—in terms of business—as it is estimated that about 18 million documented and undocumented Mexicans have about $450 billion in purchasing power. Other Latin American countries with significant numbers of their citizens based in the United States, including Guatemala and Peru, are developing their own marticulas.

Private industry also runs the risk that terrorist groups will steal or craft fake identification tags that could provide a terrorist with unauthorized access to company facilities (e.g., offices, factories, and warehouses). For instance, terrorists could use false documents to enter water filtration or nuclear power plants.

Drug Trafficking

Terrorist groups finance some other operations through the drug trade, including the transfer of cocaine, hashish, and opium. Hizballah and al Qaeda are active in financing their operations through the cultivation and sale of hashish and opium, respectively. In Afghanistan in 2003 over $2 billion was earned from the cultivation and sale of opium, a portion of which made its way to al Qaeda. Antonio Maria Costa, director of the UN Office on Drugs and Crime, asserted that the war on terrorism cannot be won until Afghanistan gets a better handle on its opium economy.

Drugs are used as currency to purchase armaments for terrorist operations. In September 2002, Hong Kong authorities arrested three men, including a U.S. citizen, following their intention to purchase four Stinger anti-aircraft missiles for ultimate use by al Qaeda. They sought to trade five tons of hashish and half a ton of heroin to fund the transaction.

Numerous other terrorist groups participate in the drug trade to fund their activities including, for example:

- The Kurdistan Workers' Party (PKK) was active in narcotics trafficking, including heroin, in Europe. The PKK used illegal drug sales as its principal source of funding.
- The Revolutionary Armed Forces of Colombia (FARC), National Liberation Army (ELN), and United Self-Defense Forces/Group of Colombia (AUC) in Colombia have connections—of varying degrees—to the drug trade. In 2000, some 70% of AUC's funding was derived from the cocaine trade. FARC, likewise, finances a principal amount of their activities by protecting cocaine smugglers and collecting taxes.

Some 90% of cocaine supplied to the United States originates from Colombia.

- Sendero Luminoso (Shining Path), based in Peru, reportedly imposed levies on drug traffickers.
- The Islamic Movement of Uzbekistan (IMU) is reportedly involved in drug trafficking in Central Asia.
- The Loyalist Volunteer Force, a terror groups in Northern Ireland, is believed to have attempted to smuggle 750,000 ecstasy pills from the Netherlands in one deal interrupted by Dutch and Northern Ireland authorities.
- Terror groups and criminal gangs operating in the Golden Triangle (Burma-Laos-Thailand) are involved in the opium, marijuana, and heroin trade in the region. The Tamil Tigers, based in Sri Lanka, have strong links to drug traffickers in Burma.

U.S. and Canadian law enforcement authorities are investigating the links between Mexican drug trafficking organizations and Arab-American organized-crime groups in both countries. Under this multi-national criminal scheme, Arab gangs in Canada smuggle pseudo-ephedrine (a component of cold medicine) into the United States. Subsequently, pseudoephedrine is sold to Mexican gangs who use it to manufacture methamphetamines. About $10 million of the operation's profits were sent to the Middle East, including some funds to Hizballah.

Terror groups are alleged to participate in counterfeit prescription and over-the-counter drug trade. Involvement in such activities aids terror groups to generate funds. Various terror groups, such as al Qaeda and Hizballah, allegedly have participated in the counterfeit drug trade in the following countries: Germany, Lebanon, Netherlands, Pakistan, Philippines, South Africa, Thailand, and the United States.

On the link between drug traffickers and terrorist groups, Juan C. Zarate, deputy assistant secretary, Terrorism and Violent Crime, U.S. Department of the Treasury, noted that their relationship provides the former military training and weapons supplies, while the latter gain revenue and experience in transferring and laundering money.

Extortion

In the Middle East (e.g., Saudi Arabia), Asia (e.g., the Philippines), Europe (e.g., Spain and Northern Ireland), and Latin America (e.g., Colombia) various terrorist groups extort money from businesses, politicians, and nongovernment citizens. The terrorist group's fee or protection-money affords victims' freedom from physical violence, at least temporarily.

Among terrorist groups that have demanded protection or revolutionary taxes in order to ward-off such attackers are: ETA (Spain), Abu Sayef (Philippines), Tupamaros (Uruguay), and ERP (Argentina). Terrorist groups in Colombia account for nearly 50% of the several thousands of kidnappings taking place there annually.

Other coercive activities include blackmailing military and police officials to either collaborate in criminal activity (e.g., drug trade) or suffer death. Likewise, terrorists force farmers based in FARC- or ELN-controlled lands to grow coca on portions of their farms. ELN and FARC also raise funds by demanding protection money from illegal drug laboratory operators in Colombia. The New People's Army in the Philippines extracted payments from bands undertaking illegal logging operations.

In the Basque region of Spain, ETA extorted money from businessmen and small businesses. ETA is supplied the names of potential targets and forwards a letter that requests a particular contribution—from tens of thousands to hundreds of thousands of dollars—to support the Basque people's "struggle," against Spain. The entity being extorted either pays the amount (or an installment thereof) or awaits further communication, often accompanied with a threat to comply or face death or injury. Also, ETA has "requested," shopkeepers to provide financial support to ETA's jailed members.

There are allegations that al Qaeda obtained millions of dollars of "protection money" from Saudi government and private sources. These funds temporarily assuaged al Qaeda members from attacking Saudi interests at home and abroad.

As evidenced by escalating attacks against Saudi and foreign interests in the Kingdom of Saudi Arabia, particularly in 2003, protection money safeguards victims only until the perpetrator feels other steps are more beneficial. Another lesson is that Saudi appeasement of al Qaeda—both directly and indirectly—actually strengthened the group's capabilities within Saudi Arabia and elsewhere.

Terrorist groups and their sympathizers bribe government officials worldwide, particularly in less-developed countries, in order to have more autonomy in conducting their terrorist operatives. Examples of this include al Qaeda's use of funds to gain favors and protection from the Taliban in Afghanistan and regimes in Sudan.

Commercial Espionage

A terrorist, sleeper, or sympathizer can be posted in a company that will be a future target of a terrorist incident. A terrorist based at an employer could provide information as to the vulnerabilities at a factory or office. The perpetrator could assist in undertaking operations that destroy company or third-party assets.

An attacker can cause damage secretly, such as poisoning water supplies or damaging computer systems. A naturalized American citizen, who served as a truck driver, was arrested in the United States in 2003 on allegations that he scoped out potential terrorist targets including bridges. Alternatively, a disguised terrorist could obtain information as to when a key employee is traveling at home or abroad, hastening a prospective kidnapping.

Conspiracies and Criminals

Some individuals aid terrorists groups by conspiring with sleeper cells. Such individuals provide explosives materials or collaborate in planning attacks. Terrorist groups (e.g., al Qaeda and Hamas) establish web sites worldwide and communicate through the Internet. Often they use encryption software and code words. Terrorist manifestos and calls-to-action are also released through the Internet, telephone, fax, letters, and in person.

Terrorist groups use third parties, including the media, to proliferate their propaganda and messages worldwide. A number of Arabic-language television stations and newspapers released al Qaeda messages. Other broadcasters, in their quest for ratings and given a message's "newsworthiness," have often followed suit. In addition, terrorist groups, such as Hizballah, have used their own television channels, radio networks, and newspapers to propagate their doctrines.

UNITED STATES

In February 2003, the FBI projected that there were several hundred U.S.-based Islamic militants connected to al Qaeda. Furthermore, it is believed that al Qaeda has established an infrastructure in this country that will facilitate another terrorist attack here.

Other militant Islamic groups, such as Lebanese Hizballah and Hamas, are reported to already have a substantial U.S. base that allows for recruitment and fundraising avenues. The FBI contends that such groups are not expected to undertake operational attacks in the United

States because such activities would put at risk their other important functions (e.g., fundraising and recruiting).

Al Qaeda and other terrorist groups either recruited or secreted "sleeper operatives" into the U.S. military. Collaborator soldiers were involved in conducting actual attacks against U.S. targets (e.g., grenade attacks killed several soldiers in Iraq) and espionage (e.g., translators allegedly attempted to smuggle sensitive information from Guantanamo Bay, Cuba, to enemy agents).

In September 2003, U.S. authorities investigated Ahmad Halabi, a Syrian-born translator with the U.S. Air Force based in Guantanamo Bay, Cuba, on suspicion of espionage. More specifically, the government alleged that Halabi transmitted sensitive and classified information to unauthorized individuals and entities, including Syrian government officials, about terrorist detainees held there.

Ahmed Mehalba, a U.S. naturalized citizen and civilian translator who worked in Guantanamo Bay, was indicted in November 2003. Mehalba was charged with mishandling sensitive government information and making untruthful statements to U.S. government officials. It is alleged that he had a computer disk marked "secret," with him during his departure to visit Egypt.

Other conspiratorial acts supporting terrorists in the United States or U.S.-based actors aiding terrorists abroad include:

- In August 2001, the FBI investigated and subsequently the INS detained, Zacarias Moussaoui, a Frenchmen of Algerian descent, following concern by a Minnesota flight school about possible suspicious behavior in relation to learning how to fly commercial jets. Investigations post-9/11 led to a determination that Moussaoui was likely a member of al Qaeda and possibly was planning a September 11-like attack.
- In December 2001, Richard Reid, a British citizen of Caribbean descent, attempted to light an improvised explosive device in his sneaker on board an American Airlines flight from Paris to Miami. After a struggle, the passengers and crew subdued Reid. He subsequently pled guilty to attempting to bring down the plane—packed with nearly 200 passengers and crew—and acknowledged his membership in al Qaeda.
- In May 2003, Iyman Faris, a naturalized U.S. citizen from Kashmir, pled guilty to providing material support to al Qaeda, including investigating possible terrorist targets. Among these

targets were bridges and railroad tracks. While based in the
United States, Faris traveled to Pakistan and Afghanistan in
support of al Qaeda.

- In summer 2003, two individuals, Moinuddeen Ahmed
Hameed and Yehuda Abraham, were charged in the United
States with attempting to finance the sale of missiles to
terrorists. The men were caught during a sting operation.

- In August 2003, U.S. authorities questioned Omar al-Bayoumi,
a Saudi and former employee of the U.S. Embassy in Saudi
Arabia, in relation to his possible connection to two of the 19
hijackers in the 9/11 attacks — Khalid al-Mihdhar and Nawaf
al-Hazmi. It is believed that the aforementioned terrorists
moved to a housing facility in San Diego, where al-Bayoumi
was already living. Al-Bayoumi is also alleged to have provided
them with rent money.

- Eleven men, including nine U.S. citizens, were indicted in
Virginia in summer 2003, with reference to training and
fighting with Lashkar-I-Taiba, a group designated as a terrorist
organization by the U.S. government. Among charges filed
against the cadre were taking hostile actions against nations that
have friendly relations with the United States, in this case,
India. Lashkar-I-Taiba is a Muslim-centric, Kashmiri-based
group seeking to drive out India from a portion of Kashmir.

- In September 2003, the U.S. government arrested Serzhik
Arasappiani, an Iranian based in Florida, on allegations of
smuggling restricted aircraft parts to Iran, a state-sponsor of
terrorism.

- Abdurahman Aalamoudi, a former executive director of the
American Muslim Council, was charged in fall 2003 with
accepting hundreds of thousands of dollars from the Libyan
government, a state-sponsor of terrorism. Alamoudi was
indicted on money laundering, fraud, and connecting illegal
activities on behalf of Libyan leader Qaddafi. Prior to his arrest,
British authorities seized $340,000 in cash from Alamoudi
while he was en route from London to Syria.

- In January 2004, Mohammed Abdullah Warsame of Minnesota
was charged with providing material support and resources to al
Qaeda from March 2000 to December 2003.

- Ryan Anderson, a specialist in the National Guard based in
Fort Lewis, Washington, was charged in February 2004, in

relation to providing intelligence to the enemy, al Qaeda. Anderson's unit, which planned to leave for Iraq later that month, apparently tried to contact al Qaeda operatives — through Internet chat rooms.

Since 9/11, there have been a number of other cases against U.S.-based individuals allegedly connected to al Qaeda or other groups. A few of such cases are set out below:

- In January 2002, the U.S. government indicted John Walker Lindh, a U.S. citizen, on: conspiracy to kill U.S. citizens abroad, providing support and resources to foreign terrorist organizations (including al Qaeda), and engaging in prohibited transactions with the Taliban. In July 2002, he pled guilty to fighting for the Taliban in Afghanistan and carrying explosives. Lindh was captured in Afghanistan in November 2001.
- In Chicago, Jose Padilla, a U.S. citizen, was detained as a material witness on suspicion of involvement with a dirty bomb plot. Padilla is suspected of being a member of al Qaeda.
- In Seattle, James Ujaama, a U.S. citizen, was accused of training with al Qaeda in Afghanistan, providing material support to terrorists, and establishing a terrorist training camp in Oregon.
- In Buffalo, seven suspected al Qaeda associates and members were accused of providing material aid to terrorists. Several were suspected of receiving military training at a terrorist training camp in Afghanistan. Six of the men pled guilty to aiding a terrorist group. The seventh, Jaber Elbaneh, was captured in Yemen in January 2004.
- In Portland, six individuals were accused of supplying material to terrorists.

OUTSIDE THE UNITED STATES

Conspiratorial acts supporting terrorists outside the United States include:

- Indonesia convicted Hutumo Pamungkas of planning to commit terrorist acts. Pamungkas provided funds used to purchase chemicals and a minivan. These items were integral tools used in the Bali nightclub bombings in October 2002, which resulted in 202 deaths.

- In May 2003, Abed Abdul Razak Kamel was sentenced to death in Yemen for the murder of three American missionaries there in December 2002.
- In June 2003, Thai police arrested three individuals, including a doctor and the head of an Islamic school, in connection with planning terrorist attacks against embassies and tourist spots in Thailand. The three are alleged to be linked with Jemaah Islamiyah, an al Qaeda-aligned group in Southeast Asia.
- In summer 2003, four individuals, including a couple and their daughter, were charged in connection with twin bombings in Bombay, India, in August 2003. The attacks caused 52 deaths and many injuries.
- In August 2003, British officials arrested Hadi Soleimanpour, Iran's former ambassador in Argentina, related to his connection in the 1994 bombing of the Jewish Community Center in Buenos Aires, which killed 85 people and injured 200. The attack was believed to have been carried out by Hizballah, the Iranian-backed terrorist group.
- In November 2003, Sajid Badat, was charged with conspiring with Richard Reid (the British national involved in trying to ignited a "shoe bomb," on a Paris-Miami flight in 2001) and others to undertake terrorist attacks.
- During winter 2003, French officials held several men, including two Algerians, with reference to aiding an Afghanistan-trained al Qaeda member move through France.
- Nine individuals were charged in Turkey with belonging to and helping a terrorist organization allegedly involved in a series of suicide bombings in November 2003.
- Irish officials discovered a terrorist training camp, including weaponry and paramilitary equipment, in Ireland in 2003.
- Spanish authorities arrested three Syrians and a Moroccan for their alleged membership in an al Qaeda cell in Spain in 2003.
- During 2002–2003 two Moroccan nationals based in Germany—Abdelghani Mzoudi and Mounir Motassadeq—were prosecuted as accessories to the 9/11 attacks and belonging to a terrorist organization. They are alleged to have been in contact with al Qaeda's Hamburg cell, including 9/11 principal hijacker Mohammed Atta. Motassadeq was convicted and sentenced to 15 years. Mzoudi is awaiting trial.

Conclusion

In sum, this chapter discussed the vast means by which companies and individuals assist terrorists to achieve their goals. It is incumbent upon government authorities to adapt quickly to the evolving methodologies by which terror groups recruit personnel and obtain goods and services. The next chapter delves more closely into the numerous ways terrorist groups raise funds to finance their carnage.

4

Financing Terror

Terror groups raise money through legal and illegal means. Among criminal financing schemes terrorists have utilized include: trading in commodities (e.g., "conflict" diamonds and gold); bogus financial instruments; currency smuggling and wire transfers; drug-trafficking; extortion, money laundering; smuggling products; securities fraud; and scams. Traditional banking and alternative financial services, including hawalas, are used to distribute terror-destined funds. These methodologies contributing to funding terror are covered in this chapter.

Traditional Financial Services

Terrorists, terrorist-front companies, and individuals contributing to terrorist groups have at their disposal the vast, multinational banking system. Bankers and law enforcement officials have difficulties distinguishing account holders with benign intentions from monies earmarked for terrorist goals. Should persons with malevolent intent place their funds at offshore banks with strict secrecy rules then the challenge to uncover terrorist financing is that much more difficult. Terror groups' use of shell companies further complicates undermining terror financing.

Financing the September 11 Attacks

There is evidence that terrorist groups source part of their activities through the receipt of funds from traditional financial institutions (e.g., banks and money-service firms). According to the FBI, the 19 hijackers involved in the 9/11 attacks opened 24 U.S. bank accounts at four different, well-known banks, with an initial average deposit of $4,000.

The 9/11 hijackers received and sent wire transfers from various countries, including Germany, Saudi Arabia, and the United Arab Emirates. They had no consistent pattern of deposits and withdrawals. Moreover, traditional living expenses (e.g., rent and utilities) were not reflected in the accounts. As such, one can presume that they brought with them substantial amounts of cash or obtained additional funds in another manner (e.g., wire transfers or criminal activity).

A number of the 9/11 hijackers purchased traveler's checks overseas and used them in conjunction with credit cards and banks accounts issued by banks in Germany and the United Arab Emirates. Some of the perpetrators used money-transfer firms to wire money among some al-Qaeda supporters.

Additional Financing Activities

U.S. authorities are investigating the ties of Soliman Biheiri, a former banker of the Muslim Brotherhood (an Egyptian militant group), for his possible involvement in financing terrorism. Biheiri established an investment firm, BMI Inc. in New Jersey, with funding provided by a nephew of Osama bin Laden, a Saudi businessmen, and Islamic Resistance Movement (Hamas) leader. It is alleged that Biheiri used BMI to undertake financial transactions with terrorists. Biheiri was sentenced to one year in prison arising from immigration violations.

Hawalas and Other Informal Money Transfer Systems

Informal money transfer systems—including underground banking systems, such as the hawala (run by hawaldars) and hundi systems of the Middle East and Asia—are used for legitimate business, personal, and charitable purposes. In fall 2002, various international organizations, including the United Nations, used hawalas to move money from Pakistani banks to Afghanistan.

Under these systems, brokers based worldwide pay off one another's debts locally in cash through credit systems. The broker takes a commission for facilitating the transfer. In many Muslim nations, hawala networks are integral parts of the financial system. As such, they are not readily replaced. In Pakistan, for instance, it is projected that about $5 billion a year flows through Pakistan's hawala networks. The headquarters of the global hawala system is deemed to be the United Arab Emirates.

Unfortunately, terrorists also use hawalas to move money worldwide.

In November 2001, the U.S. Customs Service froze the assets, and raided the U.S. offices, of a hawala group, Al Barakaat in Minnesota, Washington, Massachusetts, Virginia, and Ohio. Al Barakaat, a Somali-owned group, was implicated in managing, investing, and distributing funds on behalf of terrorists. The United States also blocked the assets of another hawala, Al Taqwa.

Al Barakaat and al Taqwa are alleged to have: raised, invested, and distributed funds for al Qaeda; offered terrorist supporters Internet service and secure communications; and arranged for the shipment of armaments.

Al Barakaat, established in 1989 by Shaykh Ahme Nur Jimale, operated in 40 nations and provided telecommunications, wire transfer, Internet, and currency exchange services. The conglomerate transferred instructions, intelligence, and funding to terrorist cells worldwide.

Al Taqwa, controlled by naturalized Italian citizen, Youssef Nada, was based in four countries: Bahamas, Italy, Liechtenstein, and Switzerland. Al-Taqwa enabled al Qaeda and other terrorist groups to invest funds and transfer cash among its members.

Nonprofit Organizations

Terrorist groups have used charitable organizations and other nonprofits, including religious-affiliated institutions, to raise funds for their operations. Some charitable organizations are formed to fund terrorist activities or are coaxed into forwarding some funds to support terror instrumentalities.

Community solicitations to fund organizations and groups that have both humanitarian and terrorist wings (e.g., Hamas and Hizballah) occur worldwide. Such fundraising activities take place in the Middle East (e.g., Saudi Arabia), Southeast Asia (e.g., Indonesia), Latin America (e.g., Paraguay), Europe (e.g., Great Britain), and North America (e.g., the United States). Private donations to charitable contributions consciously targeted for legitimate humanitarian purposes are sometimes transferred to the military operations of terrorist groups, such as Hamas.

U.S. Charities

A number of U.S.-based charities are alleged to have funded terrorists groups as set out below. For example, in January 2002, the U.S.

government froze the assets of foreign charities, such as the Afghan Support Committee and the Revival of Islamic Heritage Society, allegedly linked to al Qaeda.

In spring 2002, the International Islamic Relief Organization and other Islamic charities and companies in northern Virginia were investigated in connection with: possibly supporting terrorists, conducting money laundering, and carrying out fraudulent activities. In fall 2002, the U.S. government initiated criminal actions against Texas-based Holy Land Foundation for Relief and Development for funding Hamas.

In October 2002, Enaam Arnaout, the executive director of Benevolence International Foundation (BIF), one of the largest Muslim charities in the United States, was indicted on money laundering, material support, and wire and mail fraud charges in support of al Qaeda. Previously, Arnaout was accused of misleading contributors and funneling money to terrorist organizations. There are reports that large U.S. companies unknowingly contributed to BIF because they were unaware of the charity's possible connection to terrorist financing. In February 2003, Arnaout pled guilty to diverting charity contributions to fighters in Bosnia and Chechnya. An al Qaeda member, Jamal Ahmed al Fadi, had alleged that al Qaeda planned to use BIF to fund terrorist operations worldwide.

Likewise, in October 2002, the Treasury Department announced that the Global Relief Foundation (GRF), based in Illinois, gave financial support to the al Qaeda network. Precipitating this revelation was information that an al Qaeda financier, Mohammed Zouaydi, provided over $200,000 to GRF. GRF raised $5 million in 2001.

In February 2003, Sami Omar al Hussayn, a Saudi computer student at the University of Idaho, was accused of raising and distributing funds through the Internet with the object of promoting terrorist attacks against the United States. He was indicted in connection with providing computer consulting services to the Islamic Assembly of North America, a Saudi charity based in Michigan, and transferring $300,000 to the organization. In April 2003, an immigration judge determined that al Hussayn should be deported to Saudi Arabia.

The U.S. Department of Treasury has provided some voluntary guidelines to U.S.-based charities so that they can avoid any association with terror financing. The suggestions are several-fold. First, there is a need to establish an adequate governing structure. Second, ample disclosures and transparency in relation to corporate governance and financing operations are advisable. Third, straight-forward financial practices and accountability are necessary. Fourth, requisite investigation before any funds are distributed to foreign-based organizations.

Overseas Charities

Overseas charities have been used to fund terrorist groups worldwide. Several examples of such activities are noted below. For instance, in fall 2002, U.S. government authorities investigated a U.S. office of a Saudi-linked charity, the SAAR Fund, because the organization transferred funds to Bahamian institutions linked to al Qaeda.

Following a particularly heinous suicide bus bombing in Israel in August 2003, the Palestinian Authority froze more than three dozen bank accounts of Islamic charities that were connected to Palestinian Islamic Jihad and Hamas. Hamas has obtained funding from charities in the Middle East, Europe (United Kingdom, Germany, and France), and North and South America (United States and Paraguay).

Israeli incursions into the West Bank in 2002 revealed documents detailing that the Tulkaram Charity Committee (a front organization for Hamas) provided over $500,000 to Palestinian families whose sons died during the Intifada. Among the recipients were the parents of Abdel Rahman Hamad, a suicide bomber, who killed 23 Israelis and wounded over 100 in June 2001 in an attack in Israel. The Kingdom of Saudi Arabia's Saudi Committee for Aid to the Al-Quds Intifada provided some funds to the Tulkaram Charity Committee.

Another Saudi charity, the al-Haramain Islamic Foundation, provided funds to al Qaeda representatives in Southeast Asia and in Bosnia. Saudi public and private money was also linked to funding the terrorist group Palestinian Islamic Jihad.

Government investigation of possible terrorist links to selected charities, coupled with the negative connotations associated with providing funds to some charities, has had a stifling effect on fundraising for some nonprofits. Some individuals and companies have refrained from donating to charities that are in the same sphere of ethnic, religious, or single-issue charities that are alleged to have terrorist ties.

It is important, then, to continue to probe potential wrongdoers. At the same time, legitimate government concerns should not undermine the civic work that some charities contribute to society. Moreover, donors with truly benevolent aims should not be discouraged to give alms to worthy charities.

Commodities

The intrinsic value and portability of commodities—gold and diamonds—make them particularly attractive to terrorists as forms of exchange. Commodities are used both for laundering funds (e.g., buying gold with illicit funds) and as a source of money (e.g., smuggling or illegally trading diamonds).

Al Qaeda and the Taliban in Afghanistan used gold extensively to finance their operations (e.g., selling opium and heroin in exchange for gold) and as a means to transfer assets. In summer 2002, the Taliban and al Qaeda reportedly shifted significant amounts of gold from Pakistan through the United Arab Emirates (or Iran), with the ultimate destination to Sudan, a former bin Laden base.

Wadih el Hage, a former bin Laden assistant convicted in the 1998 bombings of the U.S. embassies in Kenya and Tanzania, is believed to have used tanzanite—a blue gemstone—to finance al Qaeda operations. Several large U.S. jewelry retailers stopped trading in tanzanite (found only in Tanzania) after revelations that this commodity was linked to bin Laden's operations.

The vastness of the rough diamond sector (e.g., $8 billion annual trade), its limited oversight, and the generally untraceable nature of this asset class, has attracted terrorists to such goods. Several terrorist groups are believed to have used illicit rough diamonds to finance some of their operations.

The Revolutionary United Front of Sierra Leone made at least $25 million per year selling rough quality diamonds. The UNITA rebels in Angola also participated in trading "conflict" diamonds. Hizballah is believed to have purchased diamonds in the Congo, while al Qaeda supposedly acquired diamonds in Sierra Leone.

In fall 2002 over forty nations agreed to a certification plan for diamonds, called the Kimberly Process. Under this system, only legally mined rough diamonds—not associated with illicit sale by warring factions—should reach established markets. Unfortunately, millions of dollars worth of conflict diamonds have already been harvested. These gems now transverse among terrorist groups, their financiers, and unknowing diamond consumers.

Bogus Financial Instruments and Transactions

Juan C. Zarate, deputy assistant secretary, Terrorism and Violent Crime, U.S. Department of the Treasury, remarked that terrorist groups use international commerce to hide their funding sources by having front companies incorrectly price merchandise, double-invoice transactions, and fabricate shipments altogether to disguise or hide the flow of funds.

Terrorist groups and their proxies use bogus financial instruments (e.g., checks) and undertake financial crimes to fund their activities. For example, in July 2002, the U.S. Customs Service arrested a naturalized U.S. citizen, Omar Shishani as he arrived in Detroit from a flight from Indonesia. Shishani, who is believed to have trained at an al-Qaeda camp in Afghanistan, was carrying nine counterfeit cashier's checks totaling $12 million — two for $5 million each, two for $500,000 each, and five for $200,000 each. Apparently, the checks were sophisticated fake checks and issued by the Pomona, California, branch of West America Bank; the bank does not have a Pomona branch.

In fall 2002, Canadian officials arrested Michael John Hamdani, a Pakistani with alleged ties to terrorist groups. Hamdani was purported to have in his possession $600,000 in counterfeit American Express and Thomas Cook traveler's checks.

Both subnational groups and state-sponsors have traditionally engaged counterfeiting. For instance, Hizballah made counterfeit U.S. currency in Lebanon for use worldwide. In the aftermath of major military operations in Iraq in 2003, pro-Hussein insurgents made counterfeit old Iraqi currency and then exchanged them for new Iraqi dinars. Insurgents attacked U.S. convoys that transport new Iraqi currency. With the new funds, insurgents were able to prolong their operations, including compensating their supporters.

Currency Smuggling, Wire Transfers, and Money Laundering

Terrorists and their supporters transfer funds among themselves, using currency smuggling, licensed money transfer operations (e.g., Western Union was allegedly used by some 9/11 hijackers), hawalas (e.g., unlicensed money transfers systems), reverse money laundering (e.g., "clean" funds used to finance terrorist operations), and money laundering (e.g., processing funds raised from criminal activities).

To facilitate such activities, terrorist abettors are used, including apparently law-abiding individuals or families. Terrorist groups also established offshore entities (e.g., financial institutions and companies) and public companies to launder illegal funds.

Currency Smuggling

Terrorist groups move cash by several means, including: wire transfers of less than $4,000 (money-transfer reporting trigger) and $10,000 (bank reporting trigger); money-belted couriers; and sending envelopes of cash sent through of mail courier companies. Examples of some of such activities are:

- A money courier for suspected al Qaeda and other international terrorist groups, Mohamed Suleman Vaid, was stopped in April 2001, trying to smuggle the equivalent of $40,000 from South Africa to Swaziland.
- In July 2002, Allah al-Sadawi, an Egyptian-born imam at a Jersey City mosque, was accused of currency reporting violations. He apparently asked his parents to smuggle a suitcase stuffed with U.S. currency on a flight to Egypt.
- In December 2002, the U.S. government arrested several individuals in Michigan and Ohio in connection with the transfer of about $50 million in cash to terrorist groups.
- In June 2003, French police uncovered $1.3 million in cash at the Paris headquarters of the terrorist group People's Mujaheddin.
- It is estimated that $2 million in foreign cash is provided annually to finance terrorist operations in Kashmir. In October 2003, a couple in Kashmir was arrested with $100,000 in cash—raised in the United States—and destined to finance Islamic militants in the region.
- In December 2003, Syrian officials seized some $23 million in cash from a group of Arabs allegedly linked to al Qaeda. It is believed that such large amounts of money were smuggled, rather than sent electronically, because of greater scrutiny of traditional banking and money-transfer systems.

Wire Transfers

There is evidence that terrorists have used money-service companies to transfer funds among their operatives. Mohammed Atta, initially viewed as a principal of the 9/11 hijackers, is alleged to have used Western

Union to send $15,000 from the United States to other al Qaeda members in the United Arab Emirates. Such revelations emboldened government regulators, including the New York Banking Department, to increase the amount of information that money service customers reveal about themselves.

Now, money service firms require customers to provide their names if the transaction exceeds $3,000. New proposed rules would require customers to provide identification documents, such as a driver's license, passport number, or national identification number. Other safeguards exist as some money service providers can block transactions if an individual's name appears on the Treasury Department's list of people connected with terrorist financing.

On the matter of bulk cash smuggling, the USA Patriot Act, passed in fall 2001, makes it illegal to hide more than $10,000 in currency and move it out of or into the United States if the suspect's intent is to avoid currency reporting requirements.

In December 2002, the U.S. government charged Mohammed Albanna, an uncle of Jaber Elbaneh—an unindicted co-conspirator of six men in upstate New York charged with supporting al Qaeda—for sending $485,000 to unidentified persons in Yemen. Albanna is claimed to have violated the USA Patriot Act because he failed to register his money-transmitting company. The government is investigating whether the funds were distributed to terrorists. Elbaneh was captured in Yemen in January 2004. Likewise, in December 2002, an unlicensed Seattle money services company, Al-Shafei Family Connect Inc., and 12 U.S.-based individuals, were indicted for sending over $12 million in cash and products to Iraq, through international, third-party intermediaries.

Money Laundering

In November 2002, Broadway National Bank pled guilty to felony charges for not filing suspicious activity reports on $123 million in cash deposits as well as not having a program to deter money laundering. The cash deposits—sometimes delivered in duffel bags—were subsequently sent overseas, particularly to Latin America and the Middle East.

While these activities do not appear to be linked to any terrorist groups, there is concern that terrorist groups are replicating this modus-operandi worldwide in an attempt to launder profits from illicit activities. In the case of Broadway, criminals connected to the laundering operations admitted to working with Colombian drug traffickers.

As there are hard fast intersections between Colombian drug traffickers and terrorist groups in that country, the terrorist connection to similar money laundering activities is not far-fetched.

In January 2004 it was disclosed that U.S. authorities were examining transactions at the bank accounts of the Saudi Arabian Embassy in Washington, D.C. In particular, the American government is exploring whether there were any possible violations of money laundering rules, including the use of large amounts of cash.

There is also concern that some of the $300 million spent annually by the Saudi Embassy in the United States might be connected to U.S.-based organizations that promote terrorism. This inquiry follows upon reports that funds from a Washington, D.C.-based bank account of the wife of the Saudi ambassador to the United States, Princess Haifa al Faisal, ultimately made their way to two California-based individuals comprising the 9/11 hijacking team.

Smuggling

Some terrorist groups, such as the Real Irish Republican Army (IRA), are active in smuggling tobacco and counterfeit products. Terrorists and their sympathizers smuggle products in the United States. In June 2002, brothers Mohamad and Chawaki Hammoud of North Carolina were convicted of running a cigarette-smuggling operation. Mohamad was also found guilty of funneling money to Hizballah. The ring, which sold $7.5 million in cigarettes, also arranged for the delivery of military equipment, such as mine-detection gear, blasting equipment, and night-vision goggles to Hizballah.

Other examples of terrorist groups involvement in smuggling products include:

- The Kurdistan Workers' Party (PKK) and Revolutionary People's Liberation Party (DEVSOL) in Turkey established an active arms trafficking ring to finance their operations.
- MIRO, a front organization of al Qaeda, was involved in smuggling weapons into Kenya from Somalia. MIRO also played a role in the 1998 al Qaeda attacks against two U.S. embassies in Africa.
- In fall 2000, the United Self-Defense Forces of Colombia (AUC) received a shipment of 3,000 AK-47 rifles and five

million rounds of ammunition smuggled into Colombia from Nicaragua aboard a Panamanian vessel.

- In August 2002, government authorities in Saana, Yemen, uncovered 650 pounds of plastic explosives found in pomegranate crates.

Securities Fraud

Following the 9/11 attacks, the Securities and Exchange Commission investigated the dramatic rise in short-selling activity in 38 companies during the days preceding the terrorist incidents. Unusual trading and subsequent disproportionate drops in stock prices of airlines, insurers, securities firms, and other companies during the week before the incidents included: AMR Corp., UAL Corp., U.S. Airways, Chubb Corp., MetLife Inc., and Morgan Stanley. Some of the affected companies were major tenants at the World Trade Center or in sectors that would be directly harmed in case of such an attack. The U.S. Secret Service contacted bond traders regarding large purchases of five-year Treasury notes before the attacks. Investigators are examining whether terrorists, or people affiliated with terrorist organizations, bought five-year notes.

Initial reports suggest that the spikes in trading prior to 9/11 were not spurred by terrorist groups. Nevertheless, the reaction of financial markets, particularly segments that are particularly vulnerable (or may "benefit," through increased demand), to terrorist threats or actual attacks, make currencies, stocks, and bonds potentially exploitable by terrorist groups and their financiers.

The Financial Action Task Force on Money Laundering, a UN entity, reported that criminal organizations and terrorist groups also use the securities industry to launder money as well as to generate revenue for their organizations. Also, drug traffickers have been known to manipulate stock prices, including the use of pump and dump schemes (e.g., generate interest in a stock while disseminate misinformation, and then selling the stock prior to the price declining).

Terrorist groups may mislead online investors to unwittingly download a mischievous computer program called Beast. The program apparently enables characters typed on a computer to be relayed to a hacker/terrorist operative. The hacker/terrorist operative would then be able to acquire log-in information and passwords from unsuspecting online investors.

Scams and Bank Robberies

Terrorists raise tens of millions of dollars annually in the United States through scams such as illegally redeeming huge quantities of grocery coupons and collecting fraudulent welfare payments. Terrorist organizations obtain coupons in bulk from recyclers, steal some from printing plants, and counterfeit others.

The coupons are then submitted for redemption by unscrupulous grocers and shopkeepers. These merchants collaborate and share these ill-gotten funds with criminal gangs and terrorists. Funds obtained from redeemed coupons have been used for terrorist support in the United States and abroad, particularly in the Middle East.

Less sophisticated scams and crimes are used as well. Associates of al Qaeda operative Ahmed Ressam shoplifted, stole luggage from tourist hotels, and picked pockets in Canada and the United States. Ressam was captured prior to proceeding with his plan to bomb Los Angeles International Airport during the 2000 millennium celebration.

Dr. Nzih Khatatbeh, a senior official of the Palestinian Authority (PA) Culture Ministry at its embassy in Uzbekistan, was allegedly involved in car theft and counterfeiting (e.g., selling forged diplomatic passports and registration plates to cigarette smugglers). Terrorists may also employ the tactics known as phising, which lures unwitting customers to bogus websites. Once there, customers provide their credit card numbers but never receive any merchandise. Also, terrorist groups have staged bank robberies to obtain funding for their operations (e.g., Weather Underground, Aryan Nations, ERP, and ETA).

State-Sponsors of Terrorism

There is a long record of governments providing terror groups with direct and indirect financial and other types of support (e.g., training, intelligence, operations, and weaponry). Rogue nations utilize terrorist proxies to further their own country's interests. A government's formal, open, and direct belligerent actions would call immediate attention to state-sponsors. Instead, using terrorist groups to carry out operations—assassinations and bombings—enables government-sponsor to claim plausible deniability.

The U.S. government currently signifies several countries as state-sponsors of terrorism, including Iran, Iraq, Syria, Libya, North Korea, and Cuba. During the Cold War, the USSR and other communist countries were involved in supporting instability and terrorism in the West and elsewhere. India has accused the Pakistani government of aiding terror groups such as in Kashmiri-separatist groups.

The PLO obtained some $125 million from the Gulf States. Also, European Union funds earmarked for the Palestinian Authority made their way to establishing an arms workshop and funding members of the terror group al Aqsa Martyrs Brigades.

Hamas has received direct and indirect financial assistance from various Arab countries, including Iran, Iraq, and Saudi Arabia. It is estimated that Iran provides some $3 million annually to Hizballah.

Saudi Arabian funds, including money raised in a telethon, were forwarded to families of Palestinian suicide bombers as "compensation," for their loss. Iraqi President Saddam Hussein also awarded up to $30,000 to the families of Palestinian terrorists involved in suicide operations.

For decades different terrorist groups have learned (or improved) their murderous skills at terrorist training camps worldwide. For instance, in Afghanistan, it is estimated that tens of thousands of individuals were trained at al Qaeda-organized camps. In the a portion of the Philippine island of Mindanao, terror groups such as Jemaah Islamiah, an al Qaeda-linked organization, and the Moro Islamic Liberation Front, a Philippine secessionist terror group, have operated terror training camps. The Filipino and U.S. governments are attempting to capture operatives training there. Terrorist training camps, for groups such as Hizballah, exist in Lebanon.

U.S. Government Responses to Terrorism Financing

Comprehending the link between finance and terrorism, in September 2001, President George W. Bush issued an Executive Order on Terrorist Financing (ETOF). The executive order blocked property and prohibited transactions with persons who commit, threaten to commit, or support terrorism. The 27 terrorists, terrorist organizations, foreign businesses, and charities listed in the ETOF included: al Qaeda/Islamic Army, Osama bin Laden, Ayman al Zawahiri, and the Wafa Humanitarian Organization. Two months later, 22 other entities—all already appearing on the State Department's list of Foreign Terrorist Organizations—were deemed subject to the ETOF provisions.

In October 2001, the Treasury Department announced the creation of the Anti-Terrorist Financing Task Force, Operation Green Quest.

Green Quest sought to: identify, disrupt, and dismantle the financial operations of charities and non-governmental organizations linked to al Qaeda; infiltrate and undermine hawalas and other underground remittance systems connected with terror groups; and assist other nations to identify bank accounts linked to terrorist organizations.

Similarly, in light of the dangers of terrorism financing, the FBI established an interagency Terrorism Financial Review Group (TFRG), whose duties include: conducting full financial analyses of terrorist suspects and their global financial support structures; strengthening financial information flows from abroad; and improving capabilities to identify terror suspects.

In October 2001, the Treasury Department's Financial Crimes Enforcement Network established a Financial Institutions Hotline for financial institutions to voluntarily report to law enforcement agencies suspicious transactions that may relate to recent terrorist activity against the United States. The purpose of the Hotline, operational 24/7, facilitates the immediate transmittal of this information to law enforcement. Also, the USA Patriot Act contains numerous provisions relating to money laundering and increased responsibilities by companies to combat this threat. While such steps are beneficial, given the magnitude of daily banking transactions, it is difficult to impede the transfer of funds to terrorists.

Post-9/11 legislation—including parts of the USA Patriot Act and the International Money Laundering Abatement and Anti-Terrorism Funding Act (MLA)—provides government authorities with additional tools to combating terrorist financing. For example, the MLA provides, in pertinent part, that: foreign financial institutions with assets in the United States now need to accept broad new anti-money laundering obligations as a condition for doing business in the United States; and the government will punish domestic and foreign banks that fail to adhere to high standards to combat money laundering.

In spring 2003, the U.S. Justice Department commenced dozens of additional terrorist financing investigations. In January 2004, the Senate Finance Committee expanded its oversight over terror financing by requesting that the Internal Revenue Service provide financial and tax records of donor lists of two dozen charities and nonprofits that are alleged to have been involved in terror financing.

U.S. law enforcement officials have frozen or seized hundreds of bank accounts, cash, and other assets of individuals, businesses, and nonprofit organizations as well as over $150 million in terrorist assets in the United States since the 9/11 attacks. Such actions have harmed terrorist financing systems, leading terror organizations to shift some of their fundraising schemes to alternatives that are currently less scrutinized.

International Responses to Terrorism Financing

International cooperation in combating terrorist financing has led to many triumphs. Responses to terrorist financing have been undertaken along national, regional (e.g., European Union and Organization of American States), and international fronts (e.g., United Nations). In September 2001, UN Security Council Resolution 1373 called for the prevention and suppression of terrorist financing by means of: criminalizing the direct or indirect collection of funds for terrorists; freezing terrorist funds and those who assist terrorists; and prohibiting persons and businesses from collaborating with terrorists or those that fund them.

Subsequently, in October 2001, the 29-nation Financial Action Task Force (including the United States) adopted eight special recommendations to prevent future terrorist financing activities in their jurisdictions. Some of the improvements sought to change national legislation included: requiring nations to crack down on alternative remittance systems such as hawalas; strengthening customer identification measures for wire transfers; and ensuring that charities are not misused to finance terrorism.

More countries such as Indonesia—the largest Muslim nation (by population) in the world—are adopting stricter "know your customer," rules. Such laws, coupled with greater enforcement, should make it somewhat difficult for terrorists and their sympathizers to utilize traditional finance facilities (e.g., banks and brokerage firms) to launder money.

Some progress against terror financing has also been witnessed in Saudi Arabia, which previously directly and indirectly funded terror groups. In January 2004, the Saudi Kingdom collaborated with the United States to freeze some of the assets of branches of a leading Saudi charity, Al-Haramain Charitable Foundation. There appears to be evidence that African and Asian branches of the foundation were involved in terror financing and weapons procurement. The foundation is believed to have links with the 1998 terror attacks against the U.S. embassies in Kenya and Tanzania.

Conclusion

Terrorist financiers use both traditional and untraditional financial systems to transfer funds. Criminal activities are also used to finance terror operations globally.

Companies, foundations, and individuals that knowingly and directly assist both subnational and state-sponsored terror attacks are part of the problem of terrorism. Greater scrutiny of prospective donations and accelerated government investigations into rogue nonprofits should reduce this menace. More inquiries by individuals, businesses, and other organizations into the true nature of nonprofits will decrease another source of terror financing.

All these efforts to undermine terror financing are crucial. After all, money is the life-blood of terrorism. All steps to prevent perpetrators from obtaining funds are essential to reducing terror threats globally.

5

Security

Without a doubt, the 9/11 attacks were the principal reasons for Corporate America's increased attention to terrorism. In 2002, terrorism was ranked third as a security and management threat in a Pinkerton survey of leading corporations. The post-9/11 greater sensitivity to the threat of terrorism is in sharp contrast to the earlier perception that terrorism is only an irritant to business.

Between 1996–2000, terrorism was never viewed as a top-ten security threat in the annual Pinkerton survey. Likewise, *Security Magazine* reported that terrorism was the number one security concern in a January 2002 survey; it was not among the top ten in the previous year's survey.

The findings in a post-9/11 survey of the International Security Management Association (ISMA), which is comprised of corporate security executives at *Fortune* 500 companies, illustrate the growing importance of corporate security. Of the corporate security directors surveyed, 95% received more support from senior management and nearly 75% foresaw increases in security funding than before 9/11.

Security expenditures at ISMA companies are projected to occur as follows: access controls and physical security (52%), technology security (26%), and more staffing (22%). With reference to the existence of a biological, chemical and nuclear contamination plan, only 35% had one in place prior to 9/11; subsequently, 39% initiated a new plan.

Indeed, one of the most glaring effects of terror's impact on business has been companies' accelerated interest in corporate security issues. This chapter discusses general themes related to corporate security, beginning with its costs. It presents an overview of security service providers. Next, the chapter addresses the importance of information security, risk and vulnerability assessments, risk management, and disaster planning. Finally, it identifies some security responses in a number of industry sectors: real estate, transportation, maritime, aviation, chemicals, and sports.

Security Costs

On the issue of improving security, and the costs associated with it, Adm. James Loy, then head of the U.S. Transportation Security Administration, explained that better security often necessitates greater expenditures. According to a *Security Magazine* survey of companies, the average budget for security products and services in 2002 was $580,851, a 7.3% increase over 2001. In 2002, about 50% of companies reported an increase in spending on security, 37% of budgets stayed the same, and 13% decreased.

Firms must assess prospective threats and undertake security upgrades to reduce such threats. Defenses against terror include fortifying physical and information security. Corporate security costs often include expenditures on: technology, security, and safety equipment; employee training; modifications to logistics and other aspects of conducting business (e.g., the anthrax attacks impacted the way mail was opened); and external security consultants and security guards.

Relevant too, is the factor of return on investment as justification for prospective security measures and budget outlays. For most *Fortune* 1000 companies, security budgets as a percentage of annual corporate sales is .1% or less, Pinkerton found. Indeed, some corporate security directors complain that senior executives too often miss the significant role of securing business operations by harping excessively on the costs associated with asset protection.

As businesses allocate more financial and human capital to corporate security, there is a tension between providing sufficient security and expending exaggerated resources. If a company spends significant amounts of money on counterterrorism measures and no terrorism incident occurs, one questions whether that allocation of resources did its job—because there was no terrorist incident—or it was a waste of money—because no terrorist attack occurred. This issue is less complex if corporate security measures actually stop or reduce the damage from a terrorist attack.

Difficulties exist in responding to terrorist threats, even with adequate funding and training. For instance, business must exert 100% effort, 24-hours a day. As witnessed by terror plots stymied globally since

9/11, terrorists need to succeed only occasionally while security always needs to be at its best.

Another difficulty is the existence of a nearly unlimited number of potential business targets (e.g., offices, retail stores, factories, and warehouses), yet limited financial, human, information, and temporal resources. Thus, the role in assessing risk and protecting more likely targets over others is one seemingly sensible approach.

Should a firm not spend adequate funds on corporate security, then it runs the risk of becoming a target of terrorism. An obvious example is the September 11 attack. After all, better security at U.S. airports, coupled with better intelligence and law enforcement capabilities (and cooperation) on 9/11, probably would have prevented some of the four separate hijackings on that fateful day.

Ignoring the advantage of hindsight, inadequate security at several airports on 9/11 enabled the perpetrators access to the planes. This, in turn, led to the destruction of some 3,000 lives coupled with: billions of dollars in property damage; huge declines in equity markets; and major negative long-term effects on airlines, tourism, and hospitality sectors; military incursions in Afghanistan; and numerous other consequences.

Government expenditures aimed at reducing terrorism are manifold and run in the billions of dollars. The Department of Homeland Security's fiscal year 2004 budget was $37.6 billion. Of that total, $6.8 billion was allocated to modernize the U.S. Coast Guard, including more funding for Maritime Safety and Security Teams (MSST). MSST have 20 teams, each comprised of 90 individuals used to provide port security, particularly in relation to safeguarding bridges, nuclear power plants, passenger vessels, and ships carrying hazardous cargo. Also, $330 million was earmarked for the U.S. Visitor and Immigrant Status Indicator Technology (US-VISIT) Program, aimed at keeping better track of non-citizens as they transverse into and out of this country.

In the face of extensive terror attacks against Israel targets since 2000, that nation is building a security fence along parts of the West Bank. The proposed 450 miles of fences is projected to cost about $1.5 billion. The Israeli government envisions that these fences will result in a decline in the number of terror attacks arising from the West Bank.

Too Much Money in One Place?

Business and government tend to focus excessive attention on the most recent terrorist attack or threat. In turn, firms—sometimes spurred by government and customer pressures—spend large amounts of money and human resources on the sector that was targeted. At the same time, government and industry often fail to pay attention to similar or analogous threats (e.g., aviation security is strengthened although ground transportation is fairly weak).

Following the September 11 attacks, when commercial planes were used as instruments of terror, the government and the aviation sector called for huge improvements in aviation security. The results included hundreds of millions of dollars allocated to purchase bomb detection and other equipment. Likewise, the role of aviation security was moved from the private sector into government hands—the federalization of the workforce. New rules and methodologies were used to counter terrorist threats in the aviation context.

Unfortunately, security at other transportation modes (e.g., passenger trains and public transportation—buses, trains, and subways) remains relatively weak, despite some improvements. Several positive developments in Washington, D.C.'s mass transit system include efforts to: improve security at bus garages and rail yards; increase the number of police officers patrolling stations, trains, and buses; and install additional equipment.

Only after the multiple bombings on commuter trains in Madrid in March 2004, did U.S. and European authorities exhibit more attention to ground transportation. Additional resources—uniformed and undercover police, bomb-sniffing dogs, and metal detectors—have been deployed with greater frequency at train and subway stations in the United States and abroad.

Greater security efforts must also take place against potentially soft targets, especially at businesses where the potential for numerous civilian casualties exists (e.g., movie theaters, indoor and outdoor sports stadiums, supermarkets, and restaurants). While it may be difficult to convince some businesses to take improved security steps—due to costs or undermining the customer "experience"—their perspectives will change should customers demand better security measures once a terror attack occurs.

Security Providers

Security services have witnessed greater receptivity by corporate clients. One delineation of corporate security services includes: executive protection, risk and vulnerability assessments, advance operations, site security surveys, information security, project risks, crisis management, security audits, and incident responses.

With reference to overseas threats and travel safety, some firms offer country studies, itinerary planning, and 24-hour crisis response. As with any other service provider, it is critical for the prospective client to ensure that the engaged corporate security firm has the capabilities to carry out its assignment.

Corporate security firms, in concert with manufacturers, can provide other safeguards such as integrated electronic security systems, including: access control systems, CCTV systems, intrusion detection, electronic imaging, optical turnstiles, and custom security consoles. Security product dealers and integrators saw the largest increases in post-9/11 sales from corporate offices, utilities and communications facilities, transportation facilities, public buildings, and industrial and educational facilities, *SDM Magazine* reports.

Some firms are utilizing protective measures such as bullet-proofing boardrooms and establishing "safe rooms," at the office. Other businessmen are enrolling in courses on executive protection courses and bomb detection. Additionally, firms use security guards to protect senior executives at work, at home, and while traveling—especially abroad. Also, extraction teams and medical emergency providers have received welcome attention due to concerns about employee travel overseas. There is, however, increasing understanding that highly visible executive protection may, at times, actually invite attention (and attack) to an executive.

Other service providers aid companies with supply chain resilience processes, particularly in light of U.S. government's C-TPAT security compliance program (discussed extensively in Chapter 6). Booz Allen, for instance, assists firms in this regard by: collecting supply chain data for risk assessments; gauging supply chain resilience levels; developing company-wide exposure to supply chain resilience; identifying and implementing supply chain resilience measures; and evaluating the firm's supply chain modifications.

Cyber-security services offered by firms include: computer forensics, penetration and vulnerability testing, and incident responses and investigations. A number of organizations and companies have joined forces to craft recommendations and best practices to assuage the threats of cyberterrorism.

Further security issues involve whether to take care of the issue in-house or to use third-party service providers. The benefits of using a managed security services provider include: hiring the requisite expertise rather than trying to train it in-house; often, lower costs; 24/7 coverage without the employee costs associated with maintaining such manpower; and having an external party to "blame," if a problem should arise.

The American Society for Industrial Security (ASIS) proffers a number of antiterrorism security measures that can be introduced by firms at minimal expense. Among some counterterror recommendations are: maintain situational awareness of world events and ongoing threats; encourage personnel to take notice and report suspicious packages; require two forms of photo identification for all visitors; increase the number of visible security personnel; establish partnerships with local government authorities to craft intelligence and information sharing relationships; and review current contingency plans or develop and implement procedures thereon if none are in place.

The corporate security director (or chief security officer) actively participates in determining appropriate security expenditures. Given the importance of the position, coupled with the need for both physical and information security skill sets, it is sometimes difficult to find the right candidate for the appropriate company.

While some sectors have delayed hiring security personnel (or added these duties to employees with other primary functions) several sectors, such as financial services, pharmaceuticals, and airlines, have actively hired such professionals. Additionally, the turf wars between the roles of the chief information officer and corporate security officials are another complicating factor in this matter.

Information Security

The crucial role of technology in the modern economic system—from telecommunications to financial markets to the defense sector—justifies paying greater attention to information security. The importance of safeguarding information technology is supported in an Internet Security Alliance (ISA) September 2002 report. The study found that 90% of firms acknowledged that information security was critical to the survival of their business. Yet, 30% answered that their current plans for dealing with technology threats were insufficient, although 50% sensed a greater urgency given the post-9/11 era.

In light of such threats, the ISA issued recommended information security practices for senior managers covering issues such as: general management, policy, risk management, security architecture and design, user issues (accountability and training; adequate expertise), system and network management (access control, software integrity, secure asset configuration, backups), and authentication and authorization (users; remote and third parties).

Depending on the size of the company, the issue of information security is covered by one (or a combination) of the following: corporate security director (or chief security officer, CSO), the chief information officer (CIO), and chief information security officer (CISO). The CISO at ABN Amro North America had an $18 million technology risk management budget and 66 security employees in North America.

Risk and Vulnerability Assessments

Risk

The ramifications of the post-9/11 era, include heightened risk with regard to physical and economic damage. Measures to reduce risks at offices and businesses include: adding or acquiring security guards, surveillance equipment, metal and bomb detection equipment; and buying detectors of chemical and biological agents, and machines that can irradiate mail. Improved training of security and office employees also affect competition and profitability. Industries and companies that fail to respond to terrorist risks may save capital by not purchasing antiterrorism products and services. However, such firms also run a higher risk of human and financial costs if an incident does occur.

The unpredictability of terrorist attacks and their negative consequences in physical, psychological, and financial terms may raise the price of risk. According to Professor Howard Kunreuther of the University of Pennsylvania, manifestations of terrorist activities, such as those of 9/11, will force executives to increasingly weigh untraditional hazards and political violence in their business and risk calculations. The scope of uncertainties will make decision-making difficult for executives and investors, Alan Ackerman of Fahnestock & Company stated. Ross Perot Jr., president and chief executive officer (CEO) of Perot Systems Corp., observed that terrorism is a risk that businesses will have to weigh.

The insurance industry, hit with about $50 billion in property, casualty, and other claims as a result of 9/11, capped potential damages and set premiums at higher levels to lessen the formidable risks associated with insuring terrorist events. Corporations are responding to such risks by increasing security, building alternative sites, purchasing insurance, and modifying logistics at their firms.

Risk and Vulnerability Assessments

An integral step of improving a company's understanding of the threats and possible responses that may exist includes the use of Risk and Vulnerability Assessments. As such, below is an overview of one type of Risk and Vulnerability Assessment that would assist a company in determining what terrorist threats and political risk issues may exist relative to their activities in the United States and abroad.

A formal risk and vulnerability assessment generally takes into account the following issues: the company's size, sector, product and service lines; product and service characteristics (benign or lethal; component parts; ancillary services); types of customers (e.g., private sector, government, military); visibility of the products and services, management, investor relations (e.g., publicly-held company); location of facilities and operations; domestic and international operations; and existing corporate security and business continuity measures in place.

An analysis of existing and future trends in terrorism is worth keeping in mind, including: types of attacks (e.g., cyberterrorism), location of attacks (e.g., Asia), perpetrators of attacks (e.g., al Qaeda), impetus for attacks (e.g., kidnapping—financing and/or increasing visibility of the group), and targets of attacks (e.g., business—transportation, energy, or tourism). Analyzing these developments in relation to possible threats against a company's operations and personnel in the United States and overseas follows. Subsequently, recommendation of possible corporate security and related measures in light of the findings are provided.

Also, consulting firms offer on-site survey teams, information technology and emergency operations tests, and simulated attacks to adduce the vulnerability of high threat facilities and critical infrastructure to terror attacks.

Political Risk and Cyber Insurance

U.S. companies increasingly weigh political risk issues when conducting business abroad, particularly in emerging markets. Political risk insurance, offered by firms such as AIG Global, is designed to protect the insured against losses that result from: confiscation, expropriation and nationalization, currency inconvertibility and non-transfer, political violence, and contract frustration. Political risk and insurance specialists, including Aon, create political risk exposure analyses that combine country risk analysis with previous insurance claims.

Companies purchase political risk insurance from private companies, national entities (e.g., Overseas Private Investment Corporation), or international organizations (e.g., Multilateral Investment Guarantee Agency). The specter of terrorism may even cause selected foreign investors to consider the risk of terrorism when calculating whether to undertake an investment in the United States. The future will show whether companies will find it necessary and financially feasible to obtain political risk insurance.

Given the growing prevalence of abductions of foreign businessmen, particularly in South America and Asia, kidnapping insurance has demanded greater attention as well. Due to the risks associated with travel and doing business in some developing countries (e.g., Indonesia, South Africa, and Colombia) and newly industrialized nations (e.g., Brazil), some corporate security directors travel to such regions in person to assess for themselves whether their companies should do business in such locations. Security is particularly important to private contractors who aid U.S. armed forces in Iraq and Afghanistan. Also, journalists and other professionals who work in war zones, such as Iraq and Afghanistan, are cognizant of the utility of private security protection.

Another insurance offering relevant to corporate security is the use of cyber insurance. Cyber insurance can provide coverage for network security failures liability and financial loss resulting from data damage, destruction, and corruption. Also, cyber-extortion and cyberterrorism coverage is available. Given the increase levels of cyber attacks and cyberterrorism, the insurance vehicles may reduce company risks.

Risk Management and Disaster Planning

Given the threat of terrorism, companies are devoting more attention and resources to the creation and maintenance of effective risk management and disaster planning programs. Although the threat to any one company in the abstract may appear small, firms that prepare for crises have an easier time resuming and recovering operations if disaster strikes.

According to an IDC August 2003 poll, nearly 70% of companies reported that they are better prepared for accessing critical data than prior to the 9/11 attacks. IDC projects that information security and business continuity spending will accelerate from $70 billion in 2003 to $116 billion in 2007. An AT&T Business Continuity and Disaster Recovery Planning August 2002 Report found that a majority of business with 100 or more employees recognized the need for implementing and testing business continuity/disaster recovery planning.

Crisis management planning relates to providing immediate corporate response to acute crisis situations (e.g., safety, media, financial, and legal). Along those lines, a December 2003 American Management Association survey found that 64% of companies crafted a crisis management plan. However, only 42% undertake routine drills or simulations to test their crisis management plan. Corporate security experts underscore the need to practice crisis management plans frequently through training employees and running crisis simulations.

Gartner, the research firm, has proposed adoption of a resilient virtual organization (RSO) perspective—the intersection of resilience and virtual operations—to aid companies in case of terror attacks. RSO recommends adoption of resilience principles into its business operations, security mechanisms, people selection, workplace development, communications networks, and architecture.

Disaster recovery planning addresses the recovery of information technology that supports business processes. While business continuity/recovery planning deals with resuscitating critical non-information technology processes, offices, and supply chains as well as manual operating procedures.

Other issues related to crisis planning include: establishing and training a crisis team; designating a crisis management headquarters; having defined contingency plans; adopting notification and action procedures; creating a best practices guidelines on evacuation and business continuity matters; and undertaking post-crisis analysis.

In light of the damage inflicted during the 9/11 incidents, previously hesitant companies are investing in expensive backup sites, data storage software and services, and emergency/contingency planning. A number of banks and securities firms adopted a number, or all, of these measures following the bombings of the World Trade Center in 1993. Damage caused by the September 2001 attacks was thereby less pervasive—at some companies—due to the existence of data storage capabilities.

Oppenheimer Funds, whose 598 employees at 2 World Trade Center survived, had its computers backed up every evening at a remote location: a Denver, Colorado, office. Due to New Jersey-based backup measures, Dow Jones—based at 1 World Financial Center (all of its 800 employees there survived)—had its web sites, e-mail, and news wire services functioning even in the aftermath of the attacks. Two World Trade Center-based Aon Corp. suffered no data losses due to backup systems. Tragically, about 175 Aon employees were killed during the attacks.

The New York Stock Exchange will likely establish a second trading floor on a different power and communications grid than on the exchange's main floor. Other contingency plans might include shifting trading to other stock exchanges in the United States or abroad. The threats to physical facilities, such as stock exchange floors, may lead to greater use of electronic markets and greater reliance on technology than was the case before the attacks. More use of fortified and remote locations, in conjunction with geographical dispersal of company assets, is expected.

Instead of establishing duplicate, fully functional sites for use in case of a disaster, some entities request key personnel to regularly bring key computer diskettes and data home for safekeeping. In the future, it would be wise for businesses to pay greater attention to data storage, backup sites, contingency planning, and security software in light of the devastating consequences of catastrophic terrorist attacks. Likewise, greater cooperation among firms and with government actors will be critical to reduce the damage of exogenous factors.

A self-regulating and enforcement organization, the National Association of Securities Dealers (NASD), whose members include exchanges, broker dealers, electronic communications networks, and other organizations, set out recommendations for business continuity programs for member firms. Likewise, a fall 2002 draft interagency (Federal Reserve, Comptroller of the Currency, and Securities and Exchange Commission) report identified broad consensus on three business continuity objectives that have special importance after September 11. It was deemed necessary that firms ensure rapid recovery and timely resumption of critical operations following a wide-scale, regional disruption or during a loss a major operating location. Furthermore, firms should undertake ongoing use or robust testing of critical internal and external continuity arrangements to ensure their effectiveness and compatibility.

Unfortunately, a February 2003, General Accounting Office (GAO) report found that various financial and securities firms had not undertaken sufficient steps to safeguard the rapid resumption of trading in the event of a major terrorist attack. The report found some weaknesses in primary sites and several firms had no backup facilities.

Sector Responses

It is important to gain an appreciation of security measures undertaken by some industries since the 9/11 attacks. Some of the security matters addressed by various sectors—real estate (apartments, retail, and government buildings), transportation (ground, maritime, and aviation), chemicals, and sports—are highlighted below.

Real Estate

With reference to safeguarding real estate, a number of issues are relevant. The real estate industry would benefit from architectural, engineering, construction, and other improvements (e.g., use of gates) that make buildings more resistant to terrorist attacks. Also, safety, communication, and evacuation procedures in case of attack (e.g., improved fire systems and lighted stairways) should be revisited. There was speculation that better evacuation procedures at the World Trade Center on 9/11 would have saved many lives. Along those lines, training owners, building managers, security personnel, and tenants with reference to comprehending risks and evacuation measures is highly advisable. Sharing best practices in terms of construction, security, and evacuation costs related to fortifying buildings will be beneficial.

APARTMENT BUILDINGS

In May 2002 the FBI issued warnings of possible bombings of apartment buildings by al Qaeda operatives in the United States. Subsequently, apartment owners provided security tips and guidance to its residents. For instance, apartment residents were instructed to report suspicious people or activities at the apartment community. Due to the same threats, the National Multi-Housing Council suggested that apartment building operators verify information of prospective residents, including prior work history, visa information, prior addresses, and school registration for foreign students.

The Security Industry Association recommends a number of security products and services that might ameliorate security measures at apartment buildings. For example, at the building's entrance, landlords should install high-security locks and doors, electronic locks, CCTV cameras, two-way voice communication, biometric devices, and card readers. Adding physical barriers, fence detection systems, security officers, motion detectors and electronic beams, CCTV cameras, microwave perimeter intrusion system, and motion-triggered lighting would strengthen perimeter security. Installation of high-security locks and doors, electronic locks, CCTV cameras, two-way voice communications, biometrics, card readers, and security officers would likewise fortify a housing complex.

RETAIL

The 9/11 attacks focused attention of property managers of high-rise office buildings, particularly those with symbolic value (e.g., Sears Tower and Empire State Building). Yet, there have been numerous terrorist attacks worldwide against retail property such as shopping malls (e.g., India and Colombia) and fast-food restaurants (e.g., South Africa and Israel).

Multiple bomb threats against IKEA stores in Europe during December 2002 raised once again the need to take note of security at retail stores. National retailers acknowledged that such incidents cause the retailers to reexamine their security measures. In light of terrorist threats, the International Council of Shopping Centers warned its members to tighten security at critical points—parking facilities, access to ventilation systems, and cargo areas. Some malls have increased the quantity of uniformed security and bomb-sniffing dogs.

Unfortunately, further review of shopping security measures appears necessary both here and abroad. After all, shopping malls in the United States have few security measures in place that would prevent a terrorist attack (e.g., checking bags of all persons entering the mall and/or using metal detectors/explosives detectors). A summer 2002 police investigation found that a number of large shopping malls in southern Israel had inadequate security measures in place. For example, security guards failed to stop simulated suicide bombers, bombs, and car bombs from entering malls.

GOVERNMENT BUILDINGS

Security concerns relating to government buildings include government's tenancy in office buildings, embassies, and military sites. The Federal Protective Service (FPS), based in the Department of Homeland Security, provides security for federal government tenants. The FPS, in conjunction with the Interagency Security Committee, is collaborating with building owners and managers to establish reasonable security standards for leases issued to government tenants by private sector owners.

In November 2002, the General Services Administration discussed the possibility of creating distinct levels of security at buildings based on the type of work performed and the number of employees at particular sites. At the high-end of the security spectrum, features such as access control and blast-resistant windows would be the norm.

Many U.S. embassies and consulates have been subjected to various degrees of terrorist attacks, including suicide bombings. The simultaneous suicide bombings at the U.S. embassies in Kenya and Tanzania in 1998 illustrate well the vulnerability of some of our overseas outposts.

Subsequent to those events, the U.S. government accelerated security funding and reviewed fortifying embassies. A number of steps are relevant to strengthening embassies and protecting embassy staff, such as: instituting public access control (e.g., controlling the flow of people), establishing perimeter security program (e.g., denying penetration by mobs and intruders), maintaining adequate residential security (e.g., protecting employees and families), allowing access to armored vehicles (e.g., to protect employees going to and from work), and providing security awareness training (e.g., to help employees and their families protect themselves).

Since major combat operations in Iraq concluded in September 2003, police and military outposts have been subjected to suicide bombing and other attacks. Such incidents create awareness of the possibility that similar targets—as well as fire stations—might be targeted in the West. Such operations would undermine medical services as well as investigative and protection capabilities subsequent to an attack.

Ground Transportation

Transportation security measures relating to mass transit, motor coaches, maritime, and aviation are discussed below.

MASS TRANSIT

According to a September 2002 GAO report, mass transit agencies in the United States face major challenges in securing their systems. After all, the extensive ridership of some systems—often found in highly populated areas—makes them enticing targets: easy access, high ridership, compact area, economic importance, economic infrastructure, and minimal existing security. At the same time, fully securing the systems—with metal detectors, photo identification, and the like—is costly, time-consuming, and impractical, as mass transit characteristics include easy access and speed.

Some attacks against U.S. mass transit are inevitable should intelligence, law enforcement, and military actions fail to prevent terrorists from reaching U.S. shores and conducting such attacks. Also, prospective threats from terrorist already in the United States should not be discounted.

The main obstacle to secure transit systems is insufficient funding, the GAO proffers. Estimates of selected security improvements at only eight transit agencies would cost $711 million. An intrusion alarm and closed circuit television system for one portal of a transit agency would cost about $250,000. Customers might be required to pay a security fee to help defray such costs.

Nearly 200 deaths and about 1,500 injuries occurred following the explosion of ten bombs on Madrid's commuter train system in March 2004. This attack led to a buttressing of security measures on mass transit systems in some parts of Europe and the United States. Increased security measures included: uniformed and undercover police; "train" marshals (in the United Kingdom); bomb-sniffing dogs; surveillance cameras; incorporation of explosives, biological, chemical, radiological, and nuclear detection equipment; and requiring photo identification when purchasing selected train tickets.

MOTOR COACHES

The Transportation Security Administration (TSA) provides the following guidance to motor coach companies and employees vis-à-vis terror threats. It is incumbent upon personnel to monitor suspicious activities and items. For example, employees should look for people who: are not where they are supposed to be (e.g., in restricted areas); use video cameras and photos; abandon items and leave quickly; and possess a weapon or a dangerous item. Additionally, motor coach workers are requested to look for: abandoned and hidden items; suspicious or dangerous objects (e.g., canisters and metal boxes); items emitting gas or vapor; and devices connected to wires and timers.

Maritime

The U.S. government is having a difficult time monitoring the inflow of legal and illegal goods and human traffic along its several thousand miles of land borders between the United States and its neighbors to the north and south—Canada and Mexico, respectively. Because U.S. maritime borders are significantly larger than land borders, greater probabilities exist that terrorists and/or their weapons will enter into the United States undetected.

As the majority of U.S. trade travels by water, an instrument of business—shipping containers—might be used to "import" terrorists and their weaponry (e.g., biological, chemical, radiological, or nuclear weapons). Such a possibility gives grave cause for concern. This is particularly so when one considers that annually about 5.7 million shipping containers enter the United States by sea and only a small percentage thereof are searched.

Government measures to prevent the entrance of terrorists or their weaponry through U.S. shores include: using radiation detectors and large X-ray equipment to scan containers; identification of high-risk cargo; and use of tamper-evident containers allowing for quick recognition if there has been any tampering. Additional maritime funding has been allocated to ameliorate dockside and perimeter protection at ports, information sharing, and security training.

Also, the U.S. government seeks to forge strong security and cargo inspection agreements with 20 foreign ports that send cargo (about 33% of all U.S. imports) to the United States. Protection of ports themselves is complex as material (e.g., ships, containers, merchandise, terminal equipment, and trucks) and human assets are potentially vulnerable to terrorist attack.

As such, an expansive, multi-layered security approach is paramount. Among the items that should be kept in mind include: monitoring of authorized personnel and visitors; review and control of cargo and containers; real-time data analysis; expansive use of relevant technology (e.g., X-ray and detection equipment, CCTV, smart cards, and radio-frequency identification tags); and better intelligence and information analysis.

The U.S. government has provided some $1 billion for port security although more funding is needed to provide adequate protection at U.S. ports. By January 2004, about 2,500 port facility operators, including public port authorities and private businesses, submitted security plans to the Coast Guard. Likewise, about 10,000 vessels provided security plans to the government.

The Coast Guard's role in combating terrorism has gained greater prominence than before 9/11. The Coast Guard obtained additional funding for: ship tracking; information technology; marine-safety and security SWAT teams in major ports; infrastructure protection; increased domestic and international outreach; and maritime escort and safety patrol.

Aviation

Since the 9/11 attacks, aviation security has undergone numerous modifications. Security screening was improved and federalized. Baggage screening is more thorough. Cockpit doors were reinforced. Security training for flight crews was overhauled and improved. Pilots are permitted to carry firearms. Flight crews may use stun guns. More air marshals have been mobilized. In January 2004, air cargo pilots were recruited to commence firearms training under a new U.S. government program. Depending on the level of the nationwide terrorism threat system, airports have prohibited curbside check-in and conducted searches of vehicles entering the airport terminal.

Interaction and cooperation among personnel in airport screening, intelligence and law enforcement, and airlines have accelerated, particularly with reference to designating certain passengers as being security risks. More specifically, Delta Airlines initially agreed to participate in a new government program, CAPPS-II.

CAPPS-II affords the U.S. government access to specific data on prospective passengers, including: name, date of birth, home address and telephone number, and travel plans. Using this data, CAPPS-II designates a threat level to a passenger's boarding card (green: standard security procedures; yellow: additional security required; and red: prohibit boarding). The attributed risks are due to various factors, including whether cash was used to buy the ticker or a one-way ticket was acquired.

Delta's participation in the program led to consumer pressure, including a potential boycott of the airline. Customers had complained about the government's access to their personal data. As such, Delta decided to withdraw from the program. Rehabilitation of CAPS-II is in the works. Another airline, JetBlue, was similarly criticized for releasing passenger data to a Defense Department contractor.

In fall 2002, the Transportation Security Administration announced that it would stop the use of random security checks at boarding gates. The announcement itself seems silly in that it gives a heads-up to potential terrorists. With such knowledge, terrorists can plan to get their weapons from an accomplice at the other side of the security gate. An ingredient of effective security is not providing prior notice to terrorists of disparate safeguard measures.

The randomness of some aviation security procedures include searches without regard to age (e.g., elderly), physical capabilities (e.g. wheel-chair bound; assuming not faking malady), and other nonintelligence-based factors. Such methodologies undermine the security system. There are severe ethical and legal issues when trying to implement security based on "profiling" ethnic or racial features.

Yet, profiling based on intelligence is another matter. Intelligence-focused screening, including face-to-face interviews of selected passengers, would be constructive. In that regard the CAPPS II Program appears to be a reasonable step that would aid aviation security. Obviously, the use of metal and bomb detectors is necessary as well.

In December 2003, the European Union (EU) agreed to provide the Department of Homeland Security data on passengers flying from the EU to the United States. The information that will be provided includes the names, telephone numbers, and credit card numbers of passengers. U.S. authorities will use the information to investigate terrorist threats and other criminal activity.

Several European and Mexican flights bound to the United States were grounded due to security reasons in December 2003. Growing fear of an aviation security threat led the U.S. government to demand foreign air carriers to attach an armed foreign air marshal on selected flights should terror threats require such steps.

Another complement to border security, and thereby aviation security, was the January 2004 implementation of the U.S. Visit Program (US-VISIT). Under this framework, U.S. authorities are permitted to fingerprint and photograph selected foreign visitors at U.S. airports and ports. The program allows for the U.S. government to obtain additional information about visitors from many countries.

The data collected will be compared against domestic and international databases of terrorists and criminals. Under US-VISIT, the U.S. government will have knowledge if, and when, a foreign visitor actually leaves the country. Almost thirty, mostly European countries, are exempt from US-VISIT. Other exceptions to the fingerprinting and photographing requirement are travelers under the ages of 14 and those over 79.

The US-VISIT has resulted in a mixed response by foreign visitors: some understand the need to strengthen security in a post-9/11 environment, while others view it as unfair and humiliating. Several countries have responded to these measures by, for instance, requiring U.S. citizens visiting foreign lands to likewise be photographed and fingerprinted (e.g., Brazil). Various nations have raised visa application fees and lengthened the time it takes Americans to obtain such documents in response to greater scrutiny of their citizens' by U.S. authorities.

Chemicals

Government and industry officials have raised concerns about protecting chemical facilities as they are potentially attractive terrorist targets. The transport of chemicals and their vulnerability in transit are likewise factors that need to be included in the security parameter.

As such, the American Chemistry Council (ACC) has established a security program that requires it members to assess chemical plant vulnerabilities, including physical and cyber threats. Vulnerability assessments, including those developed by industry and government entities, consist, in part, of scenario-focused approaches (e.g., possible effects of specific types of attacks). Other industry groups, such as the Synthetic Organic Chemical Association and the American Institute of Chemical Engineers (AICE), have also participated in improving security measures in this industry.

Greater government participation in designating high-risk plants and expanding industry self-regulating measures should prove helpful. The proposed Chemical Facilities Security Act of 2003 already envisions such steps. This proposed legislation would mandate chemical firms to undertake broad vulnerability assessments and site security plans. It is worth noting that some laws already exists relative to vulnerability assessments at chemical plants that use hazardous substances.

Sports

Security has been a key planning issue of high profile sports events since the Munich Olympics attacks. At that summer 1972 event, Palestinian terrorists killed 11 Israeli athletes and coaches. At the Atlanta Olympics in 1996, violence again breached the global games when a bomb blew up in Atlanta's Centennial Park. One person died and more than 100 were injured in the attack. A dramatic rise in financial and manpower resources earmarked for international sporting events has taken place since the Munich incident. Safety and security costs during the 1980 Winter Olympics in Lake Placid were $23 million. By the 1996 Summer Olympics in Atlanta safety and security costs jumped to $101 million. Safety and security during the 2002 Winter Olympics in Salt Lake City cost $300 million and involved 10,000 security personnel.

The World Cup, one of the most televised sports events worldwide, was hosted simultaneously in South Korea and Japan in summer 2002. South Korea took several steps in light of potential terrorist and soccer hooligan activities. The South Korea security measures encompassed the following: forming a 5,000 member anti-hooligan unit; inviting 23 spotters from 14 European countries to help authorities look for hooligans at airports and stadiums; using metal detectors at stadiums; flying fighter jets over stadiums; deploying land-to-air rockets at each stadium; banning flights of nonmilitary aircraft over stadiums and nuclear power plants; and denying entry to more than 3,200 people with suspected terrorist links and 6,400 known hooligans.

The other World Cup co-host, Japan, also took extensive security measures against both terrorists and hooligans. Among numerous security actions, the Japanese government: flew aircraft over stadiums; armed police on selected domestic and international flights; brought European spotters to aid in identifying troublesome fans; and used metal detectors at stadiums. These measures and subsequent defense measures cost $18.5 million and included over 7,500 security officers.

In retrospect, these outlays were not exaggerated as the national pride, tourism revenue, and security of the host country, players, and tourists were at risk. Also, the history of violence surrounding selected domestic and international soccer matches instigated by aggressive fans is well documented. For example, during the 1998 World Cup a French policeman nearly died after being badly beaten by foreign fans. In 2002, two Leeds United (England) supporters were stabbed to death by followers of the Turkish club Galatasaray.

After the 9/11 attacks, the National Football League established a security best practices framework that called for, among other things, an audit of security at the league's thirty-two stadiums. Concerns about possible explosions at stadiums were coupled with the prospects of terrorists putting biological or chemical agents in ventilation systems. Among some adopted security modifications at stadiums included the expanded use of video surveillance and patting down of fans as they enter stadiums.

Conclusion

While corporations have a duty to provide protection to their employees and customers, it is important to remember that their actions do not appear in a vacuum. After all, it is the role of government as well—through federal, state, and local officials, law enforcement and otherwise—to prevent terrorists from entering this nation, raising funds, and conducting operations. At the same time, corporations can assist in reducing threats by cooperating with government inquiries—as permitted by law—and providing intelligence to the government of possible terrorist activities. Moreover, companies can contribute to combating terror by allocating adequate human and financial capital to strengthen security measures. Public and private sector employees can also aid in countering terror.

6

Public-Private Partnership in Combating Terrorism

The multi-faceted public-private partnership in the war on terrorism is discussed in this chapter. This dynamic can be characterized along three main themes: government supporting industry, business helping government, and challenges to further cooperation between the two.

Government Assisting Industry in the War on Terrorism

Government assists business through various means, such as: purchasing homeland security products and services; guiding industry on threats and responses; reducing industry risk; privatization of some government activities; and other issues.

Government Spending Aids Business

In the war on terrorism, government assists industry in a number of ways. The public sector purchases homeland security products and services. For our purposes, such goods and services include: defense (e.g., military aircraft, ships, missiles, and tanks); security equipment, technology, and services (e.g., biometrics, trace detection, video cameras, document authentication machines, and security services); diverse technology products and services (e.g., military-oriented telecommunications and software, security software, data mining, data storage and recovery services, and emergency management software); pharmaceuticals (e.g., antibiotics) and biotechnology products (e.g., vaccines for smallpox and antidotes for nerve gas); germ detection equipment and services (e.g. detection of biological agents, food borne pathogens, and remediation of pathogens); and survivalist gear (e.g., gas masks and bomb shelters).

During this decade and beyond, U.S. government expenditures on homeland security products and services will reach the hundreds of billions of dollars. The obvious impetus for this increased interest in such items rests on the lessons of the 9/11 attacks, including failures due to inadequate intelligence (or analysis thereof), limited security measures — including lack or inadequate homeland security goods and services — and an under-appreciation of risks. Failures witnessed during September 11 can partially be rectified by broader use of homeland security goods and services.

The Department of Homeland Security's fiscal year 2004 budget (DHS Budget) is $37.6 billion. Of the $4.6 billion allocated to the Transportation Security Administration, $400 million will be used to acquire and install explosive detection systems at airports. An additional $85 million will be used to improve air cargo security, including improving oversight of known shippers and closer scrutiny of cargo sent on passenger aircraft.

With reference to port security, about $265 million will be spent, including: $125 million for port security grants, improving perimeter and dockside security; $64 million to aid research in non-intrusive inspection technology; $62 million for the Cargo Security Initiative (deploying U.S. inspectors and analysts at twenty foreign ports and other locations to inspect containers for mass destruction weapons prior to arrival in the United States); and $14 million for the Customs-Trade Partnership Against Terrorism (C-TPAT), elaborated later in this chapter.

It is anticipated that some 20,000 goods and service providers will offer their services to the Department of Homeland Security. Business at leading government contractors, which renamed or created homeland security divisions, is projected to accelerate due to post-9/11 demand. Leading defense government contractors include Lockheed Martin, Northrop Grumman, Boeing, Raytheon, and General Dynamics.

The Pentagon has various projects with contractors to develop advanced military hardware, including: advanced infantry gear for soldiers (bullet-resistant clothing, fuel cells for batteries, and hand-held computers); and communications satellites that accelerate the capacity to transfer video and information. In November 2002, the National Research Council called upon the U.S. military to accelerate funding for development of "non-lethal," weapons (e.g., specialized lasers that would puncture tires and destroy electrical systems; and laser beams that would create a shock wave and temporary paralysis).

To improve the safety and immediate stability of commercial airlines following the 9/11 attacks, Congress approved the $15 billion Airline Transportation and Systems Stabilization Act. Part of the monies were used for reinforcing cockpit doors, improving security training of aviation personnel, hiring additional air marshals, purchasing more bomb detection equipment, acquiring non-lethal weaponry, and refining passenger profiling systems. The DHS Budget allocates $60 million to research, develop, test, and evaluate anti-missile devices for commercial aircraft.

A newly-created Air Transportation Board, established to aid airlines hurt after 9/11, guaranteed loans of US Airways and America West Airlines, totaling about $1.2 billion combined. More than a dozen airlines have applied for loan guarantees under the $10 billion backstop support system.

The Department of Health and Human Services earmarked billions of dollars for bioterrroism countermeasures, including purchasing pharmaceuticals and vaccines. The National Institutes of Health will expend millions on examining biological-warfare defenses. The Department of Homeland Security issued bids for research efforts relating to combating animal-related agro-terrorism and post-harvest food security matters.

The DHS Budget earmarks $88 million for a National Biodefense Analysis and Countermeasures Center, which will improve understanding of bioterrorism pathogens and their effects on humans and agriculture. An additional $38 million will be used to continue the deployment of the Urban Monitoring Program (BioWatch), which aids in the early detection of bio-threats.

The DHS allocates funds specifically for researching new counter-terrorism technologies, including those products that aim at defending against (or recovering from) terrorism. The DHS Budget provides $75 million to the Rapid Prototyping Program, which supports quick adaptation of commercial technologies for homeland security purposes. The trucking industry obtained $20 million in government funding for trucking security and safety. In April 2003, for instance, the Pentagon hired Electronic Data Systems in a two-year $253 million deal covering its computer networks and data storage systems so as to further safeguard and access their assets should terrorist attacks occur.

The Environmental Protection Agency funded a water company association web site to improve communications among such firms should a terrorist incident occur. The public sector likewise provided funding and elementary research to homeland security firms focusing on pathogen antidotes and explosive detection equipment. The government has implemented legislation that would complement the liability of insurance companies in case of a severe terrorist attack.

Government-owned Amtrak received funding for security and safety measures such as: additional police officers, extra lighting and fencing, bomb-detection systems, and surveillance cameras in and around stations, tracks, yards, tunnels, and bridges. Private transportation companies, including those who ran buses, requested that government provide them with financial support to cover security costs.

Prior to 9/11, In-Q-Tel, a technology-focused venture capital arm of the Central Intelligence Agency (CIA), provided funding to private firms whose products would assist the intelligence community. Following the World Trade Center attacks, In-Q-Tel adopted a greater emphasis on goods and technologies that would aid in the war on terrorism.

The war on terrorism also resulted in opportunities to firms that are not within the homeland security realm. For example, in the case of Iraq, it is anticipated that the nation will undertake huge infrastructure projects (e.g., electricity generation and sewage plants) as well as privatizations—meaning the sale of government-owned entities to the private sector. U.S. companies are expected to have the upper hand in many prospective bidding opportunities.

The government's emphasis and spending on homeland security issues is not lost on the private sector. In recognition of a different risk dynamic post-9/11, business has significantly increased its attention to homeland security. As such, business has accelerated human and financial resources to safeguard business assets and customers.

Government Guides Industry on Threats and Responses

The Department of Homeland Security exchanges information with the private sector and individuals on terror risks and responses. The public sector shares intelligence with industry and provides business with guidance on responding to terrorist threats. Since 9/11 government officials alerted various sectors—financial institutions, nuclear power plants, aviation, and housing—of possible impending terrorist attacks.

In May 2002, the Department of Health and Human Services provided guidelines for protecting ventilation systems in commercial and government buildings from chemical, biological and radiological attacks. Other businesses, including chemical companies and nuclear power plants, heightened security measures in light of government-issued threat pronouncements.

The five-color Terrorist Threat Alert System (ranging from severe, high, elevated, guarded and low risk of a terrorist attack) is modified due to shifts in intelligence reports and news events. Increases in threat levels initially engender negative responses by companies and financial markets; the opposite is often the case when tensions subside — as naturally one would expect. Financial markets and companies prefer stability and predictability and abhor uncertainty and political violence, particularly within one's own borders.

Yet, the benefits of disclosing possible threats must be couched by the risks that excessive, unfounded warnings may create hysteria and hurt sales. Moreover, excessive "false alarms," can lead to the public ignoring future credible prognostications of prospective attacks. Industry and government increasingly share information about terror threats as both their interests are served.

The government undertakes extensive training with respect to fictional terrorist attacks, including the possible use of weapons of mass destruction. During such exercises, industry often collaborates with government representatives as well as with nonprofit organizations. The repetition of such training exercises nationwide enables industry to gain significant exposure to possible threats and to test corporate readiness.

Government also provides citizens with information about terrorism by establishing a citizen preparedness campaign. In February 2003, the Department of Homeland Security partnered with the Advertising Council and Sloan Foundation to initiate a public service advertising (PSA) campaign on this subject. The PSA suggested that families garner an emergency supply kit as well as establish a family communication plan in case of terror attack. Such activities reduce some onus for businesses to prepare their employees to terrorist challenges.

Government Reduces Industry Risk

Post-9/11 legislation limited the prospective liability of certain industries arising from the September 11 attacks. For instance, airlines and others were indirectly partially shielded from liability as 9/11 victims' families relinquish rights to potential lawsuits if they participate in the September 11 Victims Compensation Fund Program.

The Terrorism Risk Insurance Act of 2002 allows for the federal government to temporarily and partially cushion insurance company claims should a terrorist attack—perpetrated on behalf of foreign interests—take place in the United States. A prospective terror act, which must be certified by the Department of Treasury, must also cause property and casualty insurance losses of over $5 million to qualify. Insurance companies would then pay a deductible of insurance premiums received. The insurance company would then pay 10% of terror claims, with the government covering the remainder 90%. Yet, government contributions kick in only when a $10 billion liability threshold (in the initial year of the program) is exceeded—rising to $15 billion level during the program's third (and last) year.

The terrorism insurance program expires at the end of 2005. The insurance legislation is expected to reduce insurance rates and spur real estate development as some projects were held in abeyance due to insufficient or costly insurance.

Under the Support Anti-terrorism by Fostering Effective Technologies Act of 2002 (Safety Act), companies that allow their products or services to be certified as anti-terrorism wares by the Department of Homeland Security face less potential legal liability than they would otherwise. The Safety Act limits, in some cases, liability arising from damage should a government-certified homeland security product or service fail to prevent a terror incident (or should harm occur during one) to a company's insurance level. At its highest level of protection, the Safety Act potentially limits a firm's liability—other than for negligent acts. The distinct protection levels relate to the types of protection a company applies for with the government. The Safety Act aims to encourage the development of homeland goods and services.

Privatization of Some Government Activities

With the rising trend of privatizing some civilian and military functions, the public sector allows business to enter into areas previously under the purview of government. For instance, in October 2002, Army Secretary Thomas White announced that the Army might shift additional support jobs from the Army to the private sector.

Millions of dollars are used to train soldiers and carry out war simulations. Private firms have even been used to attract recruits into the armed forces. The war on terrorism increasingly includes the participation of U.S. armed forces. Government contractors will surely follow troops and generate revenue for their firms. Government contractors already carry out significant functions in connection with the war on terror (e.g., private contractors participating in drug interdiction activities in Colombia; Colombian terror groups are involved in the Colombian drug trade).

This shift towards privatization of some aspects of the military can be demonstrated in activities during the Iraq conflict in 2003. By some estimates, the number of government contractors present in the region was ten times greater than during the 1991 Persian Gulf War.

Duties of government contractors are diverse and important. Whether industry is always better suited (and cheaper) to carry out particular functions requires further analysis. At a U.S. army base in Kuwait, KBR (a subsidiary of Haliburton) provides food, laundry, and garbage services. KBR was later accused of charging excessive prices in connection with providing fuel in Iraq. A number of U.S. firms have been involved in protecting Iraqi oil fields and pipelines, while others aided in putting out oil well fires, ignited by Iraqi saboteurs.

Significant business opportunities have arisen with the downfall of Iraqi President Saddam Hussein and his regime. Aside from its involvement with the obvious oil wealth of the country, U.S. private firms are likely to pursue other business ventures and investments, including participation in the privatization of Iraqi industries (e.g., telecommunications and cement).

DynCorp, another contractor, undertakes government work in several regions, including Afghanistan. Among its duties there, it provides security to Afghan President Hamid Karzai, through U.S. State Department outsourcing of diplomatic security functions.

Other Issues

Government provides business access to, and assistance from, labor resources instrumental in combating terrorism. For instance, in the case of commercial aviation, the National Guard's presence at airports deterred terrorist attacks. Government personnel's growing expertise with terrorism affords them with ample knowledge to share with private sector personnel, such as corporate security directors, facility managers, and risk operations workers.

Some intelligence and law enforcement agencies' data about suspected terrorists is shared with different businesses, including airlines. Government and military scientists collaborate with their private sector colleagues to conduct research and development relative to counterterrorism technologies and products.

Police, firefighters, and emergency medical response services are illustrative of government labor assets that aid the private sector should a terrorist strike occur. The high-visibility defensive activities of law enforcement, particularly in New York and Washington, D.C., provide businesses with a sense of security—they feel protected—and a heightened sense of vulnerability—the situation reminds them that risks exist. About 10,000 federal, state, and local security employees provided security during at the Winter Olympics in Salt Lake City in January 2002.

The public sector aids industry by offering business-friendly procedures within a homeland security-based context. Under C-TPAT, companies that follow supply chain standards, procedural safeguards, and employee background investigations and training can benefit by gaining rapid transit through customs, as exemplified by reduced inspections and designated lanes. From its April 2002 inception through June 2003, more than 3,300 companies, including the top 60 importers (by volume), participated in C-TPAT. During fiscal year 2004, the federal government allocated $14 million to strengthening C-TPAT.

Analogous to C-TPAT, the U.S. Customs Department established the Free and Secure Trade Program (FAST) that likewise allows for expedited customs and border processing for firms that adopt government-approved security measures. Companies—manufacturers, importers, and carriers—that seek to be eligible for FAST must already participate in C-TPAT. Truck drivers who desire FAST eligibility must provide the government with personal information that is used to determine the driver's potential risk.

In December 2003, the FAST Program was extended to the Southwest Border, facilitating trade between the United States and Mexico. The US/Mexico FAST Program also requires manufacturers and carriers to utilize secure seals on trailers and containers headed to the United States. FAST lanes, used along the U.S.-Canadian border since September 2002, reduce the risk of terrorist infiltration while concurrently simplifying commerce.

The public sector interacts with industry, businesses, and industry representatives on issues relating to homeland security. Numerous industry associations representing distinct industry sectors meet with the public sector to share ideas and discuss steps that will aid in deterring and responding to terrorist threats against private industry.

The Department of Homeland Security established an Office of Private Sector Liaison (OPSL) to improve the public-private partnership in the war on terrorism. The OPSL expands the dialogue between industry and government on the matters of terror threats. Also, OPSL serves as a forum in which industry can address and gain a good understanding of security challenges. Analogously, President George W. Bush appointed a Homeland Security Advisory Council of industry leaders to ensure a greater development of the public-private partnership on terrorism.

Another government-industry forum is the State Department's Overseas Security Advisory Council (OSAC). OSAC is a public-private partnership between transnational corporations and the State Department. The State Department-based entity aids firms to do business abroad as well as provides guidance on political risk matters that companies may face while conducting overseas business. The FBI-housed Infragard Program allows for public-private interaction on cyberterrorism and other security matters.

The U.S. government has undertaken efforts to relay American viewpoints on issues, ranging from democracy to U.S. culture to youth abroad. In particular, the State Department started a magazine, *Hi*, aimed at building a bridge between the United States and the Middle East. The publication, which commenced in July 2003, is geared towards the 18 to 35 year-old group. In accepting advertising, it is presumed that *Hi* will facilitate receptivity of American goods and services to consumers in the Middle East.

Industry Aiding Government in the War on Terrorism

Industry assists government in combating terrorism through a variety of means, including: furnishing homeland security goods and services, safeguarding government assets, providing intelligence, outsourcing government roles and risks, and other matters. These topics are covered below.

Industry Furnishes Products and Services

The private sector makes available to the government various products and services, collectively designated as homeland security wares, including: defense; security equipment, technology, and related services; diverse technology products and services; security services; pharmaceuticals, biotechnology, and forensics; germ detection and remediation; and survivalist merchandise. Government acquires such items on a regular basis in efforts to protect U.S. interests at home and abroad.

By having many of these items available to other businesses and the public, industry also enables the populace to strengthen their individual defenses against terrorism. This feature alleviates some of the government's onus to protect businesses and individuals.

With reference to border security, the government has acquired thousands of hand-held radiation detectors as well as mobile detection units capable of inspecting containers, trucks, and tankers for contraband. Bomb detection equipment is widely used at the nation's airports. Biometric instruments (e.g., facial recognition software and hand-readers) are used by law enforcement in many settings.

Commercial war game simulation providers aid the military in refining strategies, improving skills, and gaining expertise under diverse conditions. Providers of radio frequency identification tags (RFID) may assist the U.S. Department of Agriculture's Animal Identification Plan to track the movement of animal species. Given past cases of mad cow disease and avian flu, coupled with future prospects of bioterror attacks against U.S. agriculture, such developments are positive.

In November 2002, the CIA used missiles on a particular unmanned aerial vehicle to kill al Qaeda terrorists in Yemen. Acknowledgement of the use of this product brought with it positive ramifications. More specifically, it demonstrated quite directly the important role companies play in the war of terrorism. Yet, in identifying specific company's products in counterterror measures, terrorists may seek retribution against particular firms. While such prospects are slight, they are worth keeping in mind.

Business Safeguards Government

Industry advises government on how to reduce terror threats. Business cooperates with government to aid in ensuring the safety of government facilities and employees. Architecture, engineering, and construction firms assist government agencies to design more "terrorist-resistant" buildings, such as embassies. Firms produce bomb-resistant walls, bullet-proof glass, bio-weapon detectors, and metal detectors that serve counterterror purposes. Also, computer security, data storage, and business continuity software help to defend government electronic assets.

Industry Provides Data to Government

There are many examples of industry exchanging information with government entities, including law enforcement, health, safety, and emergency preparedness officials. Such collaboration allows for: the defense industry to craft superior weapons; the telecommunications sector to build better communications equipment; the software and hardware sectors to create improved cybersecurity capabilities; the pharmaceuticals industry to develop drugs and vaccines aimed at defending against biological agents; and germ-detection companies and bomb detection manufacturers to provide products that can spot the presence of pathogens and bombs, respectively.

Industry provides "intelligence" and information to the public sector about potential terrorist threats. In fall 2001, a Minnesota flight school notified law enforcement officials about the suspicious behavior of Zacarias Moussaoui. In the post-9/11 era, employers more readily notify the government when an employee or customer acts in a suspicious matter. Industry representatives and employees—from truck drivers to chemical factory workers—are advised to warn managers and law enforcement authorities should circumstances warrant.

Financial institutions inform government authorities of possible terrorism financing activities. Also, banks freeze the assets of suspected terrorist groups and terror financiers as required under post-September 11 legislation.

As indicated in Chapter 5, the Transportation Security Agency's new background-checking systems, Computer-Assisted Passenger-Screening II (CAPS-II), initially tested by Delta, will link all airline reservation systems and analyze financial and government databases, when one buys a ticket. Government funding for CAPS-II during fiscal years 2003 and 2004, combined, is expected to reach $70 million. Passengers will be given a risk level (green, yellow, or red). CAPS-II has also raised civil liberty concerns. It similarly exemplifies the private sector's role in becoming a quasi-state instrumentality in combating terrorism.

The Food and Drug Administration and food industry companies collaborate in ensuring food safety. Under post-9/11 legislation, food manufacturers and distributors register with government, while food importers provide notice of prospective entrance of food products into the United States.

A newly-added exemption to the Freedom of Information Act (FOIA) enables businesses to disclose to government authorities possible security breaches at their firms without fears that such information will be reported to the public. Still, some industry representatives are concerned that disclosures will not remain confidential.

After September 11 more firms undertake greater diligence of prospective partners than before. This is done to ensure that their business partners are not fronts for domestic or international terrorists. Such expanded inquiries may prove time-consuming and costly. Yet, these actions are prudent practice for firms that want to keep a clean bill of health—and potentially avoid government sanctions at the same time.

Outsourcing Government Duties

The use of private sector employees to complement government security efforts, such as private sector security guards at government buildings, is illustrative of how industry provides personnel that assists in the war on terrorism. Government contractors also provide the public sector—both directly or indirectly—with workers who undertake activities that range from detection and remediation of bioterrorism to emergency response capabilities.

In another homeland security parameter, private contractors aid the government by doing highly sensitive foreign language translation work, risk and vulnerability assessments of government-owned mass transit systems and water treatment plants, and compile time-sensitive terrorism-related data analysis. Private contractors are increasingly placed in the front lines in high-risk areas, such as Iraq and Afghanistan. While undertaking such duties, a number of them have been killed or injured, including during terrorist attacks (e.g., military contractors were killed during a terrorist attack in a Saudi Arabian expatriate housing complex in 2003).

As highlighted earlier, the gradual privatization of a number of duties at the Pentagon exemplifies how industry conducts services that were previously under the government's realm. Growing dependence by the government on the private sector has also raised some concerns. For instance, the General Accounting Office expressed its apprehension over the Pentagon's reliance on commercial satellite companies for satellite assistance with military communications.

It is important to note that by outsourcing some functions to industry, the government also shifts the risks involved in undertaking such duties. For instance, by using private contractors rather than soldiers in particular functions (e.g., preparing meals and cleaning functions in Iraq) fewer U.S. military personnel are put at risk. This is particularly so when home-country individuals are used to carry out "menial," duties (e.g., food preparation and laundry). By using native personnel, local job creation is strengthened although using non-Americans for specific functions (e.g., food preparation, garbage removal, and laundry services) can also create risks (e.g., food poisoning of U.S. troops in Afghanistan was suspected in 2002).

Other Matters

The private sector's control over substantial parts of critical infrastructure, including telecommunications and electricity grids, makes the government concerned if these assets are inadequately protected. Moreover, as government relies on critical infrastructure, particularly during a crisis, the private sector's role in the homeland defense equation is very important.

Some newly established associations focusing on homeland security issues play a role in raising the visibility of industry perspectives on homeland security issues. For example, government security mandates, industry security standards, and government procurement possibilities, among other matters, are discussed. Other industry groups also undertake lobbying and homeland security related consulting work.

There is also a growing interaction between the private sector and government regarding the organization of seminars, training programs, and trade shows relating to homeland security and emergency preparedness. Such forums allow for government and industry to exchange information and contribute to the cross-fertilization between the two groups.

Industry also provides expertise and helps shape policy on homeland security matters as it relates to business in general, and respective industry verticals, in particular. Industry insights into the unique challenges that their sector faces are helpful when policy-makers attempt to craft rules and guidelines affecting business.

Sources of Tension in the Public-Private Partnership in Combating Terrorism

The government-industry dynamic in the war on terror also creates friction between the two spheres. A number of challenges to the public-private partnership in fighting terrorism are addressed below.

Federalization and Privatization

Government and industry enter into areas that were previously under the control or influence of the other party. The shift from private to public screeners resulted in a significant financial hit to private security firms that had offered such services at airports (although some companies now complement federal airport screeners). The federalization of aviation security occurred after private screener shortfalls partially contributed to 19 hijackers boarding four planes on 9/11.

The movement towards privatizing some military functions creates some tension between government and business, including among employees from respective camps. There is also the issue of whether the private sector should carry out certain functions—no matter the possible cost savings. Other effects of the federalization-privatization dynamic include economic and political power shifts resulting from such changes.

Government Rules Affect Business

Post-September 11 laws and other government measures greatly affected the airline industry. For instance, cockpit doors were reinforced. Also, security training for flight crews was overhauled. These activities, though necessary to provide a modicum of confidence in the flying public, resulted in substantial additional costs to industry. Government aid and security fees partially covered airline security costs.

Post-9/11 government guidelines on baggage screening and parking lot placement delayed plans to modify airport terminals, roadways, and parking garages. Such government measures also raised the operating costs of airports. Government rules relating to safeguarding food supplies also increased costs relating to operating some businesses in that sphere.

Government places restrictions and oversight on business so that terrorist threats are reduced. For instance, new regulations place additional obligations on business to provide information on employees and customers who may be connected to terrorism. In the case of a national crisis, government may put pressure on companies to provide critical goods, such as pharmaceuticals, at lower prices. This was actually the case when the Department of Health and Human Services obtained favorable prices on Cipro, an antibiotic used to counter anthrax-induced illness.

An evolving definition of what constitutes the war on terrorism and what roles industry and government have in this fight (and what they are willing to give up) will impact on how the public and private sectors will interact. Relevant to the public-private partnership relationship is the role of costs in securing industry and the determination of which entity should pay what in order to safeguard companies, individuals, and the homeland at large. This is particularly relevant with regard to critical infrastructure. Such segments of the economy—electricity grids and telecommunications systems—are mostly owned by the private sector but their security is of paramount concern to the government.

In order to cover the costs associated with improved maritime security—more government agents monitoring crews and cargo—the government considered imposing additional security user fees on importers and exporters. Airline passengers are subject to a security fee that partly covers the outlays associated with increased aviation security. Rising costs related to complying with new government rules associated with "Knowing Your Customers," (e.g., avoiding doing business with terrorists), may lead to businesses, such as banks, to pass on these expenditures in the form of higher consumer prices.

Government creates new institutions (Department of Homeland Security) that affect how business is conducted. The Department of Homeland Security integrated 22 government institutions (e.g., the Immigration and Naturalization Service, Customs Service, and Federal Emergency Management Agency) plus the Transportation Security Agency. These entities interact with various players, including workers, importers and exporters, and homeland security companies. The massive shift of government staff and duties associated with the creation of the new department also impacts this public-private partnership on terrorism.

Increased Cooperation Leads to Other Risks

Companies have faced accelerated contact with law enforcement and investigative officials regarding possible illegal activities of clients, such as customers at banks. Under such circumstances, the American Banking Association instructed that banks receive valid legal documents—subpoena, search warrant, or summons—prior to releasing any confidential information. Law enforcement's expansive investigative capabilities, derived by post-9/11 legislation, foreshadow future inquiries into business activities in relation to possible terror connections of clients, business partners, and employees.

Because terrorists are expanding the use of electronic communications—cell phones, pagers, e-mail, Voice-Over-Internet-Protocol (VOIP), and instant messaging—Internet Service Providers (ISPs) and telephone companies have witnessed a rise in inquiries from investigative authorities. Furthermore, the FBI may require ISPs to collaborate and permit the agency to install monitoring software, such as DCS1000 (previously known as Carnivore) to trace suspected terrorists'

Internet activities. Private sector participation in other intelligence-sharing programs, such as information about airline passengers in the CAPS-II Program, can led to potential consumer privacy concerns, litigation, and declining revenue due to boycotts.

Significant government investigation into the activities of potential terrorists and their supporters has heightened privacy concerns in the U.S. population. A Ponemon Institute's September 2003 survey found that 43% of Americans do not believe that the Department of Homeland Security is committed to maintaining individuals' private data, 36% had the opposite outlook, while 21% were unsure.

Improperly "Using" Counterterrorism

The relatively new discipline of "modern" counterterrorism makes it sometimes difficult for companies (e.g., the suppliers) and the government (e.g., the customer) to adduce what types of products and services are appropriate. Complicating the equation further is the inherent disposition of companies to sell goods and services as rapidly as possible to many customers even if a product (or service) may need substantial improvements.

Some companies have acted improperly by offering products or services that were bogus or failed to meet government requirements. For instance, a firm was accused of providing the government with untrained bomb-sniffing dogs, making the canines irrelevant for the tasks the government hired them to undertake. Suppliers of faulty or ineffective gas masks and other critical goods threaten safety and undermine the proper elements of the counterterrorism industry. In more innocent cases, some products simply do not adapt well or perform when used in military settings, including unique weather or other conditions.

Further negative connotations follow lengthy and expensive cost overruns that may attach to private contractors. As government counterterror responses are time-sensitive, industry delays are hurtful in multiple respects. Also, some companies may see the growth in homeland security spending as a panacea for the companies.

Government's attempts to enter the private sector have their concerns. The July 2003 announcement of a Pentagon plan to establish a forum—the Policy Analysis Market (PAM)—for speculation on geopolitics, including terrorism, was short-lived. Potential alternatives to the wagered at PAM included, for instance, the length of U.S. presence in the Gulf States. Industry and government concerns over the appropriateness and utility of establishing such a market ended this government-sponsored project. Nevertheless, it was reported that a similar, private-sector scheme will be launched in 2004.

Red Tape

An overarching tension between the parties is whether government or industry should establish minimum standards for industry security, and if so, whether such measures should be mandatory. A partial resolution to this dilemma is greater cooperation between industry and government. This is particularly so with regard to critical infrastructure as 90% of these assets are in private hands.

Even when industry can produce goods helpful in reducing the impact of terrorism (e.g., vaccines), government obstacles may arise. For instance, a lengthy regulatory approval process may undermine the speedy market entry of a product (e.g., Bioport's anthrax vaccine).

Some industry associations and companies voiced displeasure at new regulations that would codify expanded security measures. Industry opposition stems from allegations of excessive government meddling, concerns about costs of new measures, increasing associated labor costs, and impediments to conduct business. For example, in July 2002, the American Bankers Association, the Securities Industry Association, and other financial trade associations objected to a proposed regulation that would require firms to gather more information on foreign institutions that open correspondent accounts in U.S. banks.

Strict federal government security compliance procedures on hundreds of labs and scientists that use biological pathogens (e.g., anthrax and plague) in their research were actually not performed as mandated by legislation. Some scientists and labs no longer focus on this type of research due to increased security measures.

Retailers and manufacturers opposed a proposal that shippers provide a day's notice prior to loading products bound for U.S. ports. Nearly six million containers arrive at U.S. ports each year. The National Food Processors Association and National Grocers Association prefer the use of voluntary information-sharing and planning arrangements with the FBI and other agencies rather than formal rules mandating levels of protection.

The government also plays a role in approving mergers and acquisitions in the defense, homeland security, and other sectors. A case in point was the Pentagon's approval of the Northrop Grumman's proposed purchase of TRW. Subsequently, the Justice Department likewise approved the transaction. Some defense industry competitors were disappointed by the government's support of the deal.

State and local agencies have delayed purchasing some homeland security products and services because they have not yet received their requisite funding from the federal government. With adequate funding, a December 2002 National League of Cities surveyed found that city officials homeland security priorities would be: equipment (70%), training (62%), and threat prevention and detection (51%). Analogously, a September 2003 U.S. Conference of Mayors survey showed particular interest in acquiring homeland security equipment and training.

The Department of Homeland Security's fiscal year 2004 budget provides $725 million for discretionary grants to high-threat, heavily-populated urban areas and $550 million for law enforcement terrorism prevention grants—80% of the funds will be made available to states. Other portions of the $4.037 billion provided to state and local funding during this period includes: $1.7 billion for grants (states receive 80%), $750 for Firefighters Assistance Grants; and $40 million for Citizen Corps grants.

Industry's Noncompliance with Government Mandates

Another phenomenon in this dynamic includes the capacity of private and—less so—public workers to ignore government mandates that affect homeland security. A case in point is the Bush administration's call to vaccinate hundreds of thousands of health workers with the smallpox vaccine. Thus far, less than 15,000 health workers complied. Therefore, several hundred thousand medical facilities declined to participate in the program. In response, the government offered those immunized to be eligible for disability and death benefits should they be injured subsequent to their inoculation.

Government's Nonadoption of Ideal Products and Services

At times the government does not use the most beneficial private sector technology. Such inadequacies can threaten national security. Government's failure to acquire particular products and services is due to: different priorities, government recently acquired inferior offerings, unavailability of items, or government's unfamiliarity with new industry goods.

Failure to update computer hardware and software was partly responsible for the government's inability to undertake adequate data mining—shifting through vast amounts of information—and obtain content relevant to a terror investigation. The government has much to learn from the private sector in this regard. After all, prior to 9/11, many federal law enforcement databases could not communicate well with each other.

Many government agencies have very antiquated computer systems, as in the case of the FBI. As FBI Director Robert S. Mueller III explained, the FBI did not have the technical capability to search FBI databases for references to flight schools. Evolving relationship and relationship management software are increasingly used by government agencies to assist in "connecting the dots."

Another dilemma in the public-private partnership occurs when there is disagreement over what product or service will provide the best solution to the perceived terrorist threat. Disagreement as to the appropriate price of such products or services further strains the relationship between the two sectors.

Labor

The role of private sector individuals, including former senior government officials, in investigating terrorist incidents or serving on national commissions on terrorism raises several issues: possible conflicts of interest that could result in disqualifying a person or providing inappropriate advice; exploitation of the industry-government revolving door; and the quest of some former officials to seek to "rewrite" history in order to cover mistakes in their own counterterrorism strategies. Still, there is a pleasant cross-fertilization of homeland security talent between government and industry.

In this vein, it is noteworthy to observe the initial appointments and subsequent resignations of several 9/11 Commission panelists, who had been charged with the responsibility of investigating the September 11 incidents. These resignations demonstrated how business interests might interfere with the government's desire to investigate and craft solutions to terror threats.

There are various ramifications to employers when the military calls up reserves. Such measures pull away people from critical roles at private firms. Calling up reserves also reminds companies that even if they chose to bring in new people, by law, the job must be available to the reserve soldier upon his return. Management and labor face greater risks as positions are increasingly based overseas as the war on terrorism expands abroad (e.g., Afghanistan, Iraq, Yemen, and the Philippines).

Since the 9/11 attacks, government has raised great scrutiny of public and private employees. Expanded security checks of truck drivers who transport hazardous cargo (e.g., explosives, flammable liquids and gases, radioactive materials, and infectious substances) will make for better employees. In the post-9/11 world, potential drivers undertake broader background checks, including fingerprint checks and investigation of criminal or immigration offenses. Other rules require hazardous materials shippers to establish extensive security plans and training programs.

Conclusion

The developing public-private partnership in homeland security must be attended to with significant resolve as economic security, national security, and public safety are at stake. In the coming years, government will continue to buttress industry by: purchasing goods and services, providing notice of potential threats, crafting laws that will simplify doing business within the post-9/11 dynamic, and shielding industry to encourage companies to contribute to the war on terrorism. Concurrently, industry will aid the public sector through: offering homeland security products and services, aiding in protection of national assets, informing of potential terror risks, assuming some greater responsibilities, and facilitating information flows between the two groups. Nevertheless, tensions will undoubtedly exist between government and business due to their occasionally disparate perspectives and actions with regard to combating terror.

7

Terror's Effects on Labor and Management

Simultaneous car bombs destroy a huge hotel-casino in a large city, killing hundreds of gaming industry workers and their patrons. An explosion at a high-end jewelry chain kills dozens of jewelers and their customers. Hundreds of first-responders (e.g., police, firefighters, and emergency medical technicians) rush to aid victims of a bioterrorism attack at an office building, but perish during a subsequent series of explosions near the initial incident.

Any prospective terrorist attacks in the United States or abroad will victimize labor: whether they are at work or wherever they find themselves—at the wrong place, at the wrong time. Similarly, American armed forces and civilian contractors that aid the military in their duties abroad will face the consequences of terror.

Given these grave circumstances, it is incumbent to address terror's impact on labor-management relations so that we can better assess how to respond to this menace. This chapter addresses terror's victimization of labor, including physical and emotional costs. Employer and governmental aid during crises, terror's consequences on military personnel, workforce risks and opportunities, and post-9/11 employer matters are analyzed.

Terror Victimizes Labor

September 11, 2001, Terrorist Attacks

Nearly 3,000 persons were murdered during the September 11, 2001, incidents including: 246 persons (excluding the 19 hijackers) on the

4 hijacked planes; 125 persons at the Pentagon (excluding those on the plane that crashed into the building); and the remaining at the World Trade Center. The ages of the victims ranged from age two to eighty-two.

Many of the World Trade Center victims worked at domestic and international companies from all sectors of the economy as well as governmental and nongovernmental organizations. The fatalities represented over 80 nationalities, all races, and numerous religious faiths.

Terrorist attacks can harm all levels of the labor force equally: a terrorist bomb does not distinguish among upper management, middle management, entry-level managers, and clerical workers. A broad attack can harm all sectors and skill sets.

As was witnessed on 9/11, significant terrorist incidents can nearly instantaneously erase thousands in a particular sector's warfare. About 2,000 people who worked in the financial industry died as a result of the attacks on the World Trade Center. On that fateful day, the airline sector lost eight pilots and twenty-five flight attendants.

The brutality at the World Trade Center decimated particular companies and organizations especially hard, including: Cantor Fitzgerald/eSpeed, which lost about 670 employees; the New York City Fire Department, which lost over 300 members. The victims at the Pentagon included military personnel, contractors, and civilian employees.

The American Federation of Labor-Congress of Industrial Organizations (AFL-CIO) reported that hundreds of union workers were killed on 9/11, including firefighters, police officers, teachers, airline pilots, flight attendants, carpenters, electrical workers, machinists, office and professional employees, plumbers, painters, and pipe fitters.

It would be an oversight not to mention the survivors of the World Trade Center and Pentagon attacks. They were left with physical injuries that ranged from slight abrasions and bruises, broken bones that will heal, scars from burns that will instill agony and imprints for a lifetime, and severely crippling ailments that will lead to permanent disability. These walking wounded signify that terrorism's damage lasts long after the event concludes.

Fall 2001, Anthrax Cases in the United States

In fall 2001, a number of anthrax-tainted letters and subsequent anthrax exposures occurred throughout the United States. By November 21, 2001, four U.S. workers — 2 U.S. Postal Services employees in Washington, D.C.; an employee of American Media of Boca Raton, Florida;

and a worker at the Manhattan Eye, Ear, and Throat Hospital—and one retiree died as a result of complications stemming from separate anthrax attacks, which are still under investigation. By that date, too, at least 13 people were infected with anthrax in Florida, New York, and Washington, D.C. By mid-November 2001, anthrax spores were found in locations in Florida, Indiana, Maryland, Missouri, New Jersey, New York, Virginia, and Washington, D.C.

A number of federal office buildings in the Washington, D.C., area—mostly mail rooms and ancillary offices—tested positive for the presence of anthrax spores, including: Congress, the Central Intelligence Agency, State Department, Justice Department, Supreme Court, Food and Drug Administration, Voice of America, Veterans Administration, and Walter Reed Army Institute of Research.

In turn, during October 2001, 32,000 employees in the private and public sectors were administered antibiotics, such as Cipro and doxycycline, as a safety precaution against anthrax. Other employees underwent anthrax testing in order to determine whether antibiotics were necessary.

Additional Victimization

As highlighted elsewhere, since 2001 many Americans have been killed in overseas terrorist incidents. A number of examples of such victimization is set out below:

- An American teenager was stoned to death during a terror incident in Israel in 2001.
- A terrorist threw a parcel bomb into a busy shopping area, killing one U.S. citizen and wounding two others, in Saudi Arabia in 2002.
- Daniel Pearl, a American *Wall Street Journal* reporter, was abducted and later murdered in Pakistan in 2002.
- Two Americans, Barbara Green and Kristen Wormsley, were killed when grenades were thrown into a church in Pakistan in 2002.
- In 2002, five Americans were killed during a bombing at a cafeteria at Jerusalem's Hebrew University.
- Seven U.S. citizens died during a series of bombing at a several nightclubs in Bali in 2002.
- Bonnie Denise Witherall, an officer manager/nurse, was killed at a church-run health facility in Lebanon in 2002.

- Laurence Foley, an administrator of the U.S. Agency for International Development based in Jordan, was killed as he left his home in Amman in 2002.
- Three U.S. citizens were killed at a Baptist missionary hospital in Yemen in 2002.
- During a 2003 terrorist attack at an expatriate housing complex in Saudi Arabia, nine American employees of Vinnell Corp. (a subsidiary of Northrop Grumman) died and three American workers from Boeing Co. were injured.
- In 2003, a worker employed by the U.S. firm Kellog, Brown and Root was killed by a bomb while trying to deliver mail to American troops in Baghdad, Iraq.
- In 2003, a bomb exploded underneath a car carrying security guards in the Gaza Strip, killing three DynCorp employees and injuring another. The firm, a homeland security contractor, provided security services to U.S. government interests in Israel.
- In 2003 a roadside bomb near Baghdad killed two employees of U.S.-based EOD Technology. The workers' duties encompassed aiding the U.S. military to defuse and destroy Iraqi military armaments.

The growing shift towards using government contractors may result in significant victimization of industry employees. Likewise, the expanding internationalization of American business, which involves overseas work and travel, forebodes more threats against U.S. workers abroad.

Following the 9/11 attacks thousands of airline, airport, and hotel employees were fired. In January 2004, Cargill announced it would lay-off over 500 employees at beef-processing plants in the United States following mad cow disease discovery in Washington state. Should a terror attack cripple a component of the agricultural sector or food industry, the job losses to that industry would be momentous.

Emotional Consequences of Terror

The initial mental symptoms with which terrorist victims, their families, and co-workers may cope with include depression, anxiety, excessive stress, and other ailments. While some levels of mourning are typical, with individuals responding to the traumatic events in their own way, some workers may have after-effects that do not readily dissipate.

The negative emotional impact of terrorist attacks on victims, rescuers, and bystanders—from watching people die to observing bleeding body-parts strewn about, to hearing victims' last words gasping for help or hope—cannot be underestimated. As such themes are replayed, they can have an impact on labor to undertake distinct actions, such as: to change jobs, leave professions, move to other parts of the country, or continue their previous positions in memory of their fallen brethren.

The baleful, emotional consequences of terrorism range from denial of the event; mild forms of confusion, stress, and anxiety; to profound manifestations of depression, schizophrenia, and post-traumatic stress disorder (PTSD). The time, mental anguish, physical illness, and large strains on personnel departments and health advisers weigh adversely on business in terms of productivity and human capital development.

The experience of workers in Oklahoma City, Oklahoma, home of the 1995 terrorist bombing that resulted in 168 deaths, may shed light on the possible impact of employee behavior following terrorist incidents. The behaviors and actions exhibited by some of these employees after the attack included: high absenteeism and leave-taking, large turnover, impulsive and reckless behavior, low productivity, and excessive drinking and smoking. The hurtful emotional behavior experienced by some workers in Oklahoma City lasted from several months to more than a year. Initial reports from the World Trade Center and Pentagon survivors confirm similar responses.

In terrorist incidents on the scale of the World Trade Center and Pentagon attacks, some employees may find it challenging to get back to work and pick up uncompleted projects when familiar environments, such as their offices, have been destroyed. Employees' new surroundings are often sterile, containing different environments in variant locales. Also, damaged personal items, missing business records, and destroyed telecommunications, computers, and furniture only aggravate the unpleasantness that some victims feel upon returning to work.

What might prove helpful to some employees facing emotional challenges dealing with terrorist attacks is the American Psychological Association's web site. The Association gives workers helpful hints in managing traumatic stress, such as a terrorist incident.

When labor becomes a victim of terrorism there are many actors that can provide assistance: co-workers, employer, government, professionals in the health-care industry, family, friends, community, and third-party organizations (e.g., charities, unions).

Since 9/11 the nearly daily barrage of terrorist threats has frayed on the raw nerves of employees. Multiple terror attacks worldwide against numerous sectors, and the broad array of modus operandi used, particularly suicide bombings, has exposed the public to the risks that exist.

Also, the Washington, D.C., area, sniper attacks of 2002—which resulted in over 10 assassinations but were not terrorism—illustrated the susceptibility of employees that work outdoors (e.g., parking-lot attendants, crossing guards, and highway construction crews). During 2003-early 2004, a sniper shot at highway motorists in Ohio in actions that were reminiscent—in certain respects—to the Washington, D.C., area, sniper activities.

The impact of terror on labor is not limited to the immediate victims of the attacks. Terror's "shared experience" may include workers in the same sector (e.g., commercial airlines—pilots and flight attendants; mail carriers—U.S. Postal Service and Federal Express; media—anthrax letters to CBS, ABC, NBC/Daniel Pearl kidnapping) as well as workers nationwide in numerous sectors (e.g., employees at Hewlett-Packard in San Francisco and Los Angeles were told to work from home for the day on 9/11, once events of that day became known).

Against this backdrop, a number of generalities can be proffered about the possible impact of terrorism on the psyche of selected U.S. workers. For instance, the attractiveness of a specific role or the compatibility of a particular employer may have changed. Whereas formerly, some sought to get the most prominent, high-profile job at the finest, well-respected institution—whether in industry or in government—workers may now consciously choose less prominent and risky opportunities in the name of safety.

The concern or fright that may be felt by segments of the labor force may ultimately result in their seeking employment in small cities or towns that they may consider to be less of a target to terrorists. Also, employees may try to develop additional skills outside their respective job profile or industry just in case a terrorist attack would severely undermine an industry (e.g., the airline sector) and concurrently adversely affect their job security.

Employer and Governmental Support in Crises

During the initial months following 9/11, numerous employer, governmental, and nongovernmental activities and initiatives were undertaken to help the victims and their families. The forms of assistance have included financial, psychological, and spiritual support. The calling up of military reserves as well as news of the anthrax attacks during fall 2001 further tested employer, governmental, and nongovernmental capabilities with regard to U.S. labor.

Employer Responses

American employers nationwide experienced a huge demand for emergency mental health services in the wake of the September 11, 2001, terrorist incidents. American employees, including many based geographically distant from the attacks, identified with the "direct" victims of the attacks. Companies witnessed significant requests from employees for therapy and crisis counseling.

Many employers depended on employee assistance program (EAP) counselors to address workplace fears after the attacks. The terrorist attacks hurt morale as well as productivity at some companies. Past studies have demonstrated that EAPs aid in containing costs for workers' compensation.

Because small companies are unlikely to have EAPs, management at such firms has an additional obligation to play an active role in assuaging the fears that workers may have in a post-September 11 environment. Among the steps that management undertook to soothe employees' fears and readjustment included: encouragement of workers to openly discuss their concerns; modification of established, routine procedures, such as who should open mail and how mail should be opened; attempting to keep workers focused on their daily duties; underscoring that the threat of terrorism is manageable and limited; emphasizing that living in fear is not a solution and only plays into the hands of terrorists; and stipulating that workers' financial future and the economic success of the United States depends on small companies to contribute their share to the U.S. economy.

Governmental Assistance

Governmental aid and guidance to the survivors and victims' families of the World Trade Center and Pentagon terrorist incidents was furnished. The web site of the U.S. government's human resource agency, the U.S. Office of Personnel Management (OPM) offered aid and advice regarding the September 11 attacks and its aftermath, including:

•   Relocation site information for New York City federal
    employees impacted by loss of offices

- Pay and leave guidance for federal employees affected by the attacks at the World Trade Center and the Pentagon
- Rights and benefits of reservists called to active duty
- Emergency situation hiring flexibilities and information
- Frequently asked questions about federal benefits payable to victims of the terrorist attacks of September 11, 2001, and their families
- Benefits for victims of the World Trade Center and Pentagon tragedies
- Excused absence and assistance to federal employees affected by the attacks at the World Trade Center and the Pentagon
- Relief effort for victims of the terrorist actions
- List of organizations assisting in disaster relief efforts
- Handling traumatic events: a manager's handbook
- Call for blood donation
- Emergency dismissal and closure procedures

As of January 2004, 2,925 out of 2,976 families victimized during the 9/11 terrorist attacks applied for assistance under the federal September 11 Victims Compensation Fund. Additionally, some 4,300 individuals filed injury claims. The fund is projected to provide some $5 billion in compensation. Compensation to family victims have ranged from $250,000 to almost $7 million, while assistance for injuries scaled from $500 to $7.8 million.

Terror's Effects on Military Personnel

In January 2003, over 800,000 U.S. military reserves and National Guard members comprised the Ready Reserves. They are delineated further accordingly: Army National Guard (40%), Army Reserve (24%), Air National Guard (12%), Naval Reserve (10%), Air Force Reserve (8%), Marine Corps Reserve (5%), and Coast Guard Reserve (1%). By November 2003, some 300,000 were mobilized, including 163,000 on active duty.

Prior to commencing the invasion of Iraq in March 2003, the United States had nearly 300,000 troops in the Persian Gulf, based as followed: about 170,000 in Kuwait; 75,000 at sea; 10,000 each in Qatar and Saudi Arabia; 4,000 in Turkey; 5,000 in Bahrain; 3,000 in Oman; 2,000 each in Jordan, United Arab Emirates, and Diego Garcia.

These figures illustrate the vast labor resources that the government utilizes to protect U.S. interests in the Persian Gulf. The extensive manpower and skill sets, not to mention the equipment and upkeep of such forces, is staggering. Part of this contingent is a component of the Bush administration's global war on terror. As such, it demonstrates the effect political violence can have on labor forces thousands of miles away from the initial attacks.

Operation Iraqi Freedom—commenced in March 2003—was partially launched due to the perceived threat of Iraq's possession of weapons of mass destruction. United States and other intelligence agencies believed that Iraq might use the weapons against their neighbors or furnish such arms to terrorist groups.

Furthermore, there was evidence that Iraq provided support to terror groups, threatened its neighbors, and destabilized the Persian Gulf. Another principal reason for the Bush administration's position on Iraq was their calculation that Iraqi President Saddam Hussein was a brutal, dangerous dictator that needed to be replaced.

Some politicians and commentators have suggested that American efforts in Iraq are actually undermining U.S. counterterrorism elsewhere. They argue that limited governmental resources (e.g., troops, equipment, supplies, and intelligence support) used in Iraq could be placed in greater use elsewhere to fight al Qaeda and other groups (e.g., Afghanistan and the Philippines).

U.S. military action spurred by terror attacks was particularly evident when the United States and its allies undertook actions against the Taliban regime in Afghanistan after 9/11. Al Qaeda and many of its senior leadership was based there and trained with the knowledge and support of the Taliban. American and allied forces remain there and in Iraq as of April 2004.

Increased military deployments worldwide, spurred in part by the 9/11 attacks and other terror threats, has led military officials to use stop-loss orders: requiring military personnel to extend their tours from between four to six months. By such measures, troop levels should reach about 490,000. While critical for military purposes, the extension of military deployment, particularly by reserve and National Guard units, affects labor and business.

The Civilian-Soldier Balance

Terrorism has resulted in numerous consequences on military forces and reserves: combat activities are more likely to occur; military reserves and the National Guard members will likely serve longer periods with higher risk deployments; business will lose the service of key employees for extended periods; and employees may suffer reduced income (the difference between military and civilian compensation during their military reserve duty).

Employers are legally required to permit National Guard members and military reservists to leave their jobs in order to fulfill military duties. Once the employee returns, the employer is obligated to reinstate the worker at the same salary, level, status, and retirement benefits as prior to the call-up. The 1994 Uniformed Services Employment and Re-employment Rights Act protects military personnel and reservists from retaliatory or discriminatory actions by employers arising from the employees' fulfillment of military duties.

As noted earlier, the financial strain that such employees may face includes less income during their military reserve duty. Under present legislation, an employer needs only to provide unpaid leave during a "temporary" soldier's absence, although some employers provide complete or partial pay to these individuals.

According to a September 2001, Watson Wyatt survey of 51 companies about military reservists' compensation: 6% provided full pay for a set time (average of half a year), 12% offered differential pay indefinitely, 48% gave a differential pay for a set period (average of half a year), 10% provided no compensation, and 24% were other/undecided. In a fall 2001, Challenger, Gray & Christmas survey, 30% of firms stated that they were enhancing their military leave policies.

Employers' policies toward military reservists vary widely: Boeing (differential between salary and military pay for five years), UPS and Verizon Communications (differential for 12 months), Chevron-Texaco (differential for nine months), Citigroup (differential for six months), Home Depot and Kroger (differential for three months), federal government (22 days military leave—full salary and military pay).

Interestingly enough, the federal government is the largest employer (source) of National Guard and reservists. As portions of these federal employees have functions that relate to homeland security either directly or indirectly, their temporary transfer from civilian roles has some impact on domestic security and safety.

Not all National Guard members and reservists had a smooth transition from military service to civilian jobs. In fact, some 1,300 National Guard and reservists complained to the Department of Labor that they were discriminated against (e.g., missed promotions and were not reinstated) during October 2002–September 2003. This figure showed an almost 50% increase over the 900 complaints filed during the previous fiscal year.

With reference to university members of the National Guard or reserves, they are not guaranteed refunds of tuition or fees. Nevertheless, the U.S. Department of Education directed lenders and colleges to postpone student loan payments for reassigned or activated guard members and reservists. Also, the USO Worldwide Operations solicited donations for the USO Fund for Freedom's Finest to support U.S. armed forces in the United States and abroad.

Workforce Challenges and Opportunities

The 9/11 incidents, fall 2001 anthrax terrorist attacks, and counterterror military operations in Iraq, Afghanistan, and the Philippines have some employees reassessing their priorities. Civilian employees perspectives include taking more vacations, working fewer hours, volunteering less for complex and high-profile assignments, and spending more time with friends and family. Military servicemen and women, including reservists and National Guardsmen, are cognizant that armed forces demands will keep them busy for years to come.

The calling up of military reserves and National Guard for service in Iraq and Afghanistan, coupled with attacks U.S. contractors abroad, have injected further retrospection among U.S. workers. The high risks and opportunities that exist in private and public sector jobs in the homeland security context also give U.S. workers pause for self-analysis of what their roles entail.

The anthrax scare hit U.S. Postal Service's 800,000 workers particularly hard as anthrax spores were identified in a variety of postal distribution facilities in seven states and Washington, D.C. Moreover, as two postal service workers died following exposure to anthrax, with others falling ill, the sensitivity and concern of postal workers and others to future terrorist incidents are clearly understandable.

Terror's effects on U.S. labor can be seen as well through the disruption to basic worker routines previously scheduled to take place that fateful day of September 11. For example, within hours of the 9/11 attacks, the federal government sent home 260,000 workers in the Washington, D.C., area. Subsequently, many local governments and businesses closed for the day and numerous events were cancelled.

Workers in New York City—particularly Manhattan—were severely impacted: Wall Street suspended trading, numerous buildings throughout the city—including structures of the United Nations—were evacuated, and subway lines and Grand Central and Penn Stations were closed. Nationwide, airplanes were grounded and thousands of airline business travelers were stuck at airports. Spain was in a state of shock in the days following the 3/11 attacks in Madrid.

Labor expects employers to serve roles in addition to providing a job and wage. After 9/11, labor may view the employer as playing a semi-paternalistic/quasi-government role: provide physical security, emotional assistance, and guidance in times of catastrophe. Whether such new demands by some segments of the labor force are warranted—or even could be properly filled by employers—only time will tell.

Another perspective on labor's response to terrorism was witnessed when the *Wall Street Journal* announced its plans to return to its offices at the World Financial Center in lower Manhattan about nine months after 9/11. At the time, nearly three-quarters of reporters and editors responding to a survey desired that the newspaper find a permanent space elsewhere.

In anticipation of the impending war with Iraq in 2003, the Pentagon offered a media boot camp at a Marine base urban combating training campus. The training was aimed at elevating journalists' comfort level with placement of U.S. troops during a war, including basic first aid and land mine recognition. A number of American and foreign journalists were killed or injured while covering military action in Iraq in 2003.

Analogously, labor may undertake to file suit against terrorist groups, state-sponsors of terrorism, and those companies or individuals that facilitate or assist terrorist groups to carry out their activities (e.g., suppliers of weapons and funds).

Employment Discrimination

Terror can indirectly result in an increase in discrimination against an ethnic or single-issue group whose selected, fringe members—a tiny fraction of the group—are connected with political violence. More specifically, this occurs when innocent individuals of a particular ethnic group attempt to enter the job market and face employment discrimination. Those already in the workforce may encounter bias based on ethnicity. In addition, discrimination—at the extreme—can lead to violence against workers.

A negative effect of the 9/11 attacks was the nearly 200 hate crimes against Arab Americans (or persons mistaken to be of Middle Eastern or Asian—Afghani or Pakistani—descent) investigated by the FBI within several months of the September 11 incidents. Among the alleged hate crimes were: about 110 personal threats or attacks; and over 80 attacks or threats against institutions and property.

While all 19 hijackers involved in the September 11 incidents were Arabs, and the current leadership of al Qaeda consists of members of this group as well, millions of innocent Arab Americans—as well as millions of others including U.S. citizens of Sikh, Pakistani, and Afghani ancestry—were unjustly painted by racists with the same broad brush as the perpetrators of the terrorist attacks. An example of violence against minority workers (and mistaken identity) includes the October 2001 murder of a Shell employee of Indian descent in Texas, who was killed by a man who sought to retaliate against Arab Americans.

The Council on American-Islamic Relations reported that in 2002, the number of incidents of discrimination against Muslims reached 602 incidents, a 15% increase over the previous year. The most frequent types of anti-Muslim actions involved alleged employment discrimination. Numerous Muslims have also complained about negative ramifications of having Muslim- or Arab-related affiliations on their resumes.

The Equal Employment Opportunity Commission (EEOC) found that workplace complaints by Muslim workers increased by almost 100% during the fiscal year ending September 30, 2002. EEOC investigations into these matters led to employer penalties of several million dollars since September 11.

Immigration

According to the Northeastern University Center for Labor over 13 million documented and illegal immigrants came to the United States from 1990 to 2001. Of that figure, eight million immigrants joined the labor force, representing half of all new workers during the period. The total number of foreign-born workers in the United States in 2001 was 27.2 million, or 14%, of all workers in the United States. This figure provides a large base from which terrorists with a foreign-affinity could be tapped.

U.S. workers may end up facing reduced competition from documented foreign workers in the wake of the September 11 attacks, given greater concern of foreign workers' possible political, terrorist, and military affiliations. From October 2001 through June 2002, about 60,500 people were approved to work under H-1B (foreign professional) status. More than twice that figure (130,700) were approved during the previous nine-month period.

The cap for H-1 B visas is supposed to decline to 65,000 annually from fiscal year 2004. At the same time, the number of L-1 visas, which allows for inter-company transfers for up to seven years, declined slightly, from nearly 60,000 in 2001 to some 55,000 in 2002.

These developments should be viewed in light of a January 2004 Bush administration proposal—conceived prior to 9/11—to allow about eight million undocumented immigrants to live in this country under a temporary legal status (e.g., renewable three-year term), provided they can find employment.

Another twist on foreign workers relates to the tens of thousands of service jobs that have been outsourced abroad. Such outsourcing makes Americans' sensitive personal and financial data more available for possible exploitation by foreign terror groups and their operatives than were the data made available to U.S. domestic workers. Also, foreign-made products might be susceptible for tampering than U.S.-made goods. (I am assuming that American workers have U.S. interests more at heart than foreign workers).

TRAVEL VISAS

Tightening immigration procedures since 9/11 has resulted in more scrutiny of prospective foreign visitors. As such, there has been a consequent downward shift in travel by foreigners to the United States.

Against that backdrop, it is worth noting the implementation of the National Security Entry/Exit Registration System. It requires foreign visitors to notify U.S. immigration authorities about their whereabouts; it took effect in fall 2002. This new scheme, required selected nationals—initially, from Iran, Iraq, Syria, Libya, and Sudan—to be photographed, fingerprinted, and provide their itinerary to U.S. officials.

During July 2003, the Department of Homeland Security (DHS) reviewed a program that enables individuals to fly into the United States without a visa should they be passing through this country with a final destination in another nation. Analogously, from August 2003, the majority of foreign travelers to the United States that require a visa for their visit have been required to undertake an interview at a U.S. consulate. Since 2004, other security features include the photographing and fingerprinting of travelers from selected countries. While such developments discourage some foreign visitors and foreign workers, they are important components of an effective counterterrorism strategy.

Closer analysis of foreigner visa applications has resulted in less travel by foreign businessmen, researchers, and tourists to this country.

Between fiscal years 2001 and 2003, the number of nonimmigrant visa applications declined from 10.5 million to 6.9 million, while visas actually issued fell during that period from 7.6 million to 4.9 million. The number of visa-related FBI background checks rose by nearly 78% between fiscal years 2001 to 2003, reaching 250,000 in the latter case.

STUDENT VISAS

Post-9/11 government scrutiny of foreign students, including tougher visa requirements, led to fewer students at English-language programs in the United States. The decrease of some 40% in the number of summer English-language courses from 2001 to 2003 will weaken demand for U.S.-based instructors.

In fall 2003, the DHS announced plans to charge foreign students $100 each to cover costs arising from the Student and Exchange Visa Information Service. There are some 800,000 foreign students in the United States enrolled in about 8,000 institutions. This measure will defray some costs of closer inspection of student visa applicants.

This is an example of government passing on some of its homeland security costs directly to individuals. In other circumstances, the government's homeland security costs are subsumed internally, forwarded directly, or passed on indirectly to consumers and the private sector.

Employment Opportunities

TRANSLATION SERVICES

Enhanced language capabilities in the native tongues and dialects of Afghanistan, Pakistan, India, Philippines, Saudi Arabia, Iraq, and Iran are important for U.S. military and antiterrorism efforts. The limited number of Arabic-speaking U.S. soldiers has required American forces to somewhat rely on local Iraqi translators, who may have anti-American perspectives or even collaborate with U.S. enemies. U.S. citizens and other U.S.-based individuals with excellent oral and written skills in such languages will be in demand in the coming years.

The scarcity of people with non-Western language skills working in the U.S. translation business was evidenced by the fact that in fall 2001 only 120 Arabic-, 21 Farsi-, 6 Dari-, 6 Azeri-, and 1 Pashto-speaking professional translators were members of the American Translators Association. A number of U.S. government units, including the Department of Defense, CIA, and the FBI, increasingly seek to recruit native speakers of Arabic, Farsi, Dari, Pashto, Hindi, Urdu, and Uzbek.

Given the demand for people with foreign language skills, there has been an upsurge in college students who train to become specialists in these languages. This is welcome news as a 1998 study of U.S. college students indicated that far fewer students took Arabic than many other languages: 656,590 enrolled in Spanish; 199,064 enrolled in French; and only 5,505 studied Arabic.

The scarcity of Arabic-speaking professionals in the United States has resulted in more courses in that discipline being offered at language schools, including university professional development programs. For example, the George Washington University's Center for Professional Development offers an "Introduction to Arabic Translation and Interpretation." Since 9/11, Arabic is the leading language course at the U.S. military's prestigious Defense Language Institute.

OTHER "HOMELAND SECURITY" POSITIONS

There is growing appeal among recent university graduates for government service roles. This premise is supported by a fall 2001 poll in which 32% of university students nationwide expressed an interest in public service. Post-9/11 university student fascination with possible public service attacks was designated as a component of Generation 9/11.

Interest in government service by recent college students and older workers includes roles at the CIA, FBI, INS, State Department, Congress, U.S. Customs Services, U.S. Border Patrol, and Federal Air Marshals. Competition to be hired by a U.S. intelligence agency or the Foreign Service is intense. Between October 2001–September 2002, only about 1% of applicants to the FBI, National Security Agency, and the State Department's Foreign Service were hired. Likewise difficulty in being hired is projected at the CIA.

Career opportunities in the government sector advertised in 2003 included: Special Agents (FBI, in Washington, D.C.), Counter-Terrorism Analysts (CIA in Washington, D.C., area), and Transportation Security Screener (Nationwide). Other government agencies, including the Food and Drug Administration, are increasingly appealing to applicants. After all, the importance of emergency medical preparedness, health issues, medicines, and vaccines in the fight against terrorism is widely appreciated.

A number of homeland security companies—defense, security equipment and services, and germ detection—are experiencing a rise in business activity, which also bodes well for employment at such firms. Corporations are increasingly adding chief security officers and network security positions nationwide. Some positions are established to focus on homeland security opportunities in the government space.

Among other types of homeland security positions advertised with greater frequency include roles such as: Arab Linguist/Broadcaster (SAIC Inc., Virginia), Senior Bioterrorism Expert (ICF Consulting in Virginia), Weapons of Mass Destruction Specialist (Booz Allen Hamilton in Virginia), Counter-Intelligence Analyst (Management Technology Inc. in Virginia), and Emergency Management Analyst (Titan Systems Corp., Virginia). More traditional security roles include Industrial Security Specialist (Advanced Resource Technology in the Washington, D.C., area) and Access Control Officers (MVM Inc. in Virginia).

More funding earmarked for security management roles has resulted in a rising demand for seasoned executives with such skills. Recruiting firm Korn/Ferry International reported a significant increase in requests for candidates with security expertise. Security Management Resources Inc. cited strong demand for security executives since the 9/11 attacks. Candidates with prior military and security experience, coupled with security clearances, are highly desirable candidates. The unpleasant reality that terrorism may threaten the United States for years to come should only prolong demand for persons with significant military and security experience.

Of relevance to the labor market was the creation of the DHS in 2003, which integrated 22 agencies (plus the Transportation Security Agency) and about 170,000 employees under one roof. It is foreseeable there will be some personnel shifts in light of the creation of the DHS.

Development of the DHS personnel system, which includes 17 unions, will be complex and lengthy. The OPM will establish new civil service rules comprising: performance appraisals, job classifications, pay, labor, management, discipline and employee appeals.

If a specific industry were to be targeted by frequent terror incidents (e.g., suicide attacks on buses in the United States), there would likely be more hiring of security guards by that industry. Numerous suicide bombing attacks against Israeli buses led to the use of bus security guards. In March 2003, Israel's Transportation Minister told an Israeli bus cooperative, Egged, to hire another 500 security guards for public buses.

Delays in training and attaching such security personnel stemmed from disagreements over whether the government or the bus cooperatives (Egged and another firm, Dan) should bear that portion of the costs. In the meantime, limited security did little to deter numerous suicide bombs from carrying out their attacks. While additional security forces would not eliminate suicide bombs, they would reduce the lethality of such attacks.

Following the 9/11, military recruiters saw a significant rise in interest by prospective soldiers. However, some applicants fail to make the initial cut into the military services due to minimal educational background and the lack of physical fitness. Operation Iraqi Freedom led to further recognition that military forces will need more individuals joining ranks in the future. Yet, the significant number of U.S. military casualties in Iraq and Afghanistan has caused some concern from selected prospective recruits, enlisted soldiers, and their families.

U.S. operations in Afghanistan and Iraq have led to other job opportunities. Demand grew for defense contractor personnel and traditional government contractor services. Other roles exist for individuals to assist with, for instance, the development of local democracy in Iraq. RTI International, based in North Carolina, sought individuals experienced in local government services and community-based organizations for assignments in Iraq.

Post–September 11 Employer Issues

Security

Due to the perception of growing terrorist threats, employers undertake additional security efforts, such as: heighten security awareness at office buildings and manufacturing facilities, erect barriers near building entrances, and install fences; acquire security and other equipment (metal detectors, mail irradiation, special ventilation, and germ detection); contract with security personnel services for general duties and specific assignments, such as body guards for senior management; enlist corporate security and disaster specialist consultants; and issue mailroom employees gloves and masks. Also, Corporate America comprehends the need to provide employees with emergency and safety preparedness training for moral, morale, and potential liability purposes.

A March 2003 Gallup poll found that 57% of employees believed their employer did nothing to improve security, 27% cited minor improvements, while 16% remarked security improved greatly. Some companies have undertaken emergency drills in anticipation of possible terror attacks. In such an environment, the insight of the corporate security director has received greater resonance than before the September 11 attacks.

As anthrax attacks severely affected the U.S. Postal Service, mail delivery, and U.S. postal workers, in fall 2001, the U.S. government ordered 4 million masks and 86 million disposable gloves for postal workers to use while on the job. Also, the U.S. government is irradiating some mail, killing potentially harmful biological agents in turn. The U.S. government purchased additional irradiation machinery in late 2001 to reduce the threat of pathogen-laced parcels.

Postal employee unions and postal workers strenuously complained that the response to the slightest chance of exposure to anthrax in the Congress resulted in much more rapid public health and investigative responses than anthrax exposures at postal facilities. In late October 2001, Postmaster General John Potter denied that the U.S. Postal Service ignored postal worker safety at the Brentwood postal facility in Washington, D.C. (Two postal workers who worked there died of anthrax inhalation.)

In any case, the tension between postal workers and senior management may be replicated as employers must balance responding to threats to employee safety while concurrently trying to run a business in an ever-increasingly competitive environment. The employers' assessments on such matters are further complicated by the fact that employers may have limited or faulty investigative and health data critical in making decisions that weigh worker safety with running a profitable business. Miscalculations on either spectrum could lead to death of employees at one extreme, and to financial ruin at the other. As employers and employees gain additional experience with and understanding of this tension, better decisions are expected.

Additional security and training costs, disruptions to business operations, investments in data storage and emergency preparedness, lower productivity of employees, and other strains on employers are associated with the post-9/11 environment. As such, companies must find ways to reduce costs elsewhere: through job cuts, less investment in research and development, decreased spending on marketing, less investment in infrastructure and capital goods, and curtailed training of employees. Also, firms may pass along these costs to their customers in the form of higher prices, additional fees, or both.

Monitoring and Investigating Employees

Employers are using more internal reviews to monitor employees' use of the Internet, telephone, and fax communications to ensure that their workers are not involved in any: illegal activities, anti-employer actions (e.g., destroying files), corporate espionage, nor support of terrorist groups (.e.g., disclosing data or recruiting personnel).

Investigations into the possible collaboration of several U.S. military personnel in Guantanamo Bay, Cuba, with al Qaeda (or other foreign enemies) illustrates the possible risks that employers—particularly military and defense contractors—face. Penetration by terror groups into the U.S. military and defense industry provides them with: insights into potential weaknesses, access to further recruits, opportunities to sabotage assets, and exposure to intelligence and weaponry.

Terror group operatives are secreted into private sector jobs and recruited from such ranks. In May 2003, Iyman Faris, a truck driver, pled guilty to conspiring to give material aid to a terror group, al Qaeda. Among Faris' duties as an al Qaeda operative was to investigate potential targets, including bridges and tunnels.

At the extreme, then, employers need to be concerned about whether an employee is investigating a future terror target, rather than simply taking an extended lunch break! For these and other reasons companies are undertaking more background checks prior to hiring new employees and closely monitoring their activities at work (e.g., Internet and video). Nevertheless, employers' limited resources as well as the costs and inefficiencies that arise from such oversight limits robust monitoring and investigations.

Potential Liability

Employers are very interested in the potential liability of their employees in connection with a terror incident. Concern arises whether the employee is harmed at the office or carrying out functions on behalf of the employer outside of the office. Depending on the circumstances, of course, workers generally would only obtain workers' compensation payments, rather than obtain punitive damages in a civil suit.

Health Matters

Employers may face escalating mental health expenses. The harmful financial consequences to business are significant because recent studies and mental health experts concluded that depression and high stress topped the list of the leading factors resulting in heightened medical expenses for employers. Workers who had high stress had 46% larger medical costs than employees without such ailments.

In addition to the direct financial costs of mental illness, affected employees may experience reduced levels of productivity, drive, and creativity in conjunction with high incidents of absenteeism. In trying to soothe particularly troubled employees, bosses may defer urgent projects, reassign duties and projects to other employees, or readjust business plans based on the sensitivities and recovery speeds of key employees.

Other health issues relate to government mandates that military personnel take specific vaccines such as anthrax. In January 2004, a federal court ruling upheld the permissibility of the Pentagon requiring U.S. military personnel to take anthrax shots even without their consent. The consequences to employees who fail to respond to employer demands, such as vaccinations, can result in their termination or other punishment. In actuality, refusal to get anthrax vaccines has resulted in the court-martial of various servicemen.

U.S. military activities in places such as Iraq, Afghanistan, and the Philippines may also result in accelerated demands for mental health support to soldiers who served in those places. There have been reports that wounded soldiers and physically unscathed troops suffer some long-lasting effects.

Conclusion

These recent trends illustrate the inescapable reality that terrorism's effects on labor are profound. It is anticipated that future labor and management relations will continue to experience shifts due to terrorism. Should terrorists conduct attacks against various business sectors (e.g., financial, energy, and maritime), other segments of the workforce will rush to their aid (e.g., first-responders). In the post-9/11 environment, workers are expected to continue their important roles in the economy while being more vigilant of possible expanding threats. After all, retreat and fear in the face of terror will not eliminate it, but actually, will encourage more terror.

8

Additional Perspectives on Terror's Impact on Business

A discussion of initial trends arising from terror's impact on business is critical given global terror threats against industry, government, and the public. This chapter addresses the broad consequences of political violence on business accordingly: the initial impact of large-scale terror attacks on business, subsequent industry responses, and long-term structural issues affecting business.

The short-term effects of catastrophic terrorism are discussed in terms of economic and sector responses, including ramifications on financial markets and effects on business activity. Industry responses crafted thereafter include: shifts and flexibility within and among business sectors, development and expansion of homeland security companies, funding such firms, and mergers and acquisitions in that sector. The diverse forces that terror injects on business are addressed as follows: costs in terms of outlays and rising transaction costs; security at a business location; interactions with customers; ramifications on sourcing, inventory, and logistics; and legal issues.

Initial Impact of Catastrophic Terrorism

Economic and Sector Consequences

The initial economic impact of the 9/11 attacks was acute and negative, exemplified by: substantial declines in stock markets and, thereby, the value of public companies (e.g. airlines, travel businesses, and insurance); and closure of stock and bond markets for several days due to damage near those locations.

The Dow Jones Industrial Average (DJIA) and Nasdaq Composite Index declined by 7.13% and 6.83%, respectively, on the day the market reopened (September 17, 2001). On that day, airline and travel stocks dropped significantly in value, falling between 30%-60%. In the five days after trading resumed, the DJIA declined by 14.3%, the largest weekly fall since 1933. During the nearly two week period after the September 11 attacks, the Bank for International Settlements reported global equities lost some $3 trillion—about 12% of their value.

In the months subsequent to the 9/11 incidents, U.S. economic growth waned and unemployment rose, while consumer spending and confidence dropped. Commodity prices, such as oil and gold, spiked. The Federal Reserve Board injected liquidity into the money supply and reduced interest rates over subsequent months.

Moreover, the September 11 attacks resulted in: millions of dollars of damage to buildings and infrastructure (e.g., telecommunications, electricity, and subway lines); billions of dollars of lost economic output; some $50 billion in insurance liability; the demise of thousands of talented workers; $5 billion in government-sponsored victims' compensation fund; and billions of dollars in homeland security outlays by government and industry.

New York City spent some $825 million in World Trade Center-related costs, including about $350 million in removing debris in the six months following the 9/11 incidents. According to the New York City Partnership, New York City's economy would lose nearly one hundred times the overall cleanup costs—about $83 billion. A November 2001 National League of Cities study predicted that the 9/11 attacks would cause municipal revenues to decline by $11.4 billion.

Corporate America suffered severe initial damage to particular sectors, including airlines, tourism, hospitality, and insurance. Other sectors that witnessed some declines—in certain regions—were real estate, energy, technology, and entertainment. The Washington, D.C., area and Manhattan were hurt particularly hard as demonstrated by declines in tourism and hospitality revenue.

Other negative ramifications of the 9/11 attacks, besides the deaths and injuries, was the perception that the United States was no longer immune to catastrophic terror attacks on its soil. Also, by attacking American symbols of economic and military power American vulnerability to terrorism was exposed.

The impact of 9/11 on the world economy was likewise negative. This was particularly true in Japan and Europe, that were already experiencing recessions prior to the attacks. U.S. neighbors, Mexico and Canada, suffered in the subsequent economic downturn, particularly in the aviation, tourism, and hospitality sectors.

It is extremely difficult to predict prospective economic and sector consequences in the event of another catastrophic terror attack. Yet, it is probable that immediate financial market shocks will be coupled with declines in the affected sector(s). The severity and breadth of a future catastrophe—whether limited to a city, region, or broader in scope— will weigh on the severity of the attacks. With that said, significant improvements in corporate security and government counterterror efforts should lessen the negative implications of future attacks.

Although some sectors were severely damaged, other industries strengthened following the September 11 incidents. Demand for homeland security products and services expanded almost immediately. In this regard, when the principal U.S. stock markets opened on September 17, 2001, the stock price of some defense, security (e.g., bomb detection and corporate security) and technology firms (e.g., providers of video-conferencing) actually rose by over 100%. Prospects of huge government expenditures to support the newly declared war on terrorism provided some of the impetus for the rise in homeland security stock prices.

On March 11, 2004, multiple bombings on commuter trains in Madrid killed 190 and injured 1,500 people. On that day, European stock market benchmarks were hit particularly hard, with the European Dow Jones Stoxx 600 Index declining by 2.67%. Spain's stock market index fell by 2.18%. Likewise, U.S. stock markets were negatively affected, evidenced by decreases in the DJIA (1.64%) and Nasdaq Composite (1.03%). Travel-related stocks in the United States and Europe declined significantly. International stock markets, as referenced in the Dow Jones World Index, fell by 1.58%.

After the 3/11 incidents, there was widespread concern of a possible al Qaeda link to the attacks. Those concerns were confirmed fairly quickly as a Spanish and Moroccan law enforcement officials picked up operatives linked to radical Islamic groups. These developments only exacerbated declines and volatility in international stock markets during subsequent weeks.

Transactions Cancelled, Delayed, and Business Interrupted

Shortly following the World Trade Center and Pentagon attacks, various companies announced that they would put on hold their previously planned investments. Manpower Inc., the nation's largest supplier of temporary workers, canceled plans to open 40 new offices. Eastman Chemical, a leading supplier of material for plastics and paint, announced that new investments would be postponed. C.R. England Inc., a family-owned trucking company with 2,500 tractor-trailers, stated that the attacks would discourage the firm from making further investments in the immediate future.

The 9/11 incidents caused some companies to reconsider the appropriateness or timing of certain investments and transactions. Berkshire Hathaway apparently cited a clause in a contract enabling termination of an agreement in the event of "war or armed conflict," less than a week after the attacks. More specifically, it was reported that Berkshire Hathaway rescinded its offer to purchase up to $500 million of Finova Group's 7.5% senior-secured notes. A number of airlines contacted Boeing Co. to request delaying the delivery of several dozen airplanes, valued in total at several billion dollars.

The attacks also derailed very advanced merger negotiations between Keefe, Bruyette & Woods and BNP Paribas in a deal expected to be worth between $300 million to $400 million. It was reported that the parties may resume discussions in the future. Keefe, Bruyette & Woods lost about one-third of its employees during the World Trade Center attacks. Also, the attacks apparently interfered with initial merger discussions between the investment firms of Lehman Brothers Holdings Inc. and Lazard LLC.

A substantial number of conventions and conferences were canceled or rescheduled nationwide as people were concerned about traveling during the weeks following the 9/11 attacks. Leisure travel, including to aviation-dependent locations, such as Las Vegas and Miami, declined significantly (e.g., Miami lost $15 million in revenues daily in the days following the attacks).

Firms delayed construction of high-rise office buildings and condominiums as terror concerns and rising insurance weighed on future developments. New products and long planned advertising campaigns were put in abeyance, as the public needed time to grieve the September 11 incidents. Cross-sector business initiatives were frozen as firms considered what impact the attacks would have on their bottom line.

Commercial airports experienced severe declines in flights and passengers following 9/11. Reduced traffic led to abated aircraft landing fees. Fewer passengers resulted in less income to airports parking-lot operators, stores, restaurants, and ground transportation concessions.

Despite amazing resilience by business and the public after 9/11, there was still some apprehension as to whether such attacks—or worse—would be replicated in other parts of the country. There was understandable confusion whether a state-sponsor of terror would assist al Qaeda (or other groups) in providing support for superterrorism attacks against the United States. Resolve against terror, coupled with a modicum of uncertainty, marked preliminary industry responses to the catastrophic September 11 incidents.

In the aftermath of the October 2003, massive car bombing of the Red Cross headquarters in Iraq, the organization decided to close its offices in Baghdad and Basra. While that response was likely hoped for by the attackers, it also eliminated the contribution of a leading nongovernment entity. Often, as in this case, an entity that was recently inflicted by terror may temporarily cease operations and evacuate personnel from a high-risk region. Were a company to shut down operations following a terror attack, the firm would lose revenue, incur other costs, while the host country losses jobs and prestige as foreign investment likely declines.

Subsequent Industry Responses

Impact on Sectors

OVERVIEW

Significant terrorist attacks may negatively impact several sectors simultaneously (e.g., commercial aviation, insurance, hospitality, and tourism) during an early period while creating and expanding opportunities in other industries (e.g., corporate security, defense, biometrics, and explosive detection equipment). Product lines may be removed from the market or limited in their preference depending on the severity of the attack. Terrorism insurance coverage became scarce and costly after 9/11, though later, offerings in that space expanded. During the initial coverage of September 11 major television networks did not run any commercials in honor of the victims.

Terrorist attacks using the instrumentality of one sector (e.g., public mail carriers) can create negative results on the same sector (e.g., public mail carriers). Concurrently that same attack can fuel demand in other unrelated sectors (e.g., pharmaceuticals—Cipro; and electron beam irradiation machine-mail and germ detection equipment).

As indicated in Chapter 7, during fall 2001, a number of anthrax-tainted letters were sent by unknown assailant(s), causing five deaths and over a dozen injuries. The anthrax incidents led to the temporary closure of selected government and private offices. Also, the events injected panic into some segments of the American public relative to the safety of the U.S. mail system.

In light of such threats, the U.S. Postal Service purchased eight electron beam systems (machines to irradiate mail) from industry. The U.S. government planned to purchase several hundred devices, totaling additional government outlays of over $1 billion.

A serious terrorist incident can result in future investments being temporarily delayed or canceled. Likewise, a major attack can shut down segments of an industry for days. This was exhibited when commercial aviation was grounded temporarily and U.S. stock markets were closed for several days after 9/11.

A terrorist incident on one portion of an industry, such as commercial airlines in the transportation industry, can have positive ramifications on other segments of the same industry, such as corporate jets and charter services. The significant downturn in the use of commercial airlines immediately following 9/11 spawned greater interest in the use of trains, buses, and rental cars as alternative modes of transportation. Initial declines in airline, tourism, and insurance stocks after September 11 were countered by accelerated demand for homeland security firm equities.

A severe terrorist incident, even if not directly affecting the target industry, may nevertheless result in hastening the demise of already weak firms. This was witnessed in fall 2001 when Renaissance Cruises and Aladdin Gaming, two large companies in the tourism and hotel industries, filed for Chapter 11 bankruptcy. During November 2001, ANC Rental Corp., owner of Alamo and National rental cars, filed for bankruptcy due to declining demand fueled by weak commercial aviation travel in fall 2001.

If terrorists use pathogens, such as anthrax, to infect the mail system, at the same time that they engage in sniper-like attacks, then two modes of commerce — in-person purchases and online purchases (e.g., delivery of products via the mail systems) — would be affected. A severe cyberterror attack against principal e-commerce sites would likewise undermine online purchases.

Consequences of the 9/11 attacks on specific industries, such as insurance and aviation, are being played out more than two years after the incidents. Another effect of terror threats—in this case bioterrorism—is accelerated investment in biotechnology companies and pharmaceutical firms that have applicability to countering bioterrorism.

In attacking the tourism sector, numerous business are harmed simultaneously: hotels, restaurants, and transportation (e.g., aviation, car rentals). By attacking the tourism sector of the economy, an important source of revenue is lessened, creating more unemployment and dissatisfaction with the government. Terror attacks can lead to such dissatisfaction with the ruling party as to cause regime change or a shift in government policies aligned with the terror group's goals (e.g., March 11, 2004, terror attacks in Spain contributed to a Socialist Party victory in national elections).

Attacks against tourist interests have occurred worldwide. For example, in Egypt in 1993, tourists were targeted in multiple attacks, including: a bomb was hurled at a bus carrying 15 South Korean tourists in Cairo; and gunmen fired shots at boats carrying 44 British passengers and 22 French tourists along the Nile during two separate incidents. In Egypt, between 1992–1994, there were nearly 130 terrorist attacks. The incidents resulted in the deaths of nine tourists and injuries of about 60. Between 1992 and 1993 the number of tourists visiting Egypt declined by 21.8%.

The Irish Republican Army (IRA) has targeted the coastal resort areas of England. The Kurdish Workers' Party (PKK) has been responsible for bombing tourist hotels as well as kidnapping tourists and holding them as pawns in their political negotiations with the Turkish government. Terrorist attacks have discouraged tourism in Corsica. In Spain, the Basque Fatherland and Liberty terrorist group (ETA) claimed responsibility for setting explosive devices at tourist hotels on the Mediterranean coast. The bombings of two Bali nightclubs—resulting in some 200 deaths—in 2002 marked a recent example of terrorist groups targeting tourists.

While the impact of a large-scale terrorist attack can be severe, as witnessed on 9/11, it is also correct to suggest that economies and businesses can withstand substantial pain. The post-September 11 U.S. economy was remarkably resilient despite some initial shocks. Firms nationwide have largely adjusted to the new risk dynamic endemic in the post-9/11 business environment.

The American economy's capacity to rebound from the 9/11 attacks was due to various factors. First, rapid, decisive government and industry responses took hold. Second, employees in the public and private sectors displayed courage and dedication, leading in some cases to sacrificing their lives to aid others (e.g., firefighters and police). Third, consumers contributed to the recovery by continuing to shop although sales in many spheres declined in the initial weeks after the attacks. Fourth, sector-specific laws were enacted to soften the impact of the attacks. Fifth, intelligence and law enforcement success in rounding up terrorists at home and abroad gave the impression—partially true—that the U.S.-based component of the war on terrorism was proceeding fairly well. Sixth, the lack of a subsequent large-scale terrorist attack on U.S. soil—as of March 2004—aided U.S. economic and business resilience.

SELECTED SECTOR: REAL ESTATE

Before the 9/11 attacks, telecommuting was seen as a stagnating trend, as bosses decided it was too difficult to manage a network of dispersed, remote workers. Employees felt stigmatized if they were not seen around the office. But the September 11 attacks caused many workers to reevaluate their priorities, and some companies are exploring this option.

Companies now view home-based employees as a defensive measure if their offices become inaccessible. As American Express Co. offices were damaged during September 11, hundreds of employees worked "virtually," as the company sets up temporary locations in New Jersey and Connecticut. Firms located outside New York, such as Charles Schwab Corp. (San Francisco) and ABN Amro North America (Chicago) acknowledged exploring telecommuting options with great vigor.

The above shift could result in a slight reduction in traditional commercial leasing to smaller-scale commercial developments as well as technologically enhanced residential models. Also, consultants advising on establishing virtual offices and the companies that assist in establishing their telecommunications networks should benefit from this trend.

There has been an initial downturn in larger real estate projects due to higher property insurance as well as reluctance by some lenders and prospective employees. Concurrently, there has been increased interest in smaller development projects, including duplicative offices for sensitive business locations (e.g., trading facilities and backup operations facilities).

Companies with decentralized real estate set-ups—various units spread out among disparate cities or regions—may become a growing trend among selected firms that seek to reduce the impact of a massive terrorist attack. Some companies have already adopted the decentralized paradigm. A decentralized approach reduces vulnerability should one severe terrorist attack strike one location. Such schemes also raise costs as duplicate facilities and multiple personnel (including persons trained for additional job functions) are necessary.

Some architects and urban planners argue that in light of possible massive terrorist attacks during this century, it is preferable to construct future office developments separated by parks and sports stadiums. Whether such perspectives will be adopted nationwide depend on various factors, such as costs, aesthetic appeal, practicality, and the perception that large-scale terror threats are genuine.

The threat of terrorism on U.S. soil adds further challenges to landlords of large-scale retail centers, such as shopping malls. Landlords of such developments must balance the need for great security measures without concurrently scaring away customers who might perceive such steps as confirming that shopping malls are imminent terrorist targets.

With that in mind, some shopping centers have undertaken a number of security measures: hired additional security guards, improved safety and security training for property management staff, tightened restrictions on truck deliveries of merchandise and foodstuffs, and broadened parking restrictions. However, searching all shoppers prior to them entering a shopping mall is not envisioned in the United States—at least for now.

Development and Expansion of Homeland Security Companies

In the post-September 11 era, numerous products and services of companies in selected industries (or niches within a specific sector) experienced additional demand as the business community was further mobilized in the fight against terrorism. The period has also spawned frequent use of terms or buzz words, such as: companies helpful in the war on terrorism, counterterrorism companies, and homeland defense firms. Companies adopted names with the word "homeland" to give them cache in the post-9/11 era. Analogously, companies created subsidiaries and expanded business units focusing on homeland defense products and services.

Below is a discussion of some products and services in the homeland security space. Goods and services comprising this group include: traditional defense equipment; non-lethal weaponry; germ detection and remediation; biometrics, trace detection, technology, and document authentication; aviation security; security services; technology products and services; pharmaceuticals, biotechnology, and forensics; and "survivalist" merchandise. It is important to underscore, however, that inclusion or omission of any sector herein neither implies any endorsement nor judgment on the products, services, capabilities, and financial attributes of any firm.

TRADITIONAL DEFENSE EQUIPMENT

U.S. military operations against terrorist groups worldwide include Afghanistan, Iraq, Yemen, and the Philippines. U.S. clandestine activities in other nations are believed to occur elsewhere. Due to such developments, the defense industry experienced additional growth in specific sub-sectors. This trend is likely to continue as long as America counter-terror policy includes a proactive posture and government funding of such activities is maintained.

Traditional defense industry wares include: fighter, transport, and unmanned aircraft; bombs and missiles; aircraft carriers; tanks; and ground combat systems. Items used during various operations include body armor, night-vision goggles, diverse batteries to power military communications and other wares, and tiles for protection of military vehicles. Delays in production of particular wares, logistics in delivery of products, and having adequate funding for defense equipment are also items worth noting.

NON-LETHAL WEAPONRY

The military has considered (and in some cases used) various nonlethal weapons including: calmatives (incapacitating gases that immobilize the target; one type, Fentanyi, was used by Russian special forces during a fall 2002 hostage-rescue in Moscow). Demand for distraction and dis-orientation products (e.g., loud noises, infrasounds leading to hallucinations, and malodorants or noxious smells), irritant foams, smoke; and stunning instruments is expected to accelerate as such tools may prove useful in defensive and offensive operations.

GERM DETECTION AND REMEDIATION

In light of the fall 2001 anthrax attacks, the February 2004 ricin discovery in the U.S. Senate, and other biological terror threats, germ detection and remediation products and services could play a larger role in the future.

BOMETRICS, TRACE DETECTION, TECHNOLOGY, AND DOCUMENT AUTHENTICATION

The 9/11 terrorist attacks and subsequent terror incidents have brought to the forefront diverse products and services. Such items enable government and businesses to better monitor and safeguard locations (e.g., airports and office buildings). Facial recognition software can match an image against a database of criminals and terrorists. Iris-scanning cameras authenticate that a particular individual is the person he claims to be.

Trace detection machines and metal detectors are used at security checkpoints in the United States and abroad. These devices operate in airports, embassies, police stations, prisons, nuclear power plants, and other tight security environments worldwide. Government funding has been earmarked for developing sensor and other devices to stop the illegal transport and use of radiological and nuclear materials.

Surveillance cameras and closed circuit television (CCTV) are used at airports, government buildings, military facilities, factories, shopping malls, and increasingly throughout other U.S. locations. It is interesting to note that several hijackers involved in the World Trade Center and Pentagon attacks were caught on surveillance cameras at ATM machines, stores, and airports, facilitating the investigation of the terrorist incidents. With better timing, more accurate databases, and a little luck for law enforcement, perhaps some of the attacks on 9/11 could have been prevented.

Companies producing identity documents, border management, and passenger information systems as well as machine-readable travel and identity documents exhibited further demand following 9/11. Government funding of projects in this domain is projected to be strong. Smart card businesses are exploring how to adapt their technology, already implemented in mass transit cards, to limit access into secure areas.

AVIATION SECURITY

Some companies are focusing on upgrading physical security measures on planes, such as steel-reinforced cockpit doors and arming pilots with guns and stun guns. Additionally, companies are exploring the development of complete autoflight capabilities that theoretically enable jets to be guided safely without interference from the cockpit. Such systems are expected to prevent a suicide pilot from crashing a plane if airport control knows of a hijacking.

Adapting and installing anti-missile systems on commercial airlines has gained greater resonance since the attempted downing of several aircraft in Kenya, Saudi Arabia, and Iraq in 2003 by attackers using shoulder-fired missiles. Reports of possible aviation terror plots against U.S.-bound planes portend that protection of this sector will remain a principal government objective.

SECURITY SERVICES

Research firm Freedonia Group reported that the future of private security services looks bright. Demand for U.S. private security services is expected to rise 7.3% annually through 2006, reaching $48 billion that year. The private security services rubric includes: guarding, alarm monitoring, investigations, armored transport, correctional facilities, systems integration, security consulting, and pre-employment screening.

The large number of employees required to staff security checkpoints at transportation facilities, businesses, shopping malls, universities, and government installations worldwide should result in growth for security service companies. The demand for bodyguards, armored cars, sentries, background checks, and identification screening rose significantly since the 9/11 attacks.

Due to such threats, some business leaders also seek counterterrorism training for executives, bodyguards, and other protection products and services. At the extreme, executives seek armored cars with specially trained and armed drivers. Since 9/11 there has been an escalation in inquiries and demand for such services, especially by executives that travel overseas and companies with operations in "trouble-spots."

Private security guards have also been used to protect U.S. and foreign diplomats. U.S. military activity in Iraq and Afghanistan also spurred U.S. business activity in those countries. As such, demand increased for private security guards for U.S. businessmen and journalists traveling to those regions.

The September 11 attacks precipitated some employers to accelerate the use of background checks on employees, contractors, and potential hires. In turn, background-screening companies have experienced increased business. Potential clients' requests range from standard hiring procedure services to increasing surveillance of employees. This is particularly so for government contractors doing national security-related work.

Companies are legally bound to undertake criminal background checks for airport employees with access to secure areas. The aviation security law mandates additional background checks for other workers as well.

More hiring of military and contractors doing homeland security work accelerated demand for broad background checks. Individuals with security clearances have a big advantage over other job applicants as one obstacle to hiring—background check—is essentially eliminated.

Other security services include undertaking information analysis and infrastructure protection. During fiscal year 2004, the Department of Homeland Security (DHS) allocated $28 million for threat determinations and assessments of U.S. critical infrastructure and principal assets, including: public water systems, oil and natural gas production facilities, offshore platforms, natural gas pipelines, seaports, nuclear power plants, and dams. Another $84.2 million were earmarked for accurate mapping of U.S. critical infrastructure and major assets including: agriculture, food, public health and emergency services, government, defense industrial base, information and telecommunications, energy, and transportation, among others.

TECHNOLOGY PRODUCTS AND SERVICES

Assorted technology products and services have been in more demand since 9/11, including: military-oriented telecommunications and software; security software; data mining; data storage, recovery services, and emergency-management software; videoconferencing and teleconferencing hardware and software; wireless technology and other telephony; and personal digital assistants and hand-held computers.

Initial investigation of the 9/11 perpetrators and other al Qaeda members indicate that they employed everyday technologies (i.e., voice mail, cellular phones, and e-mail) to communicate, though often using codes, encryption, and other methodologies when exchanging operations-sensitive information. These steps were used, in part, to elude intelligence and law enforcement authorities.

In some cases, terrorists have used multiple cellular phones to evade interception: some phones only receive incoming calls; others make outgoing calls. Of particular importance is data encryption technology as the software makes it difficult for government officials to follow terrorists' communication exchanges.

Revelations about other terror groups have uncovered similar communication methodologies. More primitive methods, such as using personal representatives to relay messages personally, have been attributed to terrorists.

Security software firms offer antivirus software, firewalls, and intrusion detection, experienced greater demand from: businesses, governments, and individuals. These products and services are helpful in deterring possible damage from cyberterrorists to other cyber-criminals.

Research firm IDC projects that the market for high technology security products and services in 2005 will reach $46 billion, more than triple the figure reported in 2000. The market is comprised of: security services (e.g., security training), security software (antivirus software and secure content management technologies), and security hardware (e.g., physical and network access cards and firewall security appliances).

Data mining software enables the government to comb through hundreds of millions of intercepted e-mail messages, faxes, and phone calls in minutes. Such capabilities aid the government in tracking down suspected terrorists. Data mining systems are even able to distinguish a single voice out of thousands of cell phone conversations.

More companies now view advanced data storage, recovery services, and emergency management software as integral components of corporate security. Storage services provide different alternatives. They can furnish limited options, such as manually downloading data on magnetic tapes, followed by forwarding the tapes to an off-site storage. Storage services also provide broad options in which companies may purchase software and services that allow for data to be duplicated and transmitted to a remote location through secure, high-speed communications.

In another measure to fight terrorism, the U.S. government may require citizens, resident aliens, and others to obtain and carry a National ID. The card could be a relatively unsophisticated paper card with little information, such as a name, national identity number, and perhaps, a address. Such a card would be of little value as it could easily be forged. Without a photo of an individual's face, it would not be helpful for purposes of identification. Manufacturers and firms specializing in smart identification cards and related peripherals should benefit were the United States to adopt a national ID system.

A national ID system would partially undermine the multi-billion dollar global counterfeit and stolen document racket. Phony state driver's licenses and U.S. immigration cards sell on the black market for $25 and $500, respectively. An authentic diplomatic passport is projected to cost about $25,000. At San Ysidro, one entry point on the U.S.-Mexican border, the U.S. Immigration and Naturalization Service apprehended 52,000 people using false identification cards in the year 2000.

Business travel has declined and partially replaced by more video-conferencing, teleconferencing, and Internet-based collaboration tools. Firms in those fields have experienced a surge in business. Limited use of fixed line communications and cellular phones in New York City on September 11 led to expanded demand for satellite phones and service providers. Waterproofed and upgraded hand-held computers and personal digital assistants (PDAs) have expanded their application throughout U.S. military forces, included during counterterror operations abroad.

PHARMACEUTICALS, BIOTECHNOLOGY, AND FORENSICS

Bioterror attacks in the United States and abroad, coupled with future incidents thereof, have spurred demand for antibiotics and vaccines. Regular immunization against pathogens, such as anthrax and small-pox, may become the norm in years to come. Also, companies providing forensics investigative services may be called upon again as governmental medical and investigative teams respond to terrorist attacks.

"SURVIVALIST" MERCHANDISE

After the most horrific terrorist act on U.S. soil, some Americans took steps to fortify their homes and acquire food and medicines in anticipation of possible mass destruction violence caused by biological, chemical, or nuclear terrorism. Among the products that these persons have been purchasing since mid-September 2001 are: duct tape, gas masks, dust masks, antibiotics, emergency kits, electric generators, propane tanks, water filters, radios, flashlights, bottled water, and canned food. At the same time, a number of companies and entrepreneurs are marketing contraptions that claim to be helpful in the aftermath of a terrorist attack.

A DHS pronouncement in early 2003 encouraged Americans to stock up on bottled water, duct tape, plastic sheeting, first aid kits, and flashlights. This government guideline also spurred consumer interest in "survivalist," merchandise, even bomb shelters. As with homeland security products and services purchased by government and industry, consumers—in this case individuals and families—need to ensure that the items they buy are appropriate for their needs.

Investment in Homeland Security Companies

Avid public interest in investing in homeland security companies has taken hold. Should an individual investor partake in this development, numerous factors should be weighed. It is incumbent upon investors to take into consideration, among other things, a company's: financial data, its management, competitors, future prospects, regulatory issues, and geopolitical developments that may influence viability of a particular firm.

A thorough analysis of a particular company or sector does not obviate the fact that investing is highly risky and investors may lose all their capital. During the more than two years after the 9/11 attacks some homeland security companies witnessed significant accelerations in their stock price, while others suffered severe declines, including bankruptcies. The decline of some firms is reminiscent of the Internet boom and bust. So buyers—should you act—beware.

Over the long-term homeland security firms may become a permanent actor in the business community and not a fad. Under such circumstances, there may arise a need to create a formal, professional counterterrorism stock index to track such developments. Another way to invest in homeland security firms may occur through the establishment of a mutual fund or unit investment trust focusing on homeland security companies. Whether counterterrorism stock indices, mutual funds, and unit investment trusts are made available to consumers at all—let alone on the retail level—is another matter. The sensitive nature of terror, the possibility for manipulation in this space, and the notion of formally "monetizing terror" make creation of such products potentially unwise and unpalatable.

Venture capital firms and angel investors have accelerated investments in homeland security firms. Corporate investments in homeland security start-ups are coupled with government funding of nascent entities. Analogous to the Internet start-up investment euphoria, there appears to be extensive investment in start-up homeland security firms that offer many competing products and services. As such, there is a strong possibility that too many duplicative firms in a finite market may lead to a number of homeland security start-up bankruptcies, and consequent investment losses.

For disclosure purposes, the author has invested in homeland security companies and may do so in the future. However, the author does not recommend others to undertake such actions because investing entails substantial risk.

Mergers and Acquisitions Activities

There has been an increase in joint ventures, mergers, and acquisitions among companies helpful in the war on terrorism, particularly among defense, biometrics, and technology companies. Mergers and acquisitions are occurring, in part, to get better access to government procurement market, where the prospects for large, multi-year deals are strong. Also, firms realize that a more integrative approach—combining human and technological capabilities—would be helpful in strengthening corporate responses to terror. As in other sectors, mergers and acquisitions do not always result in the creation of stronger firms.

An increase in mergers and acquisitions in the homeland security sectors also has its hazards. Eventually, only a few companies may own a majority of key, unique defense products and services. Therefore, if a terrorist group were to attack or sabotage such a company in a major way, it would likely take significant time until an ancillary competitor could produce similar goods and services.

Some homeland security companies undertook acquisitions by using their highly priced stock instead of payment of cash. Additionally, their attractive stock prices enabled them to raise cash through stock and bond offerings more readily than prior to 9/11. The stock price of some acquired companies likewise witnessed a higher stock price even before the acquisition discussions. As noted earlier, the stock price of some homeland security firms, including the acquirer companies, dropped significantly following their initial rise after 9/11.

A number of the homeland security deals that have occurred since 9/11 are set out below:

- Northrop Grumman acquired TRW in a nearly $7 billion deal. This transaction, plus other Northrop Grumman acquisitions, enabled the company to expand its product lines to include: ships, unmanned and manned military aircraft, defense electronic systems, information technology services, military satellites, and missile defense systems.
- The $1.1 billion purchase by General Dynamics of a General Motor's unit comprised a variety of lighter wheeled armored vehicles, including: Stryker (medium-weight Army combat vehicle), LAV III (armored personnel carrier), and Piranha IV (multirole vehicle).
- Computer Sciences paid $677 million for DynCorp., a firm specializing in the military and security markets. The combined company will have 30,000 employees and $6 billion in revenue.
- Integrated Defense Technologies Inc., which offers electronic and technical equipment to defense and intelligence agencies, acquired a surveillance unit of BAE Systems North America for $146 million.
- L-3 Communications, a provider of intelligence, surveillance, and reconnaissance products, acquired two defense-related units

of Northrop Grumman: Displays-Navigation Systems (producers equipment for ships command and control centers) and Electron Devices (focuses on microwave technology used by the U.S. military for radar jamming and in its guidance missiles). The acquisition will involve about 900 employees and raise L-3's revenues by $140 million.

- Technology Management and Analysis, which provides engineering and ship-testing services to the U.S. Navy, was acquired by L-3 Communications, in a $50 million cash deal, with an additional $7 million sweetener if certain targets are met.
- CACI International, a government contractor with growing defense-related business, bought the government solutions division of Condor Technology Solutions. The acquired unit, which had about $20 million in revenues in 2001, provides consulting services (e.g., strategic planning, interactive training, and communications) to the National Guard and Department of Veterans Affairs.
- Mountain Wave, a maker of software that keeps track of potential threats across a computer network, was acquired by Symantec, a market leader of computer security programs, in a $20 million deal.
- Raytheon acquired software supplier Solipsys and communications equipment provider JPS Communications.

Not only are mergers and acquisitions in the homeland security space occurring, but also less formal steps—informal alliances, formal links, and joint ventures—take place. Collaborative steps enable firms to concentrate on their specialties while permitting for contributions of other firms in combating terrorism.

For instance, an alliance between a homeland security firm, Kroll Inc., a risk consulting firm, and a company outside this space, Cushman & Wakefield, a real estate entity, was forged. The firms agreed to collaborate on security in property management and risk management issues. Similarly, Guiliani Partners, an advisory firm, and CB Richard Ellis, a real estate company, entered into a strategic partnership under which the former firm will provide the latter company's clients security and other consulting advice.

In protecting many sectors, a multidisciplinary approach for protection is critical. In real estate, for example, more use of physical barriers and access controls, coupled with architectural, engineering, and construction modifications, ensure more terror resistant buildings.

Transcending Consequences of Terror on Business

The broad ramifications of terror on business will be discussed accordingly: terror costs in terms of outlays and rising transaction costs; security at a business location; interactions with customers; ramifications on sourcing, inventory, and logistics; and legal issues.

Costs

Terrorism is relatively easy and inexpensive to activate yet very difficult and extremely costly to counter. These costs are ongoing and likely will rise in the future.

The costs arising from the 9/11 attacks ran in the hundreds of billions of dollars if one includes direct and indirect effects. Some of the costs, such as security and military expenditures fueled by those incidents, are foreseen to increase annually. Private sector security costs alone are estimated at $100 billion yearly. *Fortune* magazine estimated that economic "friction" due to terrorism, as exemplified in higher expenditures of business—logistics, insurance, workplace security, information technology, travel and transportation, and workforce—will cost companies about $150 billion annually.

Other terror-related costs attach even though they are outside the security rubric. In fact, some expenditures are entirely defensive though not security related. For instance, the American Hospital Association projected that U.S. hospital systems will require nearly $10 billion to adequately react to a massive biological, chemical or nuclear terror attack.

Terror attacks against economic targets have resulted in significant financial costs worldwide. The Provisional Irish Republican Army (IRA) exploded a large bomb outside the Baltic Exchange in London in April 1992, killing three and injuring about 90. The incident caused damage and disruption estimated at least several hundred million dollars. A Provisional IRA bomb blast at a large shopping center in Manchester, England, injured 200, damaged hundreds of businesses, and caused some $300 million in damages.

Terrorist incidents against the Jakarta and Bombay Stock Exchanges in recent years also caused shattering financial costs. Multiple terrorist attacks against Israeli targets—transportation, entertainment, and restaurants — during the second Intifada caused a decline in tourism of some 50%.

Business, too, is cognizant that it has limited financial resources with which to reduce terrorist threats. In turn, the tension between providing sufficient security without expending excessive resources has gained greater resonance. This balancing act will plague government and business for the foreseeable future.

Businesses have made cutbacks in other departments due to greater security demands at corporate facilities, points-of-sale, and elsewhere. When possible, companies pass on disparate security costs to customers. Such fees are forwarded either directly (through a security fee) or indirectly (prices are raised but no disclosure as to the reason).

As there is now a security surcharge on airline tickets, so too, other businesses deemed soft targets of terrorism (e.g., restaurants and movie theaters) may impose security fees. Security charges were instituted at some restaurants in Israel, where numerous suicide bombers wreck heavy human and financial tolls.

Businesses face higher costs when government raises terror warnings. For instance, increased threat warnings result in increasing security forces within airports with requisite added costs.

The costs of compensating terrorist victims families are matters that will be increasingly relevant should terrorist attacks proliferate, particularly in the United States. Unlike the persons killed and injured during the 1993 World Trade Center attacks and the 1995 Oklahoma City bombing, the 9/11 victims (or their families) received compensation.

While some compensation was provided for some of the victims of the 1998 bombings of the U.S. embassies in Kenya and Tanzania, the projected $5 billion allocated to the 9/11 victims is unprecedented. As such, it is likely that some level of compensation will attach to a future, large-scale terror attack occurring on U.S. soil or overseas.

Because terrorists and their sympathizers use the economic system, businesses closely investigate their employees, customers, suppliers, and partners. These investigative activities have resulted in greater costs to companies (e.g., paying outside firms to investigate employee backgrounds or having internal staff to monitor employee e-mail and Internet use). Furthermore, these measures have led to friction between employees and employers.

Security at Business Locations

After 9/11, a business site — be it a store, office, or factory — can be characterized differently. There is now greater cognizance that the battlefront of terrorism has entered into business environs: restaurants, theaters, and malls have been bombed; office buildings have been attacked by car bombs and planes; factories and facilities have been sabotaged; and personnel have been kidnapped and assassinated.

These facts have led businesses to spend more resources—manpower, money, and time—to counter and assuage the terrorist challenge. Additional security measures external to the site (e.g., concrete barriers and fences) and within a business location (e.g., metal detectors and CCTV cameras) have introduced a better awareness that terrorist threats affect the ways businesses protect themselves.

It is difficult, though, to protect the business site against all perpetrators. This is particularly so with those masquerading as legitimate suppliers, customers, and employees. Moreover, defending against suicide bombers and those without concern for their fate post an operation is highly complex.

Increased security in transportation systems, particularly in shipping and trucking, resulted in: higher transaction costs; interference with tight production schedules as supplies are not delivered as expected; closing or decreasing production routes; and accelerating delays. Since 9/11, trucks are subject to closer scrutiny by law enforcement officials than before the attacks. Truckers' licenses and transportation manifests are examined more carefully. Bridges, tunnels, and highway toll facilities are under expanded surveillance. Public-private developments in improving logistics within a security framework have helped the situation.

Business tends to focus substantial attention on the most recent threat at a business site while often ignoring future challenges. Following the September 11 attacks, the commercial aviation sector implemented wide-reaching changes in its security framework. Unfortunately, security at other transportation modes (e.g., passenger trains, buses, and subways) has not yet received adequate attention. Sadly, only major attacks on disparate settings will initiate greater focus on less protected targets. An example of this was the increase in security at trains and subways in Europe and the United States after the 3/11 attacks.

Terror's spurring of broader security and national security concerns has other implications as well. A country may claim that accelerated security measures and requirements imposed on foreign companies are non-tariff barriers and inviolate of trade law. For example, in January 2004, the U.S. government pronounced that foreign carriers might be required to attach armed air marshals on specific U.S.-bound flights.

While trade law allows for use of safety measures to protect domestic consumers, extensive use of "terror safety," arguments may lead to future challenges. The existing trade agreements between the United States, Mexico, and Canada are affected by increased border security. Such security measures, while important—and even necessary—may indeed give rise to international challenges.

Companies that do not undertake security measures and adopt emergency preparedness procedures may lose customers. Clients may avoid doing business with companies that have sub-par, or worse, non-existent, security measures. Firms that invest in security products and services—such as shopping mall operators that place security officers at all entrances—may tout these measures to current and prospective clients. Some corporate jet service providers have cited their security features in the advertising as a way to attract customers.

The introduction (or escalation in the use) of security measures at a business site also affects the receptivity of the business to customers. A fortress-like setting could be a turn-off because it might be viewed as unattractive and difficult to maneuver within (e.g., barriers at the entrance). Some consumers may view additional security as a sign that a particular location, such as shopping malls, is a potential terrorist target.

There is some evidence to suggest that customers who may ventured to eat a restaurant or shop at a department store, may do without these services temporarily following terror attacks. Declining attendance at Israeli cafes and restaurants subsequent to suicide bombings at such establishments supports this assertion.

Such a business shift was also witnessed during the fall 2002, sniper attacks in the Washington, D.C. area. Although carried out by two individuals without apparent ties to terrorism, the attacks effectively "terrorized," the region and affected commerce. More specifically, the sniper attacks led to more home deliveries of groceries and meals. A similar change in business is conceivable should terrorists conduct sniper-like rampages in the United States and elsewhere.

Another element worth considering is whether a terrorist attack against a global retailer or restaurant chain justifies closure of all outlets within the same country, continent, or worldwide. Companies must weigh whether similar security measures should exist worldwide. Another calculation is whether political risk disparities warrant different security responses provided security thresholds exist.

Given the specter of terrorism, it seems reasonable that businesses address the issue of how they will respond in case of a terrorist attack. This is particularly important for customers (and employees) who may be present at a business or store during an incident.

Interactions with Customers

INFORMING CUSTOMER OF THREATS

Since 9/11 employers have given more attention to informing employees on how to react in case of a terrorist attack. The natural progression of such education is to instruct customers on how to respond in case of a terrorist incident. By making customers aware of how to behave in such trying circumstances, a company demonstrates several things. First, the firm acknowledges that it is aware of terror risks facing the community. Second, the company shows it is undertaking some security measures. Third, and most importantly, the firm is concerned about the safety of its customers.

The prospect of a restaurant customer reading a notice at the end of a menu—"In case of a terrorist attack, hit the floor and crawl to the nearest exit."—is rather far-fetched. However, during fall 2002, hundreds of Moscow theater-goers were taken hostage by Chechen terrorists, who stormed the House of Culture Theater. The incident demonstrated that a business—a theater in that instance—must be aware that it may become a target of terrorism. As such, firms should consider various approaches including security and public affairs components. Perhaps the term "emergency" rather than "terrorist attack," suffices in a warning instruction.

Therein lies the tension of a firm's duty to inform and aid its customers, while not unnecessarily scaring them away nor creating unreasonable tension. Even before the 3/11 attacks, the Washington, D.C., subway had public service notices requesting customers to be vigilant about suspicious objects and terrorist suspects.

By acknowledging that a customer might be at risk, the business potentially takes upon itself the obligation to provide a minimum level of security. Should a company fail to undertake security measures while a direct competitor does, and injury occurs, the plaintiff may have a stronger case than otherwise. At the same time, a customer who has knowledge of risks, and proceeds nonetheless, might not win on the merits.

CUSTOMERS AS THREATS

At first glance, a business owner does not know a whether customer is a terrorist. Depending on what product or service the customer is purchasing will warrant whether the business owner should undertake special care in investigating the customer—or at least finding out how the customer intends to use the product or service. There are also issues of what legal and moral obligations businesses have to "uncover" prospective terrorists.

A company often cannot determine whether a customer opens a bank account to obtain wire transfer from terrorist funders. Also, it is difficult to adduce if a client buys sophisticated technology or an unusual product (e.g., short-wave radio that can hear planes) for terrorist purposes. Among issues that might be considered are whether the products and services have dual uses.

Given fears of another 9/11-like aviation attack against Washington, D.C., particular security measures are imposed on customers who fly into (or from) Reagan/National Airport. For example, the "30-Minute Seat Rule" mandates that all passengers must stay in their seats for 30 minutes before arriving at that airport, and for the initial 30 minutes following departure from that airport. During these periods, passengers are not permitted to use the lavatories nor roam around the plane. Noncompliant passengers face potential arrest and pilots are required to modify their flight plans.

In fall 2002, the FBI requested colleges and universities to provide extensive information about foreign students, including: their name, citizenship, place and date of birth, address, and overseas contact information. While the U.S. Department of Education allows higher education institutions to provide some student information (e.g., name, address, telephone number, and place of birth) to law enforcement officials, other information (e.g., social security numbers, citizenship, and ethnicity) generally requires a subpoena or court order.

Educational service providers feel the tension between cooperating with their government's attempt to protect the nation and the rights of some customers—foreign students. Expanded U.S. government investigation of foreign student applications and registration requirements resulted in a decline in the number of overseas students on U.S. campuses. Failure by universities to comply with laws mandating cooperation with government investigations may result in the imposition of sanctions.

OTHER CUSTOMER ISSUES

A customer can become a terrorist victim (e.g., passenger on plane or a customer on train that is targeted by a terrorist). Given this possibility, customers place more demands on businesses to provide adequate security than they did prior to 9/11. As noted earlier, customers may reduce patronage at a victimized firm following a dramatic terror attack. Customers will find alternate products or services that reduce the possibility of subsequent threats or attacks (e.g., use of e-mail, phone, video-conferencing instead of flying). For a period, demand for more expensive (e.g., corporate jets) or even less convenient (e.g., buses) services will take hold as customers may seek to avoid the victimized provider or its sub-sector.

Customers do not expect a store where they shop will employ a terrorist sleeper cell members. Also, consumers do not imagine that a company is a front for terrorist groups. It is also relevant whether companies view protecting customers as more important than safeguarding workers.

Customers are part of the solution in that they can alert business owners of possible threats. Concurrently, customers can contact law enforcement authorities if they are concerned about a company's activities.

Sourcing, Inventory, and Logistics

Interruptions to distribution systems immediately following the 9/11 incidents caused companies to reexamine just-in-time inventory techniques (which involves delivery of parts to the assembly line only when they are needed). Still, the use of international and multiple domestic sources for manufacturing and the prevalence of just-in-time practices makes it arduous to modify these currently ingrained elements of production.

Yet, a number of corporations are increasing inventories and building additional storage facilities in light of terror threats. While raising the levels of inventories may force increased costs in such outlays, they may, concurrently, buffer firms by allowing for ample supplies of key components even in case of a major terrorist attack.

According to Joseph Martha and Sunil Subbakrisha of Mercer Management Consultants, manufacturers, retailers, and suppliers will be well advised to take into consideration a few strategies regarding sourcing, inventory, and logistics issues, such as:

- Inventory Management. Manufacturers will need to carry more buffer inventory in order to hedge against supply and production-line disruptions.
- Sourcing. Manufacturers should be more selective about where

their critical parts are coming from. A sourcing strategy will have to vary by location.

- Transportation. Manufacturers and retailers should consider broadening their shipping arrangements.

As broad security initiatives have been launched, manufacturers, shippers, and freight forwarders increased responsibility for container contents and security. Companies are called upon to conduct better investigation of customers, suppliers, and vendors. Secure transport containers with tamper-proof seals are increasingly used. Such measures may cause delays in shipping. Thereby, they may affect inventories, arrival of component parts, and assembly of final products.

Government-industry partnerships, such as the Customs-Trade Partnership Against Terrorism (C-TPAT) noted earlier, allows for securing and facilitating trade. Such steps also aid in instilling resilience in the supply chain process.

Impact on Revenues

Another related aspect is the decline in revenue that may occur as potentially suspicious transactions are eschewed—be they deposits from potentially unsavory customers to imports from emerging markets. The fear of doing business with individuals in high-risk countries may result in companies concentrating greater sales efforts in industrialized and newly-industrialized nations or utilizing foreign subsidiaries and third-parties to undertake riskier deals.

American foreign policy will always impact, to some extent, the capacity of U.S. firms to conduct business abroad. Expanded U.S. government scrutiny of foreigners as possible terrorists post-9/11 has concurrently engendered some negative feelings towards the United States and U.S. products. Also, what appears by some countries (e.g., France and Germany) as American expansionism or interventionist actions globally (e.g., Iraq and Afghanistan) could make foreign consumers less receptive to U.S. products and services.

Already, some non-U.S. enterprises have seized pent-up demand for non-U.S. products and services by developing their own brands. This was witnessed with the introduction of several alternatives to Coca-Cola. Also, products with a pan-Arab or Islamic positioning have expanded in the post-9/11 environment. Unfortunately, some anti-Americanism has been ingrained in selected overseas markets well before the post-9/11 era.

Legal Implications

There are many legal implications that relate to the impact of terror on business. Among some of these legal issues are: government procurement procedures and protests following awards of homeland security contracts; privacy concerns relating to customer information, industry's acquisition thereof, and government's interest in such data; businesses' treatment of employees, customers, and partners as inquiry into potential terrorists or their supporters widens; compliance with vast post-9/11 legislation affecting how business is carried out (e.g., doing business with DHS, importation procedures, food safety issues, and money laundering rules); adequate disclosures on the counterterror capabilities of homeland security products and services; and potential liability firms may face due to having inadequate security, crisis management, and emergency training procedures in place.

Also, it is difficult to ascribe liability and project potential recovery in the aftermath of a terror attack. A particularly interesting case involves potential recovery by the leaseholder of the World Trade Center, who contends that the two planes that crashed into the buildings constituted two separate attacks. Under such reasoning, the leaseholder would be entitled to a maximum recovery of some $7 billion from insurers, about $3.5 billion for each plane. In contrast, the insurers argue that the attacks comprised one attack, and thereby, only $3.5 billion—at the high end—could potentially be recovered. This dispute has been brought before a court but has yet to be resolved.

Potential lawsuits by 9/11 victims and their families against selected entities were partially stymied or pre-empted by fall 2001 legislation. Legislation insulated some companies and organizations that otherwise might have been subject to various levels of financial liability. The Air Transportation Safety and System Stabilization Act of 2001 (ATSSA), included language that limited damages American Airlines and United Airlines—hosts of the four hijacked planes—could suffer due to suits arising under the September 11, 2001, incidents.

Under ATSSA, victims' families were permitted to make claims under the Victim Compensation Fund. As of January 2004, the September 11 Victims Compensation Fund is expected to provide some $5 billion in compensation, with awards ranging from $250,000 to nearly $7 million for victims who perished. Awards for those injured during the September 11 incidents ranged from $500 to $7.8 million. Those who opted out of ATSSA could pursue claims, but as cited above, limits on possible awards—such as the insurance levels that airlines had on 9/11—would attach.

Other post-9/11 legislation and proposed laws contain language that restricts lawsuits and prevents punitive damages in suits arising from terrorist events. Other rules, potentially absolve or reduce liability to providers of homeland security products and services from liability should the DHS give its imprimatur on the firm's offerings.

With reference to lawsuits connected to the anthrax attacks, the families of postal workers victimized may be prevented from suing the U.S. Postal Service as the law already provides for some measures to compensate victims in such circumstances. Nevertheless, plaintiffs may pursue other suits, as in the case of the son of a Washington, D.C., postal worker who died following exposure to inhalation anthrax. More specifically, in November 2001, Thomas L. Morris III filed a $37 million wrongful-death action against Kaiser Permanente in Maryland, claiming that a Kaiser physician did not recognize and treat the anthrax symptoms of his father—Thomas L. Morris Jr.—but rather directed him to take Tylenol for his symptoms.

It is also worth highlighting that there is precedent for families of victims killed during a terrorist attack to file a civil action in U.S. courts against the perpetrators, the terrorist groups, and their state sponsors. In addition, victims' families have been successful in suing U.S.-based hate groups for crimes carried out by their members. American plaintiffs sometimes have a difficult recovering on successful claims due to sovereign immunity defenses. Nevertheless, some of such obstacles have been resolved by U.S. legislation freeing some monies for such awards.

In 2003, a U.S. court ruled that Iran must pay $313 million to the survivors of an elderly American woman killed during a suicide bombing in Jerusalem in 1997. The court found that Iran had supported the perpetrators of the attacks—the Islamic Resistance Movement (Hamas)—funding and training. Other Americans that have won judgments in U.S. courts relating to terror acts abroad including another victim of a suicide bombing killed in Israel in 1995 and an American journalist kidnapped in Lebanon in 1985.

A nearly decade long United Nations embargo was lifted on Libya in 2002, following its agreement to pay $2.7 billion in compensation to the relatives of those killed during the explosion of Pan Am 103 over Scotland and its aftermath. In January 2004, the Libyan government formally agreed to provide $170 million to the families of those killed during the 1989 downing of UTA Flight 772 in Africa.

In August 2002, some six hundred families of those killed during the 9/11 attacks filed suit against various Saudi Arabian interests, including banks, charities, and royal family members for their alleged support of al Qaeda. The suit sought hundreds of billions of dollars in damages. In another suit arising from the 9/11 incidents, plaintiffs sought over $1 trillion in damages in claims against bin Laden, al Qaeda, and Iraq.

Conclusion

The consequences of terrorism on business described here serve as a complement to analysis in earlier chapters on how terror metamorphoses business. In this chapter, we explored some influences on business following a major terror attack such as September 11. Volatility in currencies and stocks, delays and cancellations of transactions, disparate effects on labor, shaken consumer behavior, and industry hesitation are among the preliminary ramifications of catastrophic terror.

Industry responses to terror ranged from declines in demand for particular products and services to accelerated interest in certain sectors, such as homeland security companies. Consolidation among such terror-fighting firms was contrasted with weaknesses—including bankruptcies—among victimized industries. Additional effects of terrorism on business—higher transaction and security costs; new security dynamics at a business location; evolving customer-industry dynamics; effects on sourcing, inventory, and logistics; and multiple legal issues—were highlighted.

In the future, terrorism will inflict additional human casualties, financial costs, and manifold consequences on industry. Businesses, however, can contribute to lessening such dangers if serious attention and sufficient resources are deployed.

Conclusion

Threats

The frequency and lethality of conventional (e.g., bombings and kidnappings) and unconventional (e.g., bioterrorism and chemical terrorism) political violence is expected to continue worldwide for the foreseeable future. Unfortunately, suicide bombings in crowded civilian areas, explosions across the gamut of ground transportation, hijacked aircraft crashing into office buildings, sabotage of critical infrastructure, and bioterror attacks are no longer viewed as something fictional—even among those who have predicted that "it could never happen here."

To our dismay, many threats still remain. It is conceivable, for instance, that terrorists may target some of the approximately 600,000 bridges and tunnels in the United States. In 2003, an al Qaeda operative based in the United States pled guilty to aiding the group to find future terror targets, such as U.S. bridges and tunnels.

Other threats, such as attacks on industrial plants, are not beyond the pale. At least one million people would be at risk of exposure to deadly chemical vapor clouds were terrorists to target any one of major 125 U.S. industrial plants. Similarly, there are more than 700 other plants that could put at least 100,000 people at risk. Warnings about terror attacks against U.S. chemical and nuclear plants are well documented.

Additionally troubling are potential attacks against private sector infrastructures, including: information and communications; banking and finance; water supply; aviation, highway, mass transit, pipelines, rail, and waterborne commerce; and electric power and oil and gas production and storage.

Terrorists' attraction to attack ground and air transportation world-wide is another basis for worry. These sub-sectors have been hit unusually hard: from the use of the chemical agent sarin on Japanese subways; suicide bombings on Israeli buses; nearly simultaneous, remote-control bombings of Madrid commuter trains on March 11, 2004 (known as the 3/11 attacks), to the devastating results of the 9/11 hijackings. Such types of attacks are harbingers of future carnage against these modes of travel.

Terror groups' proclivity to attack soft targets—restaurants, theaters, and shopping malls—is an abhorrent trend. This development is unlikely to dissipate in the near future because of its perceived "effectiveness" (in the eyes of the terrorist), the prevalence of soft targets, and limited resources—intelligence, finance, equipment, and manpower—that can be allocated to defend against such dangers.

The rising trend of simultaneous terror incidents—multiple bombings against Shiite worshipers in Iraq (Baghdad and Karbalah) and Pakistan (Quetta) in March 2004—is further cause for concern. Multiple, closely coordinated attacks aggravate the damage that terror incidents inflict. The tactic of initiating new attacks once emergency personnel arrive at the initial terror location is another vile development in the terrorists' modus operandi.

The expansive use of suicide bombers and attackers without regard to their ultimate fate has caused damage across sectors (e.g., food, lodging, entertainment, and transportation) and globally: in Europe (e.g., Russia), Asia (e.g., India, Indonesia, Philippines, Sri Lanka), Africa (e.g., Algeria, Morocco, Tunisia), and the Middle East (e.g., Israel, Iraq, Lebanon, Saudi Arabia, Turkey). These developments have invoked concern across society about terror's "walking bombs" and ways to defend against them.

Terrorist groups' fascination to return to terror targets previously attacked (e.g., World Trade Center in New York) or failed missions (e.g., the Capitol and White House) should also be kept in mind. The internationalization of terror groups—worldwide movement of terrorists, arms, training, funding, and operations—further complicates efforts to reduce terrorism.

The unending breadth of terror groups' victimization of government, industry, and civilian targets makes the specter of future harm real and ominous. It is possible that a future catastrophic attack may include methodologies and targets that have not seriously been envisioned.

Recognition by government, businesses, employees, and consumers of such possibilities will hasten their efforts to lessen terrorist risk.

Defensive and proactive measures against terrorism at the individual level must be complemented by regulatory, policy, intelligence, and financial contributions that, as a group, only government and industry interests can muster. Weakness and appeasement of terrorists will only invite more terror, not less. This mistake seems to have occurred with Spanish voters, who days after an al Qaeda-linked attack in Madrid on 3/11, voted out the Popular (conservative) Party that placed Spanish troops in Iraq (which al Qaeda opposed), and replaced it with the Socialist Party, which called for removal of Spanish troops.

This faulty rationale blames the victim, while exculpating terrorists because their grievances supposedly justify violence. Under the same thought process, any terror group—whether al Qaeda or the Basque terror group ETA—would have been justified in committing the 3/11 attacks.

The 3/11 incidents illustrate the dangerous posture of terror groups conducting attacks in order to try to influence elections. This phenomenon appears to be fairly novel in the West, although British Prime Minister Margaret Thatcher took a hard-line posture against the Irish Republican Army during her election campaign.

Elsewhere, terror attacks have influenced various elections, such as in Israel, where a party taking more aggressive policies against terrorism— the Likud—actually prevailed over more conciliatory positions of the Labor Party.

There is speculation that, once again, terror groups might replicate their goal of creating change at the ballot box through the practice of terror. For instance, some have proffered that terror attacks will occur in the United States prior to—or on—the November 2004, presidential elections. If so, hopefully, Americans will be resolute and vote based on their perceptions of what is best for the country, and not be swayed by terrorists, who may seek victory for one party or another. After all, cowering to terror aggravates the problem; it is not the solution.

There are generic and specific factors that affect the intensity of future terrorist challenges. Generic components that contribute to terrorism include: ethnic, racial, religious, and tribal intolerance and violence; propaganda and psychological warfare; extreme nationalism; regional conflicts that defy easy solutions; intensification of criminal activities such as narco-trafficking and identity theft; population explosion, migration expansion, and unemployment; environmental challenges;

weapons developments and proliferation of conventional and unconventional arms; and increased growth of global mobility and sophisticated communication systems.

Specific factors and conditions that will encourage terrorism in the future include: the absence of a universal definition of terrorism; disagreement as to the root causes of terrorism; double standard of morality; loss of resolve by some governments to take effective action against terrorism; weak punishment of terrorists; violation of international law by, and promotion of, terrorism by some nations; complexity of modern societies; high costs of security; and disparate viewpoints on appropriate counterterrorism strategies.

These contributing variables foreshadow American vulnerability to political violence. This is particularly so with regard to economic interests, including critical infrastructure. Destruction or significant damage to power generating facilities, telecommunications systems, bridges, or stock exchanges would severely undermine the economy, create panic, and inflict substantial direct and indirect damage.

Terrorists in the Economic System and Financing Terror

Terrorists will continue to act within domestic and international economic systems to obtain financial resources, weaponry, products, services, information, and other tools that can be used against government, industry, and other segments of society. Terrorists contact product and service providers openly, secretly, and through the use of abettors. Unsuspecting companies and individuals may provide terrorists with wares for their operations. Given an improved appreciation of such possibilities, industry is better attuned to reduce complicity with terror groups. Companies will actively investigate future employees, clients, and partners to lessen the chance that malfeasance occurs.

Yet, firms' desire for profits has caused some to close their eyes to shading deals or purposely establish foreign subsidiaries to undertake "dirty deals" with terrorists, their sympathizers, or even state-sponsors of terrorism. Unfortunately, avarice at selected companies makes such negative corporate conduct likely to continue to some degree. Expanded enforcement and modification of government sanctions, in unison with pressure from investors in such public companies, should contribute to weakening another source of terror wares and funding.

For principally ideological, social, or financial reasons, terror groups are able to attract co-conspirators. Generally, academic studies on the link between an individual's susceptibility to become a terrorist and his poverty status found that limited economic resources and educational opportunities do not necessarily inspire greater participation in terrorist organization than those from a well-off and educated labor pool. In fact, terrorists from the latter paradigm have often played leadership roles in terror groups: from the multimillionaire Saudi Arabian scion, Osama bin Laden of al Qaeda to his co-conspirator, Egyptian physician Ayman al-Zawahiri; and from well-born Venezuelan "free-lance" Carlos "The Jackal" Sanchez, to Professor Abimael Guzman, founder of Peru's Sendero Luminoso (Shining Path). With that said, there are many examples of poverty-afflicted individuals who join a terror entity's ranks.

Terror groups and their state-sponsors aim their net broadly when searching for recruits, "fixers," sympathizers, and contributors. Terrorists approach the full spectrum of the labor pool for possible assistance with their evil goals, including: pilots, truck drivers, airport employees, soldiers, scientists, and businessmen. While relatively few individuals join terror ranks only several committed persons are required to conduct terror operations.

Additionally, volunteers seek out terror groups and their operatives. A number of American citizens who provided material aid or trained with terror groups actually sought out a terror affiliation. U.S. government agencies identified such American citizens while the latter were: searching for terror targets, preparing for an attack, seeking contact with real or perceived terrorists, and cooperating with co-conspirators from abroad.

Defending against "sleeper cell" employees will prove difficult as such individuals may appear to be model employees. The potential damage that a rogue employee can have within an organization and beyond must not be underestimated: whether sensitive information is stolen; or sabotage of critical assets occurs due to cyberterrorism to bombings.

Terrorist groups will likely continue to use the prison systems as another attractive recruitment sphere. Al Qaeda possibly approached Richard Reid and Jose Padilla in British and American jails, respectively. Additionally, groups and individuals generally not suspected to be associated with a particular terror organization will in fact be recruited in order to avoid law enforcement suspicion.

More recruitment of mercenaries, free agents, or proxies is foreseeable as evidenced by the use of "foreign fighters" in Iraq to undertake attacks against U.S. military personnel, and American government contractors; and Iraqi government, religious, and civilian targets. The greater use of proxies will likely be complemented by further interaction among terror groups, splinter terror groups, and former members joining other groups (e.g., an ETA member joining al Qaeda). Particularly reprehensible, though growing, is the use of children to smuggle explosives and carry out terrorist attacks.

A expanding nexus between terror groups and organized crime marks another dangerous development. Also foreboding is the trend of terror groups sharing and exchanging resources with organized crime — whether training, weaponry, logistics, funding, or understanding of local markets. The leveraging of such capabilities, spurred in part by a growing commonality of objectives, makes terror group-organized crime cooperation that much more ominous. Among their common objectives are: the destabilization of host states; acquisition of financial resources and raw power; and control — of varying degrees — over autonomous territory.

There is precedent for organized criminal groups acting alone with the intent to wreck havoc on important economic targets. For instance, in October 2002, a Brazilian criminal gang, First Capital Command, planned to bomb Sao Paulo's Stock Exchange, Bovespa. Given such developments, it appears useful to fortify business targets both from terrorists and organized crime. After all, the two seem interested in hurting national economic bases.

The demise of Saddam Hussein's regime in Iraq, coupled with the apparent "rehabilitation" of Libya's Muammar Qaddafi, removes two state-sponsors of terror from the ranks — at least for now. Analogously, countries and their citizenry that gave financial aid to terror groups often subsequently discover that their earlier contributions do not immune them from terror's wrath, even from groups they initially aided. Such is the case with early Saudi Arabian aid to al Qaeda and subsequent al Qaeda terror on Saudi soil.

With traditional and untraditional financial systems coming under intense scrutiny in the United States and abroad, terrorists will resort to more frequent criminal acts (e.g., identity theft, counterfeiting, drug and human trafficking, and extortion) to raise funds for their terror acts. As charities and other nonprofits also face increased attention by governments and potential contributors, another source of terror funding may decline.

In undermining terror sources of funding, terror groups are weakened. At the same time, limited resources may make terrorists desperate to undertake spectacular or unusually horrific attacks.

Security

Government and industry have spent hundreds of billions of dollars for homeland security products and services. Outlays in this regard are expanding both at home and abroad. At the same time, keeping security costs in check will prove challenging as threats are manifold and global.

Security is expected to steadily play a more prominent role at companies as terror threats remain. Well-known, American firms and other companies exemplifying Western economic power—banking, energy, and technology—both in their home countries and abroad will likely be objects of terrorists' evil. Also, operations that attract a large number of people in a concentrated area—buses, subways, train stations, stores, and restaurants—are likely to be targeted as well.

Security measures at prospective targets will necessitate multidimensional responses. The use of political risk analysis, traditional security products and services, risk management tools, and business continuity/disaster planning are critical variables that should be considered to reduce the risk of terrorism. Concurrently, such steps protect company assets and ensure survivability.

Intelligence gathering and analysis are crucial components of effective security practices within both government and industry contexts. Military and law enforcement are also integral to the security paradigm.

A corporation's ultimate objective is to be profitable. One would presume that any allocation of resources that directly or indirectly undermines profitability should be eschewed. It would be incorrect, though, to suggest that resources earmarked towards security necessarily takes away from a company's bottom line in the post-9/11 era. In fact, counterterror measures may likewise aid firms to protect data, prevent sabotage, and decrease theft of company assets. Political violence can literally destroy a company's operations—let alone the financial, physical, and emotional damage that can result.

Still, management wrestles with the issue of spending sufficient resources on counterterror efforts and safeguarding company's scarce resources. The prospects of terror attacks enable management to justify large expenditures on security. When the time comes that terror threats have waned (or are perceived as such), companies will examine more closely the utility of security expenditures. That day—given present conditions and future prospects—is a long time away.

Increased security measures in commercial aviation, with their requisite personnel and equipment costs, have spread globally. As a result, terrorists will actively embrace other targets, including ground and maritime transportation. This likely shift toward attacking other modes of transportation—buses, trains, subways, tractor truck, cruise ships—will likely occur in the United States as well. Therefore, legislation, funding, and manpower will be heralded to protect this sub-sector, but only after a major attack at home.

It is relatively easy, fast, and inexpensive for terrorists to modify their targets. In contrast, government, industry, and individuals have difficulties shifting their security capabilities against new potential terror sites. The likelihood that terror's offensive postures will outpace society's defensive measures makes security challenges rather steep.

Also, the sheer banality and lethality of terror makes securing citizenry at work, home, leisure, and elsewhere seemingly complex, though not impossible. With that said, there can never be 100% security vis-à-vis terrorism nor common crime. While many terrorists may be captured, and numerous attacks thwarted, terrorists need to inflict substantial damage only occasionally to achieve their goals.

Government responses to terror are also constrained by limited financial, manpower, and other resources. The public sector weighs allocating sufficient resources to terror threats with not furnishing excessive resources to this phenomenon. Levels of federal distribution of homeland security-related funds to state and local officials are also relevant.

Continued industry contributions to, and cooperation with, government in combating terror is an important aspect of security. The role of international cooperation among governments, nongovernmental institutions, businesses, and individuals in defeating terror should not be underestimated. Mobilizing citizenry to assist in combating terror—from turning in computer virus writers to disclosing the location of suspected terrorists—would be beneficial. This can be achieved without necessarily creating "witch hunts" within society.

Addressing some of the root causes of terror is likewise part of the long-term security dynamic. Efforts in this domain should occur concurrent to "traditional" security efforts. Dealing with some of the causes of terror will reduce the chance that new terrorists and their sympathizers will be created.

Public-Private Efforts in Combating Terror

Effective public-private cooperation is crucial in the war on terror. The interaction and support between these two spheres are exemplified in several ways: government aids business, industry assists the public sector, and challenges exist between the two.

In relation to government aiding industry, the public sector buys homeland security wares from companies. Through the privatization of some government duties industry gains access to opportunities that it otherwise did not possess. Government allocates monies—directly and indirectly—to companies prior to and in the wake of terror attacks. The government enacts laws that, for instance, limit firms' potential liabilities in case of a terror attack.

The public sector lends its personnel and expertise to companies prior to, during, and subsequent to a terror incident. These efforts attempted to minimize harm to company assets, including individuals. Government guides industry on terror threats and appropriate responses. The public sector aids industry by establishing rules that simplify ways to conduct business, even within a high security environment. Industry is afforded with formal and informal means of communications with government officials, allowing companies to better grasp security and business opportunities than they would otherwise possess.

Another component of government's war against terror, and indirectly another benefit to industry, is trade liberalization efforts with countries that potentially could be a base or source of terrorism. In early March 2004, for instance, the United States and Morocco entered into a free trade agreement. By reducing tariff and nontariff barriers between the countries, plus strengthening protections for investment and intellectual property rights, Moroccan and American firms will gain better access to each others' markets. Concurrently, the U.S. government injects another tool to increasing stability in the Middle East. Hopefully, such steps will lessen the chance that terrorism will continue to flourish in that region and beyond.

Coincidentally, Spanish authorities arrested about a dozen Moroccans in relation to the Madrid train bombings on 3/11. Other Moroccans, including an al Qaeda leader in Spain, were already held in Spain in connection with the 9/11 incidents.

Industry, likewise, assists government through various means: furnishing homeland security products and services; protecting government assets; providing intelligence about possible threats; taking on government roles and risks; creating forums for insight on counterterror technology and tactics; and contributing personnel to aid the public sector. In a novel development, the U.S. government purchased an abandoned town—Playas, New Mexico—from a mining firm, Phelps

Dodge, in May 2003, for ultimate use as a terrorist response training center.

The government-industry dynamic also has its difficulties. Tensions include developments in the federalization of counterterror roles juxtaposed with the privatization of government duties. Essentially, the query of whether government or industry oversteps its bounds by entering into the purview of the other is an example of such tension. Government legislation affecting security at companies, rules impacting how business is conducted, and the transformation of government institutions have—and will—cause friction between the private and public sectors.

In trying to protect society, government may force businesses to strain their relationships with customers. By attempting to earn significant profits, firms may exaggerate the benefits of their homeland security products and service—at the peril of government and society.

Companies and their employees may ignore government advisories of prospective attacks. Meanwhile, government may fail to heed the insights of industry as it relates to possible counterterror solutions. Interaction between the public and private sectors are stressed when differing interests and perspectives occur in crafting means to combat terrorism.

A severe terror attack often elicits strong government responses, ranging across legal, military, law enforcement, intelligence, and financial perspectives. That government is the principal responder to terrorism should not be lost in this discussion.

Labor

Past terror attacks have impacted labor in a variety of ways. Numerous workers have been killed or maimed. Those without physical scars carry psychological wounds that do not easily mend. Such effects on labor are expected to occur to a greater extent than before. This is so because terrorists' thirst for spectacular attacks and its concomitant carnage grow without being sated.

Many of the same tensions that terror has forced onto labor, particularly since 9/11, are likely to continue. Unfortunately, workers may be killed or injured in terror attacks while at work, traveling, socializing, or elsewhere. Employees may adjust their career goals in the face of terror threats—from leaving high-risk jobs to embracing private and public sector roles in the homeland security realm.

Demand for homeland security workers with diverse skills (e.g., military, language, technological, and analytical) will remain strong. So too, the entrepreneurial spirit addressing homeland security solutions will flourish. Yet, increased competition among firms offering such wares plus a finite demand for such items ultimately create a cap for employment in homeland security space.

With more segments of labor filling homeland security roles, workers gain a better understanding of risks inherent in terrorism. So too, exposure to counterterror principles enhances labor's capacity to combat terror. Employers more frequently provide counterterror and emergency training for their workers than they did prior to September 11. Due to such efforts, employers are better able to reduce company risks and enhance employee safety.

At the same time, U.S. military and counterterror activities abroad inherently place American labor in great physical risk. This applies to government and industry personnel. With the broad use of private contractors abroad, including places like Iraq and Afghanistan, American workers will need to be especially careful while working or traveling overseas. Significant terror attacks in Spain and Turkey during 2004 and 2003, respectively, plus terror threats in Great Britain, France, and Italy since 9/11 have made "safe" Europe riskier for American expatriates and tourists.

In order to better entice American personnel to work overseas—aside from tenets such as duty and patriotism—employers may provide various incentives. According to a summer 2003 Watson Wyatt survey, nearly 40% of employees were offered financial incentives to work in high-risk areas (e.g., parts of the Middle East and Asia).

Management is better attuned to the multiplicity of factors that impact running a business post-9/11. For instance, terror risks create business opportunities for management as firms pursue markets that heretofore were limited or nonexistent.

Management pays increasing attention to investigating prospective (and current) employees, business partners, and customers. Additionally, the onus of knowing that management decisions can ultimately affect employee and customer safety are new intricacies that previously have not been weighed with frequency.

Labor's role in contributing to its own safety is enhanced by formal and informal reporting programs. The government-organized Terrorism Information and Prevention System enables American transportation, postal, and public utility employees to notify authorities of suspicious activities connected to terrorism and crime. Other features of government's citizen engagement programs in relation to homeland security include: Medical Reserve Corps (allowing for retired health-care workers to assist during an emergency), Community Emergency Response Teams (encouraging workers to aid their communities during an emergency), and Neighborhood Watch Programs (including combating terrorism in this existing anticrime framework).

Government's role in soothing employer and employee pain in the aftermath of a catastrophic terror incident will continue. However, greater efforts will focus on preventing attacks. The financial drain on these types of government endeavors will be high.

Additional Perspectives on Terror's Impact on Business

A post-9/11 paradigm was created in many fronts: military, political, legal, social, and economic. In particular, terrorism creates many challenges to business. Concurrently, political violence elicits industry to undertake steps that contain proactive, reactive, offensive, and defensive measures. In the main, this book has analyzed multiple terror threats imposed on business and diverse industry responses in the face of those challenges.

In the aftermath of a catastrophic terror incident, severe, negative effects can undermine economies, financial markets, labor, companies, and individual investors. Stock markets often decline, sometimes sharply although some equities, from defense to gold companies, may spike upward, at least initially. Stock markets ultimately recover— whether within days, weeks, or months—depending on many factors, including some that have nothing to do with terrorism.

Currencies in the country directly affected by the terror attack tend to weaken vis-à-vis hard currencies. Oil prices may rise sharply following a major terror attack, as was in the case immediately after 9/11 and 3/11. Similar scenarios are likely to occur in stock, currency, and commodity markets should another major terror attack take place.

Depending on the type, scope, and sectors affected by a terror attack, business transactions can be delayed, cancelled, or revised during days or longer periods of time. Issues of political risk and insurance coverage thereof have become factors considered often in the post-9/11 business calculus.

Decisions on how to proceed in the aftermath of a major terror attack are relevant. Future possible steps include: whether to rebuild offices and businesses destroyed in an attack. Also pertinent are the costs involved in rebuilding a business following an attack. Concurrently, homeland security firms and other products and services that may benefit government and industry in combating terror (e.g., foreign language schools) are buttressed as demand for such items is expected to continue.

The advent of the Homeland Security Business Age certainly provides business opportunities for manufacturers and service companies. Yet, there will come a point when demand for such goods and services will wane. Nevertheless, the technological and methodological advances learned by companies in their contributions to the "War on Terrorism," will undoubtedly have many civilian uses that may spur growth in non-counterterrorism sectors.

Government costs related to overseas counterterror activities—from Afghanistan, Yemen, and the Philippines, to Iraq—also include "stabilization" expenditures from which American homeland security and other firms may benefit from through government contracts. In contrast, continuation of the war on terrorism also results in security expenditures and rising transaction costs that harm companies and economies.

Renewed interest in investing and fusing homeland security firms may arise post after a massive terror attack. This phenomenon, plus demand for homeland security products, should stimulate technological and scientific developments that otherwise might not have been forged.

Due to government's counterterror efforts—especially exemplified by military and intelligence activities—business will be pushed into negative situations and pulled into positive opportunities. Other ramifications of terror on business can be designated as transcending effects: terror costs in terms of outlays and rising transaction costs; security at a business site; interactions with customers; changes in sourcing, inventory, and logistics; and legal issues.

Terror's influences on sectors are manifold. These effects were exhibited most dramatically with commercial aviation: increased use of corporate jets and declining commercial airline travel; rising prevalence of videoconferencing instead of undertaking business travel; and more travel within the United States and neighboring regions (e.g., Caribbean) as opposed to trips to the Middle East, Europe, and Asia. These direct and indirect changes to business due to terrorism should accelerate in intensity as terrorism will likely spread and harm more sectors and workers globally.

Post-9/11 interest in all things homeland security has led many traditional businesses to reference security issues in their advertising and day-to-day operations—even when such matters are tangential to their business. Attempts to keep up-to-date on developments in political risk, terrorism, and homeland security have led to a proliferation of online and offline publications dealing with those subjects. Such publications have also attracted advertisers, including sponsored pieces. Another manifestation of the terror business boom is the multitude of counterterror conferences hastening the arrival of the Counterterror Business Age.

These developments are mindful of the Internet heydays when: great companies flourished but some firms hawked questionable products and services; experts abounded; information was flush; and the "Next Big Thing" mesmerized investors. Yet, things ultimately developed rather differently from the way that many had expected. Perhaps too, then, the same fate will arise in some aspects of the counterterror business dynamic.

Integrating the concept of terror in relation to its effects on business—both in theory and in practice—is a growing a post-9/11 phenomenon. These matters have been addressed herein. Rampant political instability, in conjunction with economic, social, and other factors, contributes to probable escalating global terror threats. These circumstances foreshadow that, unfortunately, business will confront terrorism—along these and other ways—for many years to come.

Bibliography

1. Overview of Terrorist Threats; *and*
2. Contemporary and Future Threats

Alexander, Dean C. "Maritime Terrorism and Legal Responses." *Denver Journal of International Law & Policy* 19 (1991): 529-567.

Alexander, Dean C. & Yonah Alexander. *Terrorism and Business: The Impact of September 11, 2001.* Ardsley, N.Y.: Transnational Publishers, 2002.

Alexander, Yonah, ed. *Combating Terrorism: Strategies of Ten Countries.* Ann Arbor: University of Michigan Press, 2003.

————. *International Terrorism: National, Regional, and Global Perspectives.* New York: Praeger Publishers, 1976.

————. *International Terrorism: Political and Legal Documents.* Dordrecht: Martinus Nijhoff, 1992.

Alexander, Yonah & Seymour M. Finger, eds. *Terrorism: Interdisciplinary Perspectives.* New York: John Jay Press, 1977.

Alexander, Yonah & Robert Friedlander, eds. *Self-Determination: National, Regional, and Global Dimensions.* Boulder, Colo.: Westview Press, 1980.

Alexander, Yonah & Milton Hoenig, eds. *Super Terrorism: Biological, Chemical, Nuclear.* Ardsley, N.Y.: Transnational Publishers, 2001.

Alexander, Yonah & Robert A. Kilmarx, eds. *Business and the Middle East: Threats and Prospects.* New York: Pergamon Press, 1982.

————. *Political Terrorism and Business: The Threat and Response.* New York: Praeger, 1979.

Alexander, Yonah & Eugene Sochor, eds. *Aerial Piracy and Aviation Security.* Dordrecht: Martinus Nijhoff, 1990.

Alexander, Yonah & Michael S. Swetnam, eds. *Information Warfare and Cyber Terrorism: Threats and Responses.* Dobbs Ferry, N.Y.: Oceana Publications, 1999.

————. *Usama bin Laden's al-Qaida: Profile of a Terrorist Network.* Ardsley, N.Y.: Transnational Publishers, 2001.

Alpert, Lukas. "New York City Water Vulnerable to Attack." *AP,* 20 May 2002.

"Al Qaeda Seen Planning Major Strikes—Interpol." *Reuters,* 8 November 2002.

Anderson, Curt. "FBI Director: 100 Terror Attacks Stopped." *AP,* 15 December 2002.

Anderson, John. "11 Killed by Bomb on Bus in Jerusalem." *Washington Post*, 30 January 2004.

———. "On Israeli Bus, Good Deed Turn Heroic." *Washington Post*, 11 October 2002.

"Animal Rights Activists Accused of Harassment." *Reuters*, 25 October 2002.

Baker, Peter & Susan Glasser. "Bomber Kills Five and Herself Near Russia's Parliament." *Washington Post*, 10 December 2003.

Bamber, David. "FBI Warns Britain of Al Qaeda Plot to Hijack Jetliner." *Washington Times*, 24 August 2003.

"Bandgladesh Mourns Victims of Cinema Blasts." *Reuters*, 9 December 2002.

Bennet, James. "Palestinian Subdued and Shot, yet His Bomb Kills 3." *New York Times*, 28 October 2002.

Bilefsky, Dan. "Can Shoppers Be Kept Safe?" *Wall Street Journal*, 5 December 2002.

Bindra, Satindra. "Similarities Seen between Indian Airlines, U.S. Hijackings." cnn.com, 27 September 2001.

"Blasts Rock Jakarta's Atrium Plaza." *Jakarta Post*, 24 September 2001.

"Bombers Target Genoa Police HQ." cnn.com, 10 December 2002.

"Bombing in Bogota Market Kills at Least Six." *AP*, 9 October 2003.

"Bomb Kills Four, Wounds 16 in Algeria." *Reuters*, 12 December 2002.

"Bombs in McDonald's and Car Rental Agency in Indonesia Kill Two." *AP*, 5 December 2002.

Bonner, Raymond. "Southeast Asia Remains Fertile for Al Qaeda." *New York Times*, 28 October 2002.

Bonner, Raymond & Jane Perlez. "Australia Comes to Terms with a New Sense of Vulnerability." *New York Times*, 16 December 2002.

Bradsher, Keith. "Warnings from Al Qaeda Stir Fear That Terrorists May Attack Oil Tankers." *New York Times*, 12 December 2002.

Broder, John. "Student Kills 3 Instructors and Himself at U of Arizona." *New York Times*, 29 October 2002.

Brooks, Rick & Christopher Chipello. "How Safe Is Your Subway?" *Wall Street Journal*, 19 February 2003.

Browning, John. "A Shock to the System." *Wired*, December 2001, 65.

Burgess, John. "French Defend Their Approach to Terror Threats." *Washington Post*, 28 December 2003.

"Car Bombing Injures 7 at Moscow McDonald's." *AP*, 20 October 2002.

Carr, Caleb. "Just Suppose It's Terrorism." *Washington Post*, 17 October 2002.

Chandrasekaran, Rajiv. "Car Bombs Kill at Least 35 in Baghdad." *Washington Post*, 28 October 2003.

———. "Shiites Massacred in Iraq Blasts." *Washington Post*, 3 March 2004.

———. "Suicide Bomber Kills 7 in Baghdad." *Washington Post*, 13 October 2003.

Cline, Ray S. & Yonah Alexander. *Terrorism as State-Sponsored Covert Warfare.* Fairfax, Va.: HERO Books, 1986.

―――――. *Terrorism: The Soviet Connection.* New York: Crane Russak, 1984.

Crispin, Shawn & Gary Fields. "Thai's Arrest Deepens Terror Fears." *Wall Street Journal,* 18 June 2003.

Dacey, Robert. "Critical Infrastructure Protection: Significant Homeland Security Challenges Need to Be Addressed." Government Accounting Office, 9 July 2002, GAO-02-918T.

Dao, James. "Report Finds U.S. Unprepared for New Terrorist Attack." *New York Times,* 25 October 2002.

"Dark Winter." *Wired,* December 2001, 67.

"Death Toll Hits 15 in Jakarta Stock Exchange Bomb." cnn.com, 14 September 2000.

Dugger, Celia. "Victims of '93 Bombay Terror Wary of U.S. Motives." *New York Times,* 24 September 2001.

Edds, Kimberly. "Calif. Student Is Indicted in Firebombing of SUVs." *Washington Post,* 18 March 2004.

Edmunds, Marion. "Hotels Increase Security after Terrorist Attacks." *Financial Times,* 8 April 2002.

Eggen, Dan. "FBI Failed to Classify Reports before Moussaoui Had Them." *Washington Post,* 28 September 2002.

―――――. "Pipe Bombs Appear to Be Linked, Probers Say." *Washington Post,* 7 May 2002.

Eggen, Dan & Sara Goo. "Celebrations and Precaution." *Washington Post,* 1 January 2004.

Ehrlich, Richard. "Jakarta May See More of This Terror." *Washington Times,* 11 August 2003.

Enders, Walter & Todd Sandler. "The Casuality between Transnational Terrorism and Tourism: The Case of Spain." Iowa State University (unpublished), November 1990.

England, Andrew & Tarek al-Issawi. "Car Bomb Kills 11 at Jordan's Embassy in Baghdad." *Washington Times,* 8 August 2003.

Farah, Douglas & Peter Finn. "Terrorism Inc." *Washington Post,* 21 November 2003.

"Fast-Food Rival Says He Poisoned Food." *Reuters,* 18 September 2002.

Favila, Aaron. "3 Die in Bus Bombing in Jittery Philippines." *AP,* 18 October 2002.

"FBI Concerned about Threat of Terror-Induced Blackouts." cnn.com, 4 September 2003.

Fernandez, Manny & Spencer Hsu. "Attack Could Shut 5 Landmarks." *Washington Post,* 8 March 2003.

Fields, Gary & Greg Hitt. "Protecting 'Soft' Targets." *Wall Street Journal,* 26 November 2003.

Fields, Gary & Nicholas Kulish. "Change to Terrorist-Threat Alert Comes Days ahead of FBI Report." *Wall Street Journal,* 10 February 2003.

————. "U.S. Heights Terrorist Alert, Citing Possible Overseas Targets." *Wall Street Journal,* 11 September 2002.

Fields, Gary & Stephen Power. "Authorities Assess Airports for Threat of Missile Attacks." *Wall Street Journal,* 5 March 2003.

"15 Die as Rebels Attack Sri Lanka Capital." *International Herald Tribune,* 16 October 1997.

Finn, Peter. "Audio Message Urges Muslims to Attack." *Washington Post,* 22 May 2003.

Gellman, Barton. "Al Qaeda Near Biological, Chemical Arms Production." *Washington Post,* 23 March 2003.

————. "Report Cites Al Qaeda Deal for Iraqi Gas." *Washington Post,* 12 December 2002.

Gertz, Bill. "CIA's Director Tells Hill Panel: 'We Made Mistakes.'" *Washington Times,* 18 October 2002.

————. "Sudanese Pilot Held by U.S. Authorities." *Washington Times,* 21 September 2002.

Gillis, Justin. "Power Grid More Vulnerable Daily." *Washington Post,* 17 August 2003.

Glasser, Susan & Peter Baker. "Gas in Raid Killed 115 Hostages." *Washington Post,* 28 October 2002.

Goo, Sara. "Flight 223 to Dulles Canceled—Again." *Washington Post,* 13 February 2004.

————. "Safety Grip Gets Tougher for Holiday." *Washington Post,* 31 December 2003.

————. "Terror Concerns Cancel British, Mexican Flights." *Washington Post,* 4 January 2004.

Goo, Sara & Susan Schmidt. "Memo Warns of New Plots to Hijack Jets." *Washington Post,* 30 July 2003.

Goo, Sara & David Snyder. "Student Charged in Airport Scheme." *Washington Post,* 21 October 2003.

Greenberg, Joel. "Bomber Kills 2 and Hurts 30 in Israeli Mall." *New York Times,* 5 November 2002.

Halloran, Richard. "'Chaotic Situation' Harbors Terror Groups in Indonesia." *Washington Times,* 6 August 2003.

Harper, Rebecca. "America's Most Toxic." *Wired,* April 2003.

Heinz, Jim. "Rebels Storm Moscow Theater, Take Audience Hostage." *AP,* 23 October 2002.

Hsu, Spencer. "'Dirty Bomb' Poses Threat, Study Says." *Washington Post,* 4 May 2002.

"Hungarian IKEA Reopens after Bomb Threat." *AP,* 5 December 2002.

Hunter, Thomas. "Modern Use of Chemical & Biological Weapons." *Journal of Counterterrorism & Security International,* Summer 1997, 14–16.

"India Blames Muslim Group for Bombay Blasts." *AP,* 26 August 2003.

"Islamic Extremists Reportedly Get VX." *Reuters,* 13 December 2002.

Johnston, David. "CIA Puts Risk of Terror Strike at 9/11 Levels." *New York Times,* 18 October 2002.

Kessler, Glenn & Alan Sipress. "Western Targets Bombed in Riyadh." *Washington Post,* 13 May 2003.

Khan, Zarar. "Suicide Bomb Plot against Americans Foiled, Police Say." *AP,* 15 December 2002.

Kimery, Anthony. "The Specter of SARS." *Homeland Defense Journal,* June 2003, 28–33.

Labbe, Theola. "Car Bomb Explodes outside Turkish Embassy in Baghdad." *Washington Post,* 15 October 2003.

———. "Homemade Bombs Bedevil Troops." *Washington Post,* 9 September 2003.

———. "Some Fear Blast at University Heralds New Phase of Violence." *Washington Post,* 6 September 2003.

LaFraniere, Sharon & Peter Baker. "Moscow's New Fear: Women with Bombs." *Washington Post,* 11 July 2003.

LaFraniere, Sharon. "Russian Compound Bombed in Chechnya." *Washington Post,* 13 May 2003.

Lancaster, John. "Gunmen in Pakistan Kill Scores of Shiites." *Washington Post,* 3 March 2004.

———. "Indian Police Kill Gunmen at Crowded Shopping Mall." *Washington Post,* 4 November 2002.

———. "India Shocked by Bombay Bombings, and Suspects." *Washington Post,* 12 September 2003.

Layton, Lyndsey. "Delays Ripple through Metro." *Washington Post,* 13 December 2003.

Lekic, Slobodan. "Suspect in Bombing Offers Prayers for Safety of Bin Laden." *AP,* 23 October 2002.

Lemke, Tim & Robert Redding, Jr. "Worm Hits Area Computer Systems." *Washington Times,* 13 August 2003.

Lerner, Marc. "Bus Bomb Kills 3 Filipinos; Attacks from 'Bad to Worse.'" *Washington Times,* 19 October 2002.

Lowitt, Bruce. "Terrorists Turn '72 Munich Olympics into Bloodbath." *St. Petersburg Times,* 29 December 1999.

MacFarquhar, Neil. "For Americans in Mideast, Daily Balance of Risk." *New York Times,* 31 October 2002.

"Malaysian Police Hunt Internet Scaremonger." *Reuters,* 19 December 2002.

Mapes, Timothy. "Indonesia Bombing Kills at Least 14." *Wall Street Journal,* 6 August 2003.

Mintz, John. "Alert Warns of Attacks Using Hijacked Cargo Jets." *Washington Post,* 8 November 2003.

Mintz, John & Sara Goo. "Air Travelers Told to Expect Closer Checks on Gadgets." *Washington Post,* 6 August 2003.

Mitnick, Joshua. "3 Americans Die in Bombing in Jerusalem." *Washington Times,* 1 August 2002.

Moore, Molly. "'Parallels' to Al Qaeda Cited in Istanbul Synagogue Blasts." *Washington Post,* 20 November 2003.

————. "Young Mother Kills 4 at Gaza Crossing." *Washington Post,* 15 January 2004.

Moore, Molly & John Anderson. "Israelis Intercept 'Mega Bomb.'" *Washington Post,* 6 September 2002.

————. "Suicide Bomber Kills 15 on Bus in Northern Israel." *Washington Post,* 6 March 2003.

Moore, Molly & Yesim Borg. "Istanbul Rocked by Car Bombs." *Washington Post,* 16 November 2003.

————. "It Felt Like an Earthquake." *Washington Post,* 21 November 2003.

Moore, Molly & Glenn Frankel. "Israelis Fear Bombing by British 'Tourists' Heralds New Threat." *Washington Post,* 10 May 2003.

Nakashima, Ellen. "Lethal Blast Hits Jakarta Hotel." *Washington Post,* 6 August 2003.

————. "Thai Officials Probe Tie to Al Qaeda in Attacks." *Washington Post,* 9 January 2004.

Nakashima, Ellen & Alan Sipress. "Indonesia Military Allegedly Talked of Targeting Mine." *Washington Post,* 3 November 2002.

Nason, Randall. "Working to Secure the Electric Network." *Security Technology & Design,* November 2003, 18–22.

"One Killed as Bomb Explodes at Church." *Reuters,* 20 October 2002.

"Passenger Bus Ambushed, Five Dead." *Kathmandu Post,* 9 December 2002.

"Pipeline Explosion Kills 105 in Nigeria." *AP,* 21 June 2003.

Pomfret, John. "Bombs Explode at 2 Prominent Beijing Universities." *Washington Post,* 26 February 2003.

Powell, Bill. "Still out There." *Fortune,* 11 November 2002.

Priest, Dana. "Hussein's Capture Not Likely to Harm Al Qaeda." *Washington Post,* 26 December 2003.

Priest, Dana & Sara Goo. "3 Air Routes Focus of Scrutiny." *Washington Post,* 3 January 2004.

Priest, Dana & Susan Schmidt. "Al Qaeda Threat Has Increased, Tenet Says." *Washington Post,* 18 October 2002.

Regalado, Antonio. "Scientific Data Offer No Proof of Beef Safety." *Wall Street Journal,* 26 December 2003.

Richburg, Keith. "Five Held in Madrid Blasts." *Washington Post,* 14 March 2004.

Ricks, Thomas & Peter Selvin. "Spain, U.S. Seize N. Korean Missiles." *Washington Post,* 11 December 2002.

Rosenberg, Matthew. "Kenyan Tells of Plot to Bomb Embassy." *Washington Post*, 25 October 2003.

Rubenstein, Harry. "Bus Bombing Ranks among Most Lethal Attacks." *Jerusalem Post*, 5 June 2002.

Sands, David. "U.N. Has Long History of Casualties." *Washington Times*, 23 August 2003.

Schmidt, Susan & Dan Eggen. "Al Qaeda Official Tells of Planned Attacks." *Washington Post*, 20 March 2003.

————. "Suspected Planner of 9/11 Attacks Captured in Pakistan after Gunfight." *Washington Post*, 14 September 2002.

Schneider, Howard. "Car Bomb Kills British Banker in Saudi Arabia." *Washington Post*, 21 June 2002.

Selvin, Peter. "Saudi Bombing Blamed on Al Qaeda." *Washington Post*, 10 November 2003.

Seper, Jerry. "FBI Issues Warnings of Threat to Coastal Bridges." *Washington Times*, 2 November 2001.

Seper, Jerry & Bill Gertz. "Arms Dealer Arrested in Terror Sting." *Washington Times*, 13 August 2003.

Seper, Jerry & Guy Taylor. "Muhammed Said to Forge Passports for Illegal Aliens." *Washington Times*, 11 November 2002.

Shadid, Anthony. "Blast at Italian Police Post in Iraq Kills 29." *Washington Post*, 13 November 2003.

Shahine, Alaa. "Al Qaeda Is Said to Have Weighed Nuclear Threats." *AP*, 9 September 2002.

Sharkey, Joe. "Crime: Rising Threat in Many Areas." *New York Times*, 22 October 2002.

Sipress, Alan. "Bremer Survived Ambush Outside Baghdad." *Washington Post*, 20 December 2003.

————. "Suicide Bomber Kills 17 Iraqis, Wounds 33." *Washington Post*, 15 December 2003.

Smith, Craig. "France Holds 8 in Connection with Tunisia Blast." *New York Times*, 6 November 2002.

"Sniper Victims." *Washington Post*, 21 October 2002.

"Socks Prompt Warning about Al Qaeda and Planes." *AP*, 5 December 2003.

"Spain Says ETA Planned New Year's Bombing." *Reuters*, 19 December 2002.

Tavernise, Sabrina. "Inside, Fearful Children; Outside, Frantic Relatives." *New York Times*, 24 October 2002.

"Terrorism on Wall Street." *AP*, 16 September 1999.

Thomas, Cal. "Grim Signals of More to Come." *Washington Times*, 30 October 2002.

"Turkish TV: Suspected El Al Hijacker Wanted to Crash Plane into Tel Aviv Building." *AP*, 18 November 2002.

"U.S. Indicts 2 Florida Men in Bomb Plot." *Reuters*, 18 May 2002.

Vedantam, Shankar. "Mad Cow Case Found in U.S. for First Time." *Washington Post*, 24 December 2003.

————. "U.S. Recalls Meat Linked to Wash. Slaughterhouse." *Washington Post*, 25 December 2003.

Vedantam, Shankar & Blaine Harden. "As Probe of Infected Cow Spreads, So Does Worry." *Washington Post*, 27 December 2003.

Vick, Karl. "U.S. Diplomat Is Killed by Gunman in Jordan." *Washington Post*, 29 October 2002.

Vick, Karl & Karen De Young. "Terrorism Suspected in Yemen Blast." *Washington Post*, 10 October 2002.

Wahab, Salah. "Tourism and Terrorism: Synthesis of the Problem with Emphasis on Egypt." *Tourism, Crime and International Security Issues*, 1996.

Walters, Joanna et al. "Three Held over 'Poison Gas' Bomb Plot on Tube." *Observer*, 17 November 2002.

Warrick, Joby. "Nuclear Program in Iran Tied to Pakistan." *Washington Post*, 21 December 2003.

Warrick, Joby & Glenn Kessler. "Iran's Nuclear Program Speeds Ahead." *Washington Post*, 10 March 2003.

Wax, Emily. "Jordan Arrests Iraqis in Plot to Poison Water, and Probes Others." *Washington Post*, 2 April 2003.

————. "Kenyan Police Find Bomb-Making Materials, Seek Owner." *Washington Post*, 17 December 2002.

————. "Suicide Bombers Kill 12 at Resort in Kenya." *Washington Post*, 29 November 2002.

Williams, Daniel. "Chief Envoy, at Least 16 Others Dead." *Washington Post*, 20 August 2003.

————. "Gunman Wounds 3 at Iraq Mosque." *Washington Post*, 6 September 2003.

————. "17 Killed in Attacks on Police in Iraq." *Washington Post*, 23 November 2003.

Williams, Daniel & Anthony Shadid. "Saboteurs Hit Iraqi Facilities." *Washington Post*, 18 August 2003.

Wright, Robin. "Car Bomb Explodes at Saudi Complex." *Washington Post*, 9 November 2003.

Yost, Pete. "FBI: Suicide Bombers Likely in U.S." *AP*, 20 May 2002.

Zeller, Tom. "Under the Lens: Southeast Asia Confronts Its Demons." *New York Times*, 20 October 2002.

Web Sites

www.ap.org (Associated Press).

www.aviationnow.com/awin (Aviation Week Intelligence Network).

www.bbc.co.uk (British Broadcasting Company).

www.cert.org (CERT Coordination Center, Carnegie Mellon University).

www.cia.gov (Central Intelligence Agency).
www.cnn.com (Cable News Network).
www.dhs.gov (Department of Homeland Security).
www.fbi.gov (Federal Bureau of Investigation).
www.jpost.com (Jerusalem Post).
www.mipt.org (National Memorial Institute for the Prevention of Terrorism).
www.9-11commission.gov (National Commission on Terrorist Attacks upon the United States).
www.nipc.gov (National Infrastructure Protection Center, Department of Homeland Security).
www.potomacinstitute.org (The Potomac Institute for Policy Studies).
www.reuters.com (Reuters).
www.state.gov/s/ct/rls/ (Counterterrorism Office, Department of State).
www.whitehouse.gov (White House, Office of the President).

3. Terrorists and Their Supporters Participate in the Economic System

Alexander, Yonah. "Hizballah: The Most Dangerous Terrorist Movement." *Intersec,* October 1994.
————, ed. *Combating Terrorism: Strategies of Ten Countries.* Ann Arbor: University of Michigan Press, 2003.
————. *Palestinian Religious Terrorism: Hamas and Islamic Jihad.* Ardsley, N.Y.: Transnational Publishers, 2002.
————. *Palestinian Secular Terrorism.* Ardsley, N.Y.: Transnational Publishers, 2003.
Alexander, Yonah, Michael Swetnam, & Herbert Levine. *ETA: Profile of a Terrorist Group.* Ardsley, N.Y.: Transnational Publishers, 2001.
"Al Qaeda's Wealth Still Intact, Says Swiss Official." *Reuters,* 5 September 2002.
Badolato, Edward. "South Africa: A Supermarket for Terrorists." *Journal of Counterterrorism & Security International,* Summer 1997, 10-13.
Baker, Peter. "15 Tied to Al Qaeda Turned over to U.S." *Washington Post,* 22 October 2002.
Barrett, Paul. "Idaho Arrest Puts Muslim Students under Scrutiny." *Wall Street Journal,* 28 May 2003.
Barro, Robert. "The Myth That Poverty Breeds Terrorism." *Business Week,* 10 June 2002, 26.
Benesh, Peter. "Behind Radical Muslim Discontent: Economic Failure of Modern Islam." *Investors Business Daily,* 21 September 2001.
Bernard, Tara. "Scam Targets Citibank Customers." *Wall Street Journal,* 19 August 2003.
Borrus, Amy. "To Catch an Identity Thief." *Business Week,* 31 March 2003, 91.
Browning, Lynnley. "Outsourcing Abroad Applies to Tax Returns, Too." *New York Times,* 15 February 2004.

Burg, Bob & Lori Palatnik. "The Gossip Threat." *Security Magazine,* January 2003, 34–35.

Cappello, Daniel. "The Second Man." *New Yorker,* 16 September 2002.

Cloud, David. "Long in U.S. Sights, a Young Terrorist Builds Grim Resume." *Wall Street Journal,* 10 February 2004.

Cooper, Christopher. "In Pakistani Bombing, Al Qaeda Earmarks." *Wall Street Journal,* 17 June 2002.

Crawford, David & Ian Johnson. "Pre-9/11 Germany Had Al Qaeda Cell in Sight for Years." *Wall Street Journal,* 17 January 2003.

Davis, Ann. "Some Colleges Balk at FBI Request for Data on Foreigners." *Wall Street Journal,* 25 November 2002.

DeBaise, Colleen & Yochi Dreazen. "Ring of Identity Thieves Is Broken." *Wall Street Journal,* 26 November 2002.

Dobbs, Michael. "Al-Jazeera Airs Audiotape Allegedly of Bin Laden." *Washington Post,* 5 January 2004.

Draper, Robert. "The Ones That Got Away." *GQ,* January 2004.

Duffy, Daintry. "Liar, Liar." *CSO,* January 2003, 16.

––––––––. "The Fraud Squad." *CSO,* January 2003, 34–40.

Eggen, Dan. "FBI Curbed in Tracking Gun Buyers." *Washington Post,* 18 November 2003.

––––––––. "In Plea Deal, Seattle Activist Admits Conspiring to Aid Taliban." *Washington Post,* 15 April 2003.

––––––––. "Jewelry Stores Raided in Al Qaeda–Related Probe." *Washington Post,* 9 July 2002.

Eggen, Dan & Douglas Farah. "Iranian Arrested in Florida Sting." *Washington Post,* 25 September 2003.

Farah, Douglas & Allan Lengel. "U.S. Holds Al Qaeda Trainee." *Washington Post,* 20 July 2002.

Farley, Dennis. "To Catch a Thief." *Security Magazine,* January 2003, 29–30.

Finer, Jonathan. "Prison Interpreter Is Indicted." *Washington Post,* 13 November 2003.

Garbati, Ana. "El Gobierno Vasco Acusa a Aznar de Alejar Empresas de Eusakadi." *El Periodico,* 14 Noviembre 2002.

Gertz, Bill. "Few CIA Analysts Put on Al Qaeda Case." *Washington Times,* 19 September 2002.

GlobalOptions Inc. *An Analysis of Terrorist Threats to America's Medicine Supply.* Gaithersburg, Md.: Signature Book Printing, 2003.

"Gold Theft Continues to Be a Big Business in South Africa." *Intersec,* July/August 2002, 239.

"Guardsman Charged in Al Qaeda Case." *AP,* 18 February 2004.

Harden, Blaine. "Engineer Held as Part of Portland Probe." *Washington Post,* 5 April 2003.

––––––––. "Sting Suspect Stressed Military Prowess." *Washington Post,* 14 February 2004.

Hardy, Quentin. "Inside Dope." *Forbes,* 10 November 2003.

Haughney, Christine, & Michael Powell. "N.Y. Men Are Called Al Qaeda Trainees." *Washington Post,* 19 September 2002.

Horvath, Stephanie. "U.S. Fines 86 Firms for Business with Nations on 'Enemies' List." *Wall Street Journal,* 3 July 2002.

Higgins, Alan et al. "How Al Qaeda Put Internet in Service of Global Jihad." *Wall Street Journal,* 11 November 2002.

"Internet Fraud Increased Sharply Last Year." *AP,* 10 April 2003.

"Italy and the Eco-Mafia." *Business Week,* 27 January 2003.

Jefferson, Philip & Fredric Pryor. "On the Geography of Hate." *Economic Letters* Vol. 65, No. 3 (1999): 389–395.

Kaihla, Paul. "Terror Forging." *Business 2.0,* December 2002/January 2003, 122–127.

Kessler, Glenn. "Front Firms Aided Iran Nuclear Bomb Effort, Sources Say." *Washington Post,* 19 December 2002.

Khan, Kamran. "Most-Wanted Militant Is Arrested in Pakistan." *Washington Post,* 19 September 2002.

Koknar, Ali. "The Turkey Connection: Combating Nuclear, Chemical, Biological Materials, and Narcotics Smuggling." *Journal of Counterterrorism & Security International,* Summer 1997, 18–22.

Krueger, Alan & Jitka Maleckova. "Education, Poverty, Political Violence and Terrorism: Is There a Causal Connection?" unpublished, May 2002.

Kushner, Harvey. "Financing Terrorist Activities through Coupon Fraud and Counterfeiting." *Journal of Counterterrorism & Security International,* Summer 1998, 10–12.

LaFraniere, Sharon. "A Young Gang Leader Sheds His Obscurity." *Washington Post,* 25 October 2002.

Lancaster, John & Kamran Khan. "Pakistanis Say Nuclear Scientists Aided Iran." *Washington Post,* 24 January 2004.

Marciniak, Sean. "Identity-Theft Scam Rises on Web." *Wall Street Journal,* 22 July 2003.

Markon, Jerry. "3 Wanted Men Arrested in Virginia Jihad Case." *Washington Post,* 20 July 2003.

Markon, Jerry & Susan Schmidt. "11 Indicted in Alleged Va. Jihad Network." *Washington Post,* 28 June 2003.

Masters, Brooke. "Mass Theft of Identities Alleged." *Washington Post,* 26 November 2002.

———. "U.S. Indicts 5 in Scam to Launder Drug Money through Insurance." *Washington Post,* 7 December 2002.

Masters, Brooke & Caroline Mayer. "Identity Theft More Often an Inside Job." *Washington Post,* 3 December 2002.

Mesenbrink, John. "Utility Dams Crime." *Security Magazine,* January 2003, 37.

Mintz, John. "Arab Translator Investigated for Months." *Washington Post,* 27 September 2003.

————. "Terrorism Investigators Search Company in Mass." *Washington Post*, 7 December 2002.

————. "Yemeni Likely to Face Early Trial." *Washington Post*, 11 February 2004.

Mintz, John & Douglas Farah. "Small Scams Probed for Terror Ties." *Washington Post*, 12 August 2002.

Moore, Meg. "Pillars of Your Community." *CSO*, January 2003, 45–48.

Murphy, Brian. "Members of Terror Group in Greece Found Guilty." *Washington Post*, 9 December 2003.

Nakashima, Ellen. "11 Men with Suspected Ties to Al Qaeda Arrested in Southeast Asia." *Washington Post*, 19 December 2003.

O'Balance, Edgar. "Blood Diamonds: The Insurgent's Currency." *Intersec*, June 2002, 197–199.

Powell, Michael & Christine Haughney. "Terror Cell Broken, U.S. Says." *Washington Post*, 15 September 2002.

"Public Enemy No. 1: Identity Theft." *Wired*, February 2004, 44–45.

Raa, Ivan. "Fear & Loathing in Colombia." *Intersec*, September 2001, 262–265.

Robinson, Mike. "Islamic Charity Leader Pleads Guilty." *AP*, 10 February 2003.

Roig-Franzia, Manuel. "N.C. Man Convicted of Aiding Hezbollah." *Washington Post*, 22 June 2002.

Rosen, Jeffrey. "Identity Crisis." *Wired*, January 2004, 27–28.

"Saddam Gives $260,000 to Families of Palestinian 'Martyrs.'" *AP*, 13 March 2003.

Sager, Ira. "The Underground Web." *Business Week*, 2 September 2002.

Schaefer, Sara. "Identity Theft Costs Businesses $48 Billion a Year." *Wall Street Journal*, 4 September 2003.

Schmidt, Susan. "Armed Forces Directed to Radical Muslim Web Site." *Washington Post*, 29 June 2003.

————. "FBI Issues Alert for Four Terror Suspects." *Washington Post*, 6 September 2003.

————. "9/11 Hijackers' San Diego Contacts Detailed by Lawmakers' Report." *Washington Post*, 23 July 2003.

————. "Spreading Saudi Fundamentalism in U.S." *Washington Post*, 2 October 2003.

————. "Terror Suspect's Photos Cited." *Washington Post*, 12 March 2003.

————. "Trucker Pleads Guilty in Plot by Al Qaeda." *Washington Post*, 20 June 2003.

Seper, Jerry. "U.S. Arrests Six in Probe of Money Transfers to Yemen." *Washington Times*, 19 December 2002.

Shishkin, Philip. "Europe's Unruly Chain of Terrorism." *Wall Street Journal*, 9 July 2003.

"Shoe-Bomb Suspect Seeks to Change His Plea to Guilty." *Wall Street Journal*, 3 October 2002.

Simpson, Glenn. "U.S. Details Suspicions of Islamist Funding." *Wall Street Journal,* 20 October 2003.

Sipress, Alan & Ellen Nakashima. "Al Qaeda Affiliate Training Indonesians on Philippine Island." *Washington Post,* 17 November 2003.

Sipress, Alan. "Key Player in Nuclear Trade Ring Found Hospitable Base in Malaysia." *Washington Post,* 24 February 2004.

Smith, R. Jeffrey & Amy DePaul. "Al Qaeda 'Scout' Had Low Profile." *Washington Post,* 21 June 2003.

Sterling, Bruce. "Absolute Corruption." *Wired,* December 2002, 94.

Thompson, Julian. "Explosive Terrorist Capabilities." *Intersec,* July/August 2002, 217.

————. "The FARC-IRA Connection." *Intersec,* September 2001, 262.

Thompson, Robyn. "The Threat of Corporate Espionage & Terrorism." *Journal of Counterterrorism & Security International,* Summer 1997, 34, 38–41.

"Three Tied to Al Qaeda Arrested in Hong Kong." *Washington Times,* 6 November 2002.

Tupman, Bill. "The Business of Terrorism." *Intersec,* June 2002, 186–188.

"U.S. Imposes Ban on Chinese Firm for Selling to Iran." *Wall Street Journal,* 23 May 2003.

Vick, Karl. "Turks Assert Al Qaeda Link in Bomb Arrest." *Washington Post,* 20 December 2003.

Vogel, Steve & John Mintz. "Translator Accused of Spying." *Washington Post,* 24 September 2003.

Warrick, Joby. "Smugglers Enticed by Dirty Bomb Components." *Washington Post,* 30 November 2003.

Waxman, Sharon. "Friends, Families 'Shocked' by Arrest." *Washington Post,* 6 October 2002.

Weiss, Rick. "Mail-Order Molecules Brew a Terrorism Debate." *Washington Post,* 17 July 2002.

————. "Researchers Create Virus in Record Time." *Washington Post,* 14 November 2003.

Willox, Norman & Thomas Regan. "Identity Theft: Authentication as a Solution—Revisited." National Fraud Center, 2 October 2001.

Winer, Jonathan & Trifin Roule. "Fighting Terrorist Finance." *International Institute for Strategic Studies* 44 (2002): 87-104.

Web Sites

www.ap.org (Associated Press).

www.aviationnow.com/awin (Aviation Week Intelligence Network).

www.bbc.co.uk (British Broadcasting Company).

www.cia.gov (Central Intelligence Agency).

www.cnn.com (Cable News Network).

www.csoonline.com (Resource for Security Executives, CSO Magazine).

www.dhs.gov (Department of Homeland Security).

www.doj.gov (Department of Justice).
www.fbi.gov (Federal Bureau of Investigations).
www.interpol.org (Interpol).
www.intersec.co.uk (Intersec Publishing).
www.irrc.com (Investor Responsibility Research Center).
www.jpost.com (Jerusalem Post).
www.mipt.org (National Memorial Institute for the Prevention of Terrorism).
www.9-11commission.gov (National Commission on Terrorist Attacks upon the United States).
www.potomacinstitute.org (Potomac Institute for Policy Studies).
www.reuters.com (Reuters).
www.sia.com/moneylaundering/ (Security Industry Association).
www.silkroadstudies.org/drugtrade.htm (Program for Contemporary Silk Road, Uppsala University).
www.treasury.gov (Department of Treasury).

4. Financing Terror

Alexander, Yonah, ed. *Combating Terrorism: Strategies of Ten Countries.* Ann Arbor: University of Michigan Press, 2003.
————. *Palestinian Religious Terrorism: Hamas and Islamic Jihad.* Ardsley, N.Y.: Transnational Publishers, 2002.
————. *Palestinian Secular Terrorism.* Ardsley, N.Y.: Transnational Publishers, 2003.
Alexander, Yonah, Michael Swetnam, & Herbert Levine, *ETA: Profile of a Terrorist Group.* Ardsley, N.Y.: Transnational Publishers, 2001.
"Aspects of Financial Transactions Indicative of Terrorist Funding." *SAR Bulletin,* Financial Crimes Enforcement Network, Department of Treasury, January 2002.
Beckett, Paul & Carrick Mollenkamp. "In Wake of Sept. 11, Regulators Crack Down on Money-Transfer Industry." *Wall Street Journal,* 28 December 2001.
Beers, Rand, Assistant Secretary for International Narcotics and Law Enforcement Affairs. Judiciary Subcommittee on Technology, Terrorism and Government, Senate Judiciary Committee, 12 March 2002.
Block, Robert. "In South Africa, Mounting Evidence of Al Qaeda Links." *Wall Street Journal,* 10 December 2002.
Chandrasekaran, Rajiv. "Muslim World Moves Money without Trace." *Washington Post,* 10 November 2001.
Cooper, Christopher. "How Drive to Block Funds for Terrorism Entangled Mr. Aden." *Wall Street Journal,* 6 May 2002.
Cowell, Alan. "40 Nations in Accord on Conflict Diamonds." *New York Times,* 6 November 2002.

"Crackdown on Terror Funding Is Questioned." *Los Angeles Times*, 8 April 2002.

Crawford, David & Ian Johnson. "Saudi Funds Tied to Extremism in Europe." *Wall Street Journal*, 30 December 2003.

Eggen, Dan. "3 N.Y. Men Arrested for Money Transfers." *Washington Post*, 18 December 2002.

Eggen, Dan & John Mintz. "Muslim Groups' IRS Files Sought." *Washington Post*, 14 January 2004.

Eichenwald, Kurt. "Bin Laden Family Liquidates Holdings with Carlyle Group." *New York Times*, 26 October 2001.

Farah, Douglas. "Al Qaeda Gold Moved to Sudan." *Washington Post*, 12 August 2002.

————. "Bank Data for Saudi Embassy Subpoenaed." *Washington Post*, 23 November 2003.

————. "Saudis Face U.S. Demand on Terrorism." *Washington Post*, 26 November 2002.

————. "U.S. Indicts Prominent Muslim Here." *Washington Post*, 24 October 2003.

Fields, Gary. "Four Accused of Sending Cash to Iraq." *Wall Street Journal*, 27 February 2003.

Frantz, Douglas. "U.S.-Based Charity Is under Scrutiny." *New York Times*, 14 June 2002.

Freedman, David. "Telling You: A $300,000 Con Shows How Easy It Is to Manipulate the System." *Business 2.0*, August 2002.

Greil, Anita. "Officials at Al Taqwa Companies Are Questioned on Terror Links." *Wall Street Journal*, 8 November 2001.

Johnson, Carrie & Mike Musgrove. "Student Charged with Hacking Stock Account." *Washington Post*, 10 October 2003.

Johnston, William. "Combating the Financing of Terrorism in the United Kingdom and the United States—Money Laundering." *International Bar Association Banking Law Committee Newsletter*, April 2002.

————. "Money—Dirty, Hidden, New and Clean." *International Bar Association Banking Law Committee Newsletter*, April 2002.

Krane, Jim. "U.S. Seeks to Cut Off Money to Guerrillas." *AP*, 5 December 2003.

Kushner, Harvey. "Financing Terrorist Activities through Coupon Fraud and Counterfeiting." *Journal of Counterterrorism & Security International*, Summer 1998, 10–12.

Levitt, Matthew. "Combating Terrorist Financing, Despite the Saudis." *Policywatch: Analysis of Near East Policy from the Scholars and Associates of the Washington Institute*, 1 November 2002.

————. "The Network of Terrorist Financing." *Policywatch: Analysis of Near East Policy from the Scholars and Associates of the Washington Institute*, 6 August 2002.

Lormel, Dennis, Chief, Financial Crimes Section, FBI. "War on Terrorism." Testimony before the Subcommittee on Oversight and Investigations, House Committee on Financial Services, 12 February 2002.

Masters, Brooke. "N.Y. Bank Guilty in Laundering Case." *Washington Post,* 18 December 2002.

———. "U.S. Indicts 5 in Scam to Launder Drug Money through Insurance." *Washington Post,* 7 December 2002.

McManee, Mike et al. "The Cash Squeeze on Terror Inc." *Business Week,* 17 March 2003, 38–39.

"Minneapolis Man Charged with Conspiring to Provide Material Support to Al Qaeda." Press Release, Department of Justice, 21 January 2004.

Mintz, John. "Firm Indicted in Fund Transfers." *Washington Post,* 20 December 2002.

———. "U.S. Labels Muslim Charity as Terrorist Group." *Washington Post,* 19 October 2002.

Mueller, Robert S., III, FBI Director. Testimony before the Senate Committee on Intelligence, 14 February 2003.

Perez, Evan. "Banking on Immigrants." *Wall Street Journal,* 9 May 2003.

Phillips, Michael. "Afghan Aid Flows through Dark Channels." *Wall Street Journal,* 12 November 2002.

"President Announces Crackdown on Terrorist Financial Network." Office of the Press Secretary, White House, 7 November 2001.

"President Freezes Terrorists' Assets." Office of the Press Secretary, White House, 24 September 2001.

Priest, Dana & Susan Schmidt. "Congressional Panel Links Hijackers, Saudi Financiers." *Washington Post,* 23 November 2002.

Prystay, Cris. "Malaysia's Banks Aim to Take Islamic Financing Mainstream." *Wall Street Journal,* 20 November 2002.

Reddy, Anitha. "Terrorists Are Now Targets in Money-Laundering Fight." *Washington Post,* 25 July 2002.

"Report on Money Laundering Typologies 2002–2003." Financial Action Task Force on Money Laundering, 14 February 2003.

Schneider, Howard. "Saudis See Obstacles in Freezing Accounts." *Washington Post,* 25 October 2001.

Sheridan, Mary Beth & Douglas Farah. "Jailed Muslim Had Made a Name in Washington." *Washington Post,* 1 December 2003.

Simpson, Glenn. "Probe of Saudi Embassy Widens as Bank Activity Is Scrutinized." *Wall Street Journal,* 14 January 2004.

———. "Charity Backed by Saudis Linked to 1998 Terror Attacks in Africa." *Wall Street Journal,* 23 January 2004.

———. "Report Links Charity to an Al Qaeda Front." *Wall Street Journal,* 20 September 2002.

———. "Tracing the Money, Terror Investigators Run into Mr. Qadi." *Wall Street Journal,* 26 November 2002.

_____. "U.S. Knew of Terrorist, Charity Ties." *Wall Street Journal*, 9 May 2003.

_____. "U.S. Links Scholar to Terror Funding." *Wall Street Journal*, 17 March 2003.

Sommer, Terje. "Banking Secrecy and the Treatment of Information." *International Bar Association Banking Law Committee Newsletter*, April 2002.

"Terrorism: What You Need to Know about U.S. Sanctions." Office of Foreign Assets Control, Department of Treasury, undated.

"Terrorist Assets Report Calendar Year 2002: Annual Report to the Congress on Assets in the United States of Terrorist Countries and International Terrorism Program Designees." Department of Treasury, 2003.

Tett, Gillian & Mark Huband. "'Dirty Bomb' Materials in Africa Heighten Terror Concern." *Financial Times*, 18 June 2003.

"Thailand Probes Sri Lankan Rebel Arms Smuggling Ring, AFP Says." bloomberg.com, 24 September 2003.

Toameh, Abu Khaled. "PA Embassy in Pakistan Stealing Cars, Counterfeiting Cash." jpost.com, 6 October 2002.

"Treasury Establishes Financial Institutions Hotline Relating to Terrorist Activity." Department of Treasury, 11 October 2001.

Tucker, Neely. "Muslim Charity Fights Closure." *Washington Post*, 23 April 2003.

"U.S. Department of the Treasury Anti-Terrorist Financing Guidelines: Voluntary Best Practices for U.S.-Based Charities." Department of Treasury, undated.

"U.S. Intensifies Financial War on Terrorists." *Wall Street Journal*, 8 November 2001.

Vick, Karl. "Iranian Dissident Group Labeled a Terrorist Cult." *Washington Post*, 21 June 2003.

Vistica, Gregory & Douglas Farah. "Syria Seizes Six Arab Couriers, $23 Million." *Washington Post*, 20 December 2003.

Warren, Mary Lee, Deputy Assistant Attorney General. Testimony before the Subcommittee on Oversight and Investigations, House Committee on Financial Services, 12 February 2002.

Warrick, Joby. "Iran Admits Foreign Help on Nuclear Facility." *Washington Post*, 27 August 2003.

Williams, Daniel. "Swiss Probe Illustrates Difficulties in Tracking Al Qaeda's Cash." *Washington Post*, 12 November 2001.

Winer, Jonathan & Trifin Roule. "Fighting Terrorist Finance." *International Institute for Strategic Studies* 44 (2002): 87–104.

Worth, Robert. "Bank Failed to Question Huge Deposits." *New York Times*, 28 November 2002.

Zarate, Juan, Deputy Assistant Secretary, Terrorism and Violent Crime, Department of Treasury. Testimony before the Subcommittee on Oversight and Investigations, House Committee on Financial Services, 12 February 2002.

Web Sites

www.findlaw.com (Find Law).

www.moneylaundering.com (Money Laundering Publication).

www.treasury.gov/offices/enforcement/ofac/sanctions/terrorism.html(Department of Treasury).

www.un.org/Docs/scres/1999/99sc1267.htm (United Nations).

www.un.org/Docs/sc/committees/1373/ (United Nations Counter-Terrorism Committee).

www.whitehouse.gov/afac (White House, Office of the President).

www.whitehouse.gov/response/financialresponse.html (White House, Office of the President).

www.whitehouse.gov/response/investigativeresponse.html(White House, Office of the President).

5. Security

Abboud, Leila. "Coast Guard Braces for Fight." *Wall Street Journal,* 26 June 2002.

Abelson, Reed & Jonathan D. Glater. "Businesses Finding That Good Security Is No Longer Optional." *New York Times,* 17 October 2001.

Aizenman, Nurith. "Avian Flu Cases Strike Fear in Delmarva." *Washington Post,* 11 February 2004.

Alexander, Dean C. & Seymour Rubin. "Securing Mexican Investments." *Journal of Commerce,* 12 April 1993.

Alexander, Dean C. & Yonah Alexander. *Terrorism and Business: The Impact of September 11, 2001.* Ardsley, N.Y.: Transnational Publishers, 2002.

Alexander, Yonah & Charles K. Ebinger, eds. *Political Terrorism and Energy: The Threat and Response.* New York: Praeger Publishers, 1982.

American Society for Industrial Security. *Security Industry Buyers Guide.* Alexandria, Va.: American Society for Industrial Security, 2003.

Ames, Ben. "Department of Homeland Security Asks for Private Sector Solutions." *Homeland Security Solutions,* April 2003.

Anderson, John & Molly Moore. "Two Palestinians Shot Dead, 20 Wounded in Fence Protest." *Washington Post,* 27 February 2004.

Asser, Martin. "Analysis: Soccer Violence an International Problem." *BBC News,* 19 June 2000.

"AT&T Business Continuity & Disaster Recovery Planning Final Report." *AT&T,* August 2002.

Baum, Dan. "This Gun for Hire." *Wired,* February 2003, 119-123.

Behr, Peter. "Nuclear Plants' Vulnerability Raised Attack Concerns." *Washington Post,* 21 October 2001.

Bianco, Anthony & Stephanie Forest. "Outsourcing War." *Business Week,* 15 September 2003, 68-78.

Bilefsky, Dan. "Can Shoppers Be Kept Safe?" *Wall Street Journal*, 5 December 2002.

Block, Robert & Daniel Michaels. "U.S. to Require Foreign Airlines to Add Guards on Some Flights." *Wall Street Journal*, 30 December 2003.

Block, Robert. "U.S. to Require Advance Notice on Cargo Data." *Wall Street Journal*, 21 November 2003.

Block, Robert & Stephen Power. "U.S. to Tighten Airline Screening of Passengers." *Wall Street Journal*, 13 January 2004.

Brick, Michael. "Airport Improvements Are Adrift after Sept. 11." *New York Times*, 26 June 2002.

Brooks, Rick. "Corporate Mailrooms Are First Line of Defense against Bioterrorism." *Wall Street Journal*, 15 October 2001.

"Cargill." *Washington Post*, 10 January 2004.

Catan, Thomas. "Bank Security Falls Victim to Moles." *Financial Times*, 1 March 2003.

Chea, Terence. "Security Demands May Boost Area Firms." *Washington Post*, 20 October 2001.

"Chemical Safety: Emergency Response Community Views on the Adequacy of Federal Required Chemical Information." Government Accounting Office, 31 July 2002, GAO-02-799.

Clarke, Liz. "Security Is Measured." *Washington Post*, 11 September 2002.

Clarke, Richard. "Cybersecurity Now!" *Homeland Defense Journal*, May 2003, 18–23.

Cooperman, Alan. "Secret Service Takes Blame for Waiter's Exit." *Washington Post*, 11 December 2003.

Costello, Jane. "Airport Screening: Fickle Stickler." *Wall Street Journal*, 14 May 2002.

Dacey, Robert. "Critical Infrastructure Protection: Significant Homeland Security Challenges Need to Be Addressed." Government Accounting Office, 9 July 2002, GAO-02-918T.

Davenport, Christian & Manuel Roig-Franzia. "Truckers Subject to Growing Scrutiny." *Washington Post*, 13 October 2001.

"Diffuse Security Threats: Technologies for Mail Sanitization Exist, but Challenges Remain." Government Accounting Office, April 2002, GAO-02-365.

Di Justo, Patrick. "You're Being Watched." *Wired*, December 2003, 62.

Dobbs, Michael. "U.S. Facing Bigger Bill for Iraq War." *Washington Post*, 1 December 2002.

Dooren, Jennifer. "Cargo Security Is Still Lax on Passenger Planes." *Wall Street Journal*, 16 January 2003.

Downey, Kristin & Amy Joyce. "At Work, a War of Nerve." *Washington Post*, 23 March 2003.

Duffy, Daintry. "Goal-Line Stand." *CSO*, January 2004, 24–30.

"Executive Protection: Protecting against Assassinations and Kidnappings." *Journal of Counterterrorism & Security International*, Summer 1997, 24–25.

Fabrikant, Geraldine. "Editors Rush to Revise Long-Made Plans." *New York Times,* 17 September 2001.

Feder, Barnaby. "Trying to Plan for the Unthinkable Disaster." *New York Times,* 17 September 2001.

Fialka, John. "Water Utilities Need $1.6 Billion for Upgrades." *Wall Street Journal,* 8 April 2003.

Fields, Gary. "U.S. Tightens Scrutiny of Sea Cargo." *Wall Street Journal,* 25 June 2002.

"FY2004 Budget Fact Sheet." U.S. Department of Homeland Security, 1 October 2003.

Garfinkel, Simson. "Information without Borders." *CSO,* January 2004, 51–53.

Gertz, Bill. "U.S. Eyes Pilot with Ties to Al Qaeda." *Washington Times,* 20 September 2002.

Gold, Russell. "Cities Confront High Cost of Security." *Wall Street Journal,* 24 March 2003.

Goo, Sara. "E.U. Agrees to Share Airline Passenger Data." *Washington Post,* 17 December 2003.

————. "Hundreds of Pilots Trained to Carry Guns." *Washington Post,* 27 August 2003.

————. "Ridge Sees Long-Term Role for Air Marshals." *Washington Post,* 26 November 2003.

————. "Security Rules for Charters Delayed." *Washington Post,* 20 November 2002.

————. "TSA May Try to Force Airlines to Share Data." *Washington Post,* 27 September 2003.

Goo, Sara & Amy Joyce. "U.S. Taking Photos and Fingerprints of Visitors." *Washington Post,* 6 January 2004.

Grant, Peter & Charles Gasparing. "Lehman Will Move Its Base out of Wall Street." *Wall Street Journal,* 9 October 2001.

Grimsley, Kristin. "Many Firms Lack Plans for Disaster." *Washington Post,* 3 October 2001.

Guerrero, Peter. "Mass Transit: Challenges in Securing Transit Systems." Government Accounting Office, 18 September 2002, GAO-02-1075T.

Hakim, Danny. "Bracing for Reaction When Trades Resume." *New York Times,* 17 September 2001.

Hanson, Julie. "Government Knows Best." *CSO,* January 2004, 18.

Harris, Nicole & Eleena De Lisser. "What to Expect at the Airport." *Wall Street Journal,* 27 November 2002.

Heffernan, Richards. "Security on the Move." *CSO,* September 2003, 22.

Holson, Laura. "Sudden Sense of Insecurity at Many Companies." *New York Times,* 16 September 2001.

"How Experts Grade Homeland Security." *Washington Post,* 10 September 2002.

Irwin, Neil. "Area's Preparedness Improving." *Washington Post,* 25 April 2002.

"Jersey City: 'Wall Street West.'" *Business Week,* 29 October 2001.

Jeter, Jon. "U.S. Arrivals Fingerprinted in Brazil." *Washington Post,* 4 January 2004.

Johnson, Ed. "Britain Tightens Security on Flights Across Atlantic." *Washington Post,* 29 December 2003.

Johnson, Steven. "Stopping Loose Nukes." *Wired,* November 2002, 163–169.

Kamien, David. "What Keeps Port Security Directors Up at Night." *Homeland Security,* January 2004, 10–14.

Kelly, Kate. "Blackout Put Wall Street's to the Test." *Wall Street Journal,* 18 August 2003.

Kilman, Scott. "Government Lacks Means to Thwart Agro-Terror Strike." *Wall Street Journal,* 20 September 2002.

"Knife-Wielding Man Overpowered on Jet." *Reuters,* 10 September 2002.

Koprowski, Gene. "Building a Virtual Border." *Homeland Defense Journal,* August 2003, 34–38.

Kurtz, Rod. "Safer Harbors, Higher Fees." *Inc. Magazine,* January 2004, 27.

Labbe, Theola. "U.S. Quits Fortified Hotel in Baghdad." *Washington Post,* 27 October 2003.

Levere, Jane. "As Screening Increases, Travel Light to Travel Best." *New York Times,* 15 December 2002.

Lisser, Elena de. "Countries Pile Fees, Red Tape on U.S. Tourists." *Wall Street Journal,* 22 January 2004.

Maher, Kris. "Play It Safe." *Wall Street Journal,* 23 May 2002.

Markoff, John. "Vulnerability Is Discovered in Security for Smart Cards." *New York Times,* 13 May 2002.

Maske, Mark & Leonard Shapiro. "League Awaits Word on Security Issues." *Washington Post,* 21 January 2003.

McCartney, Scott. "Airlines Will Raise Fares, Pocket Security Fees." *Wall Street Journal,* 13 May 2003.

———. "For Airlines and Flying Public, More Security Is Sole Bright Spot." *Wall Street Journal,* 11 September 2002.

———. "Money Hasn't Closed Security Gaps." *Wall Street Journal,* 9 May 2002.

McCreary, Lew. "Safe Harbor." *CSO,* April 2003, 29–35.

Meaney, Jeffrey. "Security and Business Continuity Planning at the World Trade Center." Presentation at State Department OSAC Meeting, 14 November 2002.

Mechanic, Michael. "Beyond the Wall." *Wired,* August 2003, 114–116.

Michaels, Daniel. "E.U. Sets Tougher Law for Air Security." *Wall Street Journal,* 9 December 2002.

———. "In Europe, Heists at Airports Show Holes in Security." *Wall Street Journal,* 8 November 2002.

Miller, Bill & Dan Eggen. "FBI Memo Author Did Not Envision Sept. 11." *Washington Post,* 23 May 2002.

Miller, Bill & Christine Haughney. "Nation Left Jittery by Latest Series of Terror Warnings." *Washington Post,* 22 May 2002.

Morello, Carol & David Fahrenthold. "Few Feel Rattled by Security Alert." *Washington Post,* 11 September 2002.

Nudell, Mayer & Norman Antokol. *The Handbook for Effective Emergency and Crisis Management.* Washington, D.C.: Lexington Books, 1988.

"Olympics Games: Costs to Plan and Stage the Games in the United States." Government Accounting Office, November 2001, GAO-02-140.

Pinkerton. *Top Security Threats and Management Issues Facing Corporate America.* Westlake Village, Calif.: Pinkerton, 2000–2003.

Planin, Eric. "Chemical Plants Face Oversight." *Washington Post,* 5 August 2002.

Platt, E. Alan. "Corporate Security Weaknesses and the Hidden Threats." *Intersec,* September 2002, 258–262.

Power, Stephen. "Efforts to Protect Travelers Hits Turbulence." *Wall Street Journal,* 22 May 2002.

———. "Federal Official Faults TSA Screener Testing as 'Inane.'" *Wall Street Journal,* 9 October 2003.

———. "Security Rules for Air Charters Hit Turbulence" *Wall Street Journal,* 2 August 2002.

"President Signs Anti-Terrorism Bill." Office of the Press Secretary, White House, 26 October 2001.

"President Signs Aviation Security Legislation." Office of the Press Secretary, White House, 19 November 2001.

"President Unveils 'Most Wanted' Terrorists." Office of the Press Secretary, White House, 10 October 2001.

Price, Elaine. "The Evolution of Business Continuity." *Security Technology & Design,* November 2003, 48–49.

Priest, Dana & Bill Miller. "Tenet Calls for Security Safety Net." *Washington Post,* 28 June 2002.

Pristin, Terry. "U.S. Landlords Face Post-9/11 Standards." *New York Times,* 11 February 2004.

Ramstack, Tom. "Airlines Ask U.S. to Ease War Costs." *Washington Times,* 19 September 2002.

———. "Chemical Firms Use Stricter Security." *Washington Times,* 16 October 2001.

Reel, Monte. "An Uneven Security Blanket." *Washington Post,* 30 June 2002.

Revell, Oliver. "Protective Blast and Anti-Ramming Wall Development." *Security Technology & Design,* November 2003, 40.

Rich, Motoko. "Firms, Employees Look to Home Offices Again." *Wall Street Journal,* 3 October 2001.

Roberts, Paul. "Be Careful What You Check For." *CSO,* September 2003, 16.

Romero, Simon. "Attacks Expose Telephone's Soft Underbelly." *New York Times,* 15 October 2001.

Rosen, Jeffrey. "With Liberty and Surveillance for All." *CSO,* January 2004, 38–44.

Samuelson, Robert. "Rediscovering Risk." *Washington Post,* 23 October 2002.

Scalet, Sarah. "Immune Systems." *CSO,* August 2003, 42–47.

Schneider, Greg. "Private Plane Charters: One Way One Air Security." *Washington Post,* 2 June 2002.

————. "Screening Deadline Worries Grow." *Washington Post,* 14 June 2002.

Schroeder, Michael & Kate Kelly. "U.S. May Require Backup Wall Street." *Wall Street Journal,* 22 October 2002.

Schwartz, John. "Microsoft Sets $5 Million Virus Bounty." *New York Times,* 6 November 2003.

"Security the Key to Sporting Success." *BBC News,* 15 January 2002.

Seper, Jerry. "FBI Computer System Turns into Unproductive Money Pit." *Washington Times,* 20 December 2002.

Shanley, Agnes. "The Chemical Controversy." *Homeland Defense Journal,* August 2003, 28–33.

————. "Chemical Defense on Main Street." *Homeland Defense Journal,* June 2003, 18–23.

Sharkey, Joe. "Airports Bracing for Bigger Problems." *New York Times,* 11 June 2002.

Shenk, David. "Watching You." *National Geographic,* November 2003, 2–29.

Simon, Harvey. "Companies Want to Hire Managers with Homeland Security Experience." *Homeland Security & Defense,* 14 January 2004, 4–5.

————. "DHS Rushing Low-Cost Technologies to the Field and Searching for Breakthrough Products." *Homeland Security & Defense,* 17 September 2003, 1, 3.

Simpson, Glenn. "Language Lesson for Pentagon." *Wall Street Journal,* 3 December 2003.

"Site Security Guidelines for the U.S. Chemical Industry." American Chemistry Council et al., October 2001.

"Technologies for Improvement Homeland Security." National Institute of Standards and Technology, September 2002.

"Transportation Security Guidelines for the U.S. Chemical Industry." American Chemistry Council et al., undated.

Treaster, Joseph. "Among Executives, Fear of Kidnapping Rises." *New York Times,* 2 July 2002.

Tully, Shawn. "Rebuilding Wall Street." *Fortune,* 1 October 2001.

"Uzbek Clash Causes Concern." cnnsi.com, 10 October 2001.

"U.S. Military 'To Reinforce World Cup Security.'" *BBC News,* 14 February 2002.

"Value-Added Security Solutions." Securitas. www.securitasusa.com/capabilities.

Violino, Bob. "Bonding Time." *CSO*, August 2003, 28–32.

Wald, Matthew. "Boston Airport Acts Quickly to Prepare for New Rules." *New York Times*, 19 December 2002.

———. "Guards at Nuclear Plants Feel Swamped by Overtime Deluge in the Wake of 9/11." *New York Times*, 20 October 2002.

———. "Tough Issues on Baggage Screening Remain." *New York Times*, 5 November 2002.

Waldman, Amy. "India Reports Killing 2, Stopping Terror Attack." *New York Times*, 4 November 2002.

Wall, Robert. "The Pros and Cons of Airliner Anti-Missiles Systems." *Homeland Security*, January 2004, 16–21.

Winslow, Ron. "U.S. Hospitals May Need $10 Billion to Be Prepared for Bioterror Attack." *Wall Street Journal*, 29 October 2001.

"Workplace Security." *Wall Street Journal*, 29 September 2003.

Wyatt, John. "Training in High Risk Security." *Intersec*, July/August 2002, 230–231.

Yoo, Jae-Suk. "World Cup Security a Concern among Organizers." *AP*, 18 May 2002.

Zalud, Bill. "Team Integration." *Security Magazine*, January 2003, 12–16.

———. "2002 Industry Forecast Study Security Yin-Yang: Terror Push, Recession Drag." *Security Magazine*, 23 January 2002.

Zimmerman, Ann. "Malls' Challenge: Protect Shoppers, Soothe Nerves." *Wall Street Journal*, 18 October 2001.

Web Sites

www.asisonline.com (American Society of Industrial Security).
www.aviationnow.com/awin (Aviation Week Intelligence Network).
www.battelle.org (Battle Memorial Institute).
www.buses.org. (American Bus Association).
www.businessroundtable.org/pdf/814.pdf (Business Roundtable).
www.businessroundtable.org/pdf/984.pdf (Business Roundtable).
www.businessroundtable.org/pdf/1015.pdf (Business Roundtable).
www.ci-pinkerton.com (Pinkerton Consulting and Investigations).
www.contingencyplanning.com (Contingency Planning & Management).
www.csoonline.com (Resource for Security Executives, CSO Magazine).
www.dhs.gov (Department of Homeland Security).
www.govexec.com/homeland (Government Executive, Homeland Security).
www.homelanddefensejournal.com (Homeland Defense Journal Online).
www.intersec.co.uk (Intersec Publishing).
www.isalliance.org (Internet Security Alliance).
www.krollworldwide.com (Kroll Inc.).

www.mcgraw-hillhomelandsecurity.com (McGraw-Hill Homeland Security).
www.miga.org (Multilateral Investment Guarantee Agency).
www.securitygateway.com (Security Industry News & Information, Security Industry Association).
www.securitymanagement.com/library/Counter_terror.html (Security Management, American Society of Industrial Security).
www.securitymagazine.com (Security Magazine).
www2.cio.com/ask\expert/2003/questions/question1577.html (Chief Information Officer Magazine).
www.telemussolutions.com (Telemus Solutions).
www.tsa.gov (Transportation Security Administration).
www.wackenhut.com (Wackenhut Corporation).
www.whitehouse.gov (White House, Office of the President).

6. Public-Private Partnership on Combating Terrorism

Abate, Tom. "Bioterrorism Defense Being Developed: Bay Area Companies Collaborate with Federal Agencies." *San Francisco Chronicle,* 25 September 2001.

Abelson, Reed. "In a Chorus of Caution, Some Still Chant Boldness." *New York Times,* 17 October 2001.

Aeppel, Tom. "Now Is the Time to Sell 'U.S.-Made.'" *Wall Street Journal,* 22 October 2001.

"Airports Council International-North America Calls on Congress to Focus Attention on Airports." Airports Council International, 25 September 2001.

Alexander, Dean C. & Yonah Alexander. *Terrorism and Business: The Impact of September 11, 2001.* Ardsley, N.Y.: Transnational Publishers, 2001.

Alexander, Yonah & Dean Alexander. "Complex Partnership in War on Terrorism." *Washington Times,* 25 September 2002.

Allen, Mike & John Mintz. "Homeland Department May Take a Year to Take Shape." *Washington Post,* 21 November 2002.

"Amtrak Safety Drives $1.8 Billion Package." *AP,* 18 October 2001.

Anderson, Mark. "Chaos Has Awakened Giant." moneycentral.msn.com, 1 October 2001.

Angwin, Julian. "Demand for Cipro Brings Sales—and Scrutiny—to Online Supplier." *Wall Street Journal,* 22 October 2001.

Baum, Dan. "This Gun for Hire." *Wired,* February 2003, 119-123.

"Battered but Unbroken." *Fortune,* 1 October 2001.

Bertinato, Scott & Daintry Duffy. "The Public Face of Security." *CSO,* January 2004, 47.

Bianco, Anthony & Stephanie Forest. "Outsourcing War." *Business Week,* 15 September 2003, 68-78.

"Big Increase in Real Estate Insurance Premiums on the Way, Professionals." International Council of Shopping Centers, 12 October 2001.

Bredemeier, Kenneth. "Thousands of Private Contractors Support U.S. Forces in Persian Gulf." *Washington Post,* 3 March 2003.

Brown, David. "Maker of Anthrax Vaccine to Reopen after Renovating Mich. Plant." *Washington Post,* 1 November 2001.

"Businesses Scramble to Push for Tax Breaks." *Wall Street Journal,* 10 October 2001.

Buxbaum, Peter. "Truck Industry Having Doubts on Border Program's Effectiveness." *Homeland Security & Defense,* 14 January 2004, 7.

Carey, Susan. "Airlines Install Reinforcing Bars to Secure Cockpits." *Wall Street Journal.* 3 October 2001.

Carr, Kathleen. "Safe Harbor." *CSO,* January 2004, 40–41.

Carroll, Jill & Ron Winslow. "Bayer to Slash Price U.S. Pays for Anthrax Drug." *Wall Street Journal,* 25 October 2001.

Carnahan, Ira. "Who Gets the $20 Billion." *Forbes,* 15 October 2001.

"Cepheid and ETG to Develop Biological Agent Detection Systems for Military and Other Applications." Press Release, Cepheid, 13 August 2001. www.cepheid.com/pages/press/010813.html

Chea, Terence & Justin Gillis. "Drug Firms Scramble on Scare." *Washington Post,* 18 October 2001.

"Citizen Preparedness in War on Terrorism Executive Order." Office of the Press Secretary, White House, 9 November 2001.

"Coast Guard Wants to Buy Transportable GPS Towers." *Government Security News,* July 2003, 11.

Connolly, Ceci. "Smallpox Compensation Proposed." *Washington Post,* 6 March 2003.

————. "U.S. Officials Reorganize Strategy on Bioterrorism." *Washington Post,* 8 November 2001.

Cowley, Stacy. "Preventing Disease One Mad Cow at a Time." *CSO,* March 2004, 12.

Datz, Todd. "From the Ground Up." *CSO,* March 2004, 35–40.

————. "Government Relations: Capital Ideas." *CSO,* December 2003, 34–39.

Davis, Bob. "Massive Federal R&D Initiative to Fight Terror Is Under Way." *Wall Street Journal,* 25 November 2002.

"Department of Homeland Security Institutes Operation Liberty Shield." *Security Products,* May 2003, 46–49.

"Department of Homeland Security Makes Agro-Terrorism a High Priority for Research." continuitycentral.com, 20 December 2003.

Doyle, John. "Industry Help Sought on Guarding Infrastructure." *Homeland Security & Defense,* 14 January 2004, 2.

Duffy, Daintry. "Adversaries: Underground Fears." *CSO,* December 2003, 40–45.

"Egis II Explosives Detection Systems." *Thermo Electron Corporation*. www.thermo.com/eThermo/CDA/Products/Prod.%20.%20./1,1075,14817-167-X-1-13795,00.htm

Eilperin, Juliet & Caroline Mayer. "Federal Air-Security Bill Clears Congress." *Washington Post*, 17 November 2001.

"Enhancing Aviation Safety & Security." Office of the Press Secretary, White House, 27 September 2001.

Fahey, Jonathan. "We See You." *Forbes*, 15 October 2001.

"Features of the RAPID." *RAPID*. www.idahotech.com/rapid/features.htm

Ferdinand, Pamela. "Mayors in Bind of Rising Costs of Security, Declining Revenue." *Washington Post*, 23 November 2001.

"Financial Actions." Office of the Press Secretary, White House, undated.

Freedman, David. "The De-Hijacking Swtich." *Business 2.0*, November 2001.

"From Smart to Brilliant Weapons." *Business Week*, 8 October 2001.

Godinez, Victor. "Protection Services Firms See a Surge in Demand." dallasnews.com, 23 October 2001.

Goo, Sara. "No Reclaiming Items Seized at Airports." *Washington Post*, 9 October 2003.

Goodwin, Jacob. "NYC Transit Agency and U.S. Army Prepare to Fight Subway Terror." *Government Security News*, July 2003, 1.

Gugliotta, Guy. "Tech Companies See Market for Detection." *Washington Post*, 28 September 2001.

Hedgpeth, Dana. "Marriott to Pay $115,000 to Arab American Group." *Washington Post*, 16 August 2002.

Henry, David. "Putting on a Grim New Face." *Business Week*, 15 October 2001.

Hilsenrath, Jon. "Terror's Toll on the Economy." *Wall Street Journal*, 9 October 2001.

Hitt, Greg & Martha Brannigan. "Air-Security Bill Poses Tough Challenges." *Wall Street Journal*, 19 November 2001.

Holson, Laura. "Sudden Sense of Insecurity at Many Companies." *New York Times*, 16 September 2001.

"Homeland Security Buys N.M. Town for Training." *Reuters*, 23 May 2003.

"ICSC Joins Call for Government Terror Insurance Guarantees." International Council of Shopping Centers, 10 October 2001.

"Industry Recovery and Action Plans." American Hotel & Lodging Association, undated.

Irwin, Neil. "Embassy Architects Juggle Security, Aesthetics." *Washington Post*, 2 September 2002.

Kaufman, Marc. "New Food Import Rules Issued." *Washington Post*, 2 October 2003.

Kessler, Glenn. "OMB Chief Signals New Spending Goals." *Washington Post*, 17 October 2001.

Koerner, Brendan. "The Security Traders." *Mother Jones*, September/October 2002.

Lakshmi, Rama. "Soda Giants Battle Public Panic in India." *Washington Post*, 10 August 2003.

LeDuc, Daniel. "Md. to Seek $250 Million in Anti-Terrorism Funds." *Washington Post*, 2 November, 2001.

Lee, Christopher. "Army Weighs Privatizing Close to 214,000 Jobs." *Washington Post*, 3 December 2002.

McCartney, Scott & John McKinnon. "U.S. Loan Package Doesn't Shut Out Weak Airlines." *Wall Street Journal*, 4 October 2001.

McCreary, Lew. "Why You Need a CSO." *CSO*, January 2004, 10–11.

McGinley, Laurie. "Bush Seeks More Funds to Boost Stockpiles of Anthrax Antibiotics." *Wall Street Journal*, 15 October 2001.

McGray, Douglas. "The Marshall Plan." *Wired*, February 2003, 116–117.

Merle, Renae. "U.S. Probes Military Use of Commercial Satellites." *Washington Post*, 6 December 2002.

Miller, Bill. "Outdated Systems Balk Terrorism Investigations." *Washington Post*, 13 June 2002.

Mintz, John. "U.S. Fails to Certify Many Labs That Use Pathogens." *Washington Post*, 12 November 2003.

Morgan, Dan. "Expenses Covered by Emergency Fund Rising Rapidly." *Washington Post*, 2 October 2001.

———. "House Panel Allocates $1.67 Billion for Pentagon Counterterrorism Bid." *Washington Post*, 9 November 2001.

"New Counter-Terrorism and CyberSpace Security Positions Announced." Office of the Press Secretary, White House, 9 October 2001.

"Northrop Grumman Lands Major Postal Contract." *Government Security News*, July 2003, 34.

"Office of Homeland Security." White House, undated.

Oster, Christopher & Michael Schroeder. "Carriers Plan Lower-Cost Terror-Insurance Pool." *Wall Street Journal*, 8 November 2001.

Peck, Michael. "Successful War Games Combine Both Civilian and Military Traits." *National Defense*, November 2003, 24–27.

Pianin, Eric & Bill Miller. "Businesses Draw Line on Security." *Washington Post*, 5 September 2002.

Pianin, Eric & Ellen Nakashima. "U.S. Seeks to Boost Security, Soothe Public." *Washington Post*, 18 October 2001.

"Port Security Grants." Transportation Security Administration, 10 August 2003. www.portsecuritygrants.dottsa.net

"President Authorizes Transfers from Emergency Response Fund." Office of the Press Secretary, White House, 5 November 2001.

"President Bush Releases $5.1 Billion in Emergency Funds." Office of Management and Budget, White House, 21 September 2001.

"President Commends House for Passing Airline Security Bill." Office of the Press Secretary, White House, 1 November 2001.

"President Establishes Office of Homeland Security." Office of the Press Secretary, White House, 8 October 2001.

"President Issues Military Order." Office of the Press Secretary, White House, 13 November 2001.

"President Signs Anti-Terrorism Bill." Office of the Press Secretary, White House, 26 October 2001.

"President Signs Aviation Security Legislation." Office of the Press Secretary, White House, 19 November 2001.

"President's Letter to the Speaker on Airline Stabilization Funds." Office of the Press Secretary, White House, 25 September 2001.

"Procedures for Compensation of Air Carriers." Office of the Secretary, Department of Treasury, 2001.

Raghavan, Anita et al. "Banks and Regulators Drew Together to Calm Markets after Attack." *Wall Street Journal,* 18 October 2001.

Reddy, Anitha. "An Eye toward the Big Leagues." *Washington Post,* 16 February 2004.

Reich, Robert. "Subsidies Aren't a Wartime Necessity." *Wall Street Journal,* 16 October 2001.

"Remarks by the President at Photo Opportunity with House and Senate Leadership." Office of the Press Secretary, White House, 19 September 2001.

"Ridge Unveils Advisory Council." *Government Security News,* July 2003, 11.

Roberts, Paul. "Lights, Camera, Grandma." *CSO,* December 2003, 16.

"A Ruinous Day for Insurers." *Business Week,* 24 September 2001.

Scarlet, Sarah. "Ways to Fight ID Theft." *CSO,* March 2004, 46–52.

Schwartz, Nelson. "The Pentagon's Private Army." *Fortune,* 17 March 2003.

"SEC Request Relating to Information Pertaining to the Terrorist Attacks." Securities and Exchange Commission, 18 October 2001.

Seper, Jerry. "FBI Issues Warning of Threat to Coastal Bridges." *Washington Times,* 2 November 2001.

"September 11: Here Come the Trial Lawyers." *Business Week,* 12 November 2001.

Shaver, Katherine. "A Dramatically Different Way to Travel." *Washington Post,* 5 September 2002.

Simon, Harvey. "Central DHS Procurement Office to Make Purchases for 14 Agencies." *Homeland Security & Defense,* 17 September 2003, 4.

———. "DHS Rushing Low-Cost Technologies to the Field and Searching for Breakthrough Products." *Homeland Security & Defense,* 17 September 2003, 1, 3.

Stratford, Mark. "Covert Surveillance: 'Spy' Technology." *Intersec,* July/August 2003, 244–245.

Thompson, Cheryl. "Audit Finds INS Mismanaged $31 Million Automation Project." *Washington Post,* 12 November 2001.

Thompson, Erica. "Visage Identity Verification Technology for Law Enforce-
ment Sector Delivering Results Nationwide," *Security Products*, May 2003, 14.
"Top Billing." *CSO*, January 2003, 18.
"TSA Divvies $2.3 Billion in Security Fees among 66 U.S. Airlines." *Govern-
ment Security News*, July 2003, 22.
VandeHei, Jim & Milo Geyelin. "Bush Seeks to Limit Liability of Companies
Sued as Result of Attacks." *Wall Street Journal*, 25 October 2001.
"Washington Tries to Spell Relief." *Business Week*, 8 October 2001.
Weisman, Jonathan & Anitha Reddy. "Spending on Iraq Sets Off Gold Rush."
Washington Post, 9 October 2003.
"Working with DHS." Department of Homeland Security, 3 April 2003.
Yim, Randall. "National Preparedness: Integration of Federal, State, Local,
and Private Sector Efforts Is Critical to an Effective National Strategy for
Homeland Security." Government Accounting Office, 11 April 2002,
GAO-02-621T.
Zellen, Barry. "Border Technology & Policy Innovation at U.S. Ports." *Intersec*,
July/August 2003, 231–236.

Web Sites

www.aviationnow.com/awin (Aviation Week Intelligence Network).
www.dhs.gov (Department of Homeland Security).
www.govsecinfo.com (Government Security Expo & Conference).
www.9-11commission.gov (National Commission on Terrorist Attacks upon
the United States).
www.whitehouse.gov (White House, Office of the President).

7. Terror's Effects on Labor and Management

"AFT Members among Victims of Terrorist Attacks." *American Federation of
Teachers*, 3 October 2001. www.aft.org/news/aft_victims.html
"Airline Pilot Association, Pilots Reaching Out." Press Release, *AIPA*, 27 Sep-
tember 2001. www.alpa.org/Pilots_Reaching_Out.htm
"Airline-Security Chief May End Random Checks." *AP*, 24 September 2002.
Aizenman, Nurith & Edward Walsh. "Immigrants Fear Deportation after
Registration." *Washington Post*, 28 July 2003.
Alexander, Dean C. & Yonah Alexander. *Terrorism and Business: The Impact of
September 11, 2001*. Ardsley, N.Y.: Transnational Publishers, 2001.
Alexander, Yonah & Dean Alexander. "Business Climate of Terrorism." *Wash-
ington Times*, 27 June 2002.
Allen, Mike. "Bush Proposes Legal Status for Immigrant Labor." *Washington
Post*, 8 January 2004.
Appleby, Julia. "Bioterrorism Changes How Health Care Works." *USA Today*,
31 October 2001.
"Army, Navy to Alert Reservists." *Washington Post*, 15 December 2002.

"Ashcroft: Ohio Trucker Admits to Terror Ties." cnn.com, 19 June 2003.

Atlas, Riva & Geraldine Fabrikant. "After Havoc, Reviving a Legacy." *New York Times,* 29 September 2001.

Becker, Maki & Greg Gittrich. "Weapons Still Fly at Airports." *New York Daily News,* 4 September 2002.

Behr, Peter. "Bond Firm to Aid Kin of Terror Victims." *Washington Post,* 11 October 2001.

Blum, Justin & Manny Fernandez. "Area Postal Workers Undergo Anthrax Screenings." *Washington Post,* 22 October 2001.

Blustein, Paul. "Economy Showed Resilience after 9/11, but Costs Remain." *Washington Post,* 10 September 2002.

"Boeing Security Head Warns of Surveillance." *AP,* 24 May 2003.

Brown, DeNeen. "A Scholar Confronts 'Ugly Face of America.'" *Washington Post,* 11 November 2003.

Burkeman, Oliver. "For Some It Is a Day to Grieve, for Some a Day to Dread, for Others a Day to Hide Away." *Guardian,* 11 September 2002.

Cha, Ariana. "Peril Follows Contractors in Iraq." *Washington Post,* 14 November 2003.

Chaker, Anne Marie & David Bank. "For Regular Charities, There's Little Relief after Terror Attacks." *Wall Street Journal,* 8 October 2001.

Cherney, Elena & Marjorie Valbrun. "EEOC Sues Hotel, Prepress Firm Charging Bias against Muslims." *Wall Street Journal,* 1 October 2003.

Cody, Edward. "Israel's Economy Hit by a One-Two Punch." *Washington Post,* 19 May 2002.

Cohn, D'Vera. "Immigrants Account for Half of New Workers." *Washington Post,* 2 December 2002.

Colin, Michelle et al. "When the Office Is the War Zone." *Business Week,* 19 November 2001.

Curl, Joseph. "Terrorism Insurance Bill Signed into Law." *Washington Times,* 27 November 2002.

"Defining the CSO." *CSO.* www.csoonline.com/career/descriptions.html

Doty, Cate. "Reservists Are Getting More Than They Bargained For." *New York Times,* 19 January 2003.

Eaton, Leslie. "Yet Another Beginning on Heartbreak Street." *New York Times,* 6 May 2003.

Eggen, Dan. "Top FBI Counterterror Official Announces Retirement." *Washington Post,* 9 October 2003.

―――. "Tougher Rules on U.S. Visas Bring Fears of Long Waits." *Washington Post,* 24 May 2003.

Eilperin, Juliet. "Debating the Limits of Liability." *Washington Post,* 17 November 2001.

Ellin, Abby. "Traumatized Workers Look for Healing on the Job." *New York Times,* 30 September 2001.

"Faces of the Fallen." *Washington Post,* 20 March 2004.

"Flight Attendants Testify before Congress on Aircraft Security Issue." Association of Flight Attendants, 25 September 2001. www.alpa.org/ Pilots_Reaching_Out.htm

"Foreign Students Could Pay $100 Tracking Fee." *Washington Post,* 23 October 2003.

Fowler, Geoffrey. "The Price of Patriotism." *Wall Street Journal,* 30 April 2002.

Golden, Daniel. "After Sept. 11, the CIA Becomes a Force on Campus." *Wall Street Journal,* 4 October 2002.

Goo, Sara. "Agency Tackles Visa-Program Threat." *Washington Post,* 31 July 2003.

————. "Armed Pilots Must Put Guns in Lockboxes." *Washington Post,* 26 February 2003.

Greenberger, Robert. "Saudi Bombing Hits U.S. Firm Hard." *Wall Street Journal,* 14 May 2003.

Haughney, Christine. "Respiratory Ills Plague Ground Zero Workers." *Washington Post,* 16 September 2002.

Henry, Shannon. "INS Sees Big Drop in High-Tech Visas." *Washington Post,* 16 August 2002.

Hockstader, Lee. "Army Stops Many Soldiers from Quitting." *Washington Post,* 29 December 2003.

————. "Post-9/11 Visa Rules Keep Thousand from Coming to U.S." *Washington Post,* 11 November 2003.

Hopkins, Jim. "Executives at Small Firm Don Another Hat: Therapist to Workers." *USA Today,* 31 October 2001.

Hsu, Spencer & Lyndsey Layton. "Scattershot Spending in Terror Fight." *Washington Post,* 10 September 2002.

Irwin, Neil & Michael Barbaro. "Getting Back to Business." *Washington Post,* 25 October 2002.

Jackson, Maggie. "Contingency Plans to Fill Reservists' Shoes." *New York Times,* 10 October 2001.

Johnson, Carrie. "Requests for Skilled-Worker Visas Fell Short of Limit." *Washington Post,* 5 November 2001.

Joyce, Amy. "More Jobs Than Security Clearances." *Washington Post,* 19 May 2003.

Kirkpatrick, David. "Some at Wall St. Journal Fear Return to Manhattan." *New York Times,* 18 June 2002.

Konrad, Rachel. "Visa Program Robs U.S. Technology Workers of Jobs, Dignity." *Washington Times,* 11 August 2003.

Kronholz, June. "For Reservists, Tales of Interrupted Lives." *Wall Street Journal,* 11 September 2002.

————. "Patriot Act Riles an Unlikely Group: Nation's Librarians." *Wall Street Journal,* 28 October 2003.

Lee, Christopher. "OPM Begins Sorting Security Personnel." *Washington Post,* 9 December 2002.

Loeb, Vernon. "Army Expansion Could Last 5 Years." *Washington Post*, 30 January 2004.

———. "Judge Reverses Anthrax Ruling." *Washington Post*, 8 January 2004.

Loeb, Vernon & Theola Labbe. "Civilian Convoy Attacked in Iraq." *Washington Post*, 26 October 2003.

Martinez, Barbara. "Anthrax Victim's Son Sues Kaiser Facility His Father Consulted." *Wall Street Journal*, 14 November 2001.

Merle, Renae. "For U.S. Contractors, a Reminder." *Washington Post*, 14 May 2003.

———. "U.S. Contractors Are Targets Overseas." *Washington Post*, 16 October 2003.

Merritt, Jennifer. "Sorry, the Boss Is in Baghdad." *Business Week*, 17 February 2003.

Miller, Bill. "National Guard Awaits Niche in Homeland Security Plan." *Washington Post*, 11 August 2002.

Moore, Molly & John Anderson. "Bomb Kills 3 Americans in Gaza Strip." *Washington Post*, 16 October 2003.

Murphy, Caryle. "Post–Sept. 11 Study Finds Increase in Bias Complaints by Muslims in U.S." *Washington Post*, 16 July 2003.

Nakashima, Ellen. "Potter Defends USPS Response to Anthrax Fears." *Washington Post*, 31 October 2001.

Newman, Barry. "U.S. Visa Rules Deter Students from Abroad." *Wall Street Journal*, 29 July 2003.

"98 Percent of Eligible Families Seek 9/11 Aid." *Washington Post*, 17 January 2004.

Nusbaum, Marci. "Another Duty Calling: Military Service." *New York Times*, 24 November 2002.

"Off the Job." *Fortune*, 27 October 2003.

"One Year: Special Memorial Section." *Washington Post*, 8 September 2002.

"Paying Reservists." *Business Week*, 26 November 2001.

Pierre, Robert. "Victims of Hate, Now Feeling Forgotten." *Washington Post*, 14 September 2002.

Power, Stephen & Stephanie Horvath. "U.S. Seeks Women for Air-Security Jobs." *Wall Street Journal*, 24 July 2002.

Puente, Maria et al. "Stories and Faces Personalize Victims." *USA Today*, 13 September 2001.

Richburg, Keith. "Suicide Bomb Survivors Face Worlds Blown Apart." *Washington Post*, 31 January 2004.

Salmon, Jacqueline. "Red Cross Distributing $100 Million." *Washington Post*, 26 September 2001.

Salmon, Jacqueline & Ann O'Hanlon. "For Pentagon Families, Grief and Paperwork." *Washington Post*, 18 November 2001.

"Security Jobs, Not Jobs Security." *Washington Post*, 4 October 2002.

"Security Poor at Malls." *Itim News Agency*, 5 August 2002.

Sheridan, Mary Beth. "Muslims in U.S. Feel Targeted by Anti-Terror Business Policies." *Washington Post,* 9 July 2003.

Simon, Harvey. "Companies Want to Hire Managers with Homeland Security Experience." *Homeland Security & Defense,* 14 January 2004, 4–5.

Simpson, Glenn. "Language Lesson for Pentagon." *Wall Street Journal,* 3 December 2003.

Singer, Mark. "Home Is Here." *New Yorker,* 15 October 2001.

Singletary, Michelle. "Reservists Need Financial Readiness." *Washington Post,* 24 November 2002.

Siwolop, Sana. "A Legal Tightrope for Employers after Attacks." *New York Times,* 24 October 2001.

Snyder, David & William Branigin. "Jobs Put Some Workers in Vulnerable Spots." *Washington Post,* 19 October 2002.

Strauss, Valerie. "Mastering Arabic's Nuances No Easy Mission." *Washington Post,* 28 May 2002.

"This Is Going to Leave a Huge Scar on All of Us." *Fortune,* 1 October 2001.

"300 Arrested at Wal-Mart." *Reuters,* 23 October 2003.

"Too Big a Helping Hand?" *Business Week,* 29 October 2001.

Treaster, Joseph. "Industries Welcome U.S. Aid on Terror Insurance." *New York Times,* 21 November 2002.

Tully, Shawn. "Rebuilding Wall Street." *Fortune,* 1 October 2001.

"U.S. Office of Personnel Management: Post-Disaster Guidance and Other Information." *OPM.* www.opm.gov/guidance/index.htm

"UAW Contributes $250,000 to Relief Efforts, Urges Additional Fundraising by UAW 63." United Auto Workers, Press Release, 18 September 2001.

Valbrun, Marjorie. "More Muslims Claim They Suffer Job Bias." *Wall Street Journal,* 15 April 2003.

Valbrun, Marjorie & Scott Thurm. "Foreign Workers Will Soon Get Fewer U.S. Visas." *Wall Street Journal,* 1 October 2003.

Van Drehle, David & Christine Haughney. "Memories of 9/11 Add Perspective." *Washington Post,* 17 August 2003.

Van Gelder, Lawrence. "The Last Hurdle to Work: Security." *New York Times,* 24 November 2002.

"The Victims." *Washington Post,* 14 September 2001.

"The Victims." *Washington Post,* 27 September 2001.

Vost, Pete. "FBI: Suicide Bombers Likely in U.S." *AP,* 20 May 2002.

White, Erin & Suzanne Vranica. "Military Recruiting Gets Personal." *Wall Street Journal,* 1 November 2002.

Williams, Daniel. "Bridging a Divide, but Only in Language." *Washington Post,* 27 November 2003.

Web Sites

www.americanexpress.com (American Express).

www.cantor.com (Cantor Fitzgerald).

www.fredalger.com (Fred Alger).
www.monster.com (Monster Worldwide).

8. Terror Impacts on Business

Abate, Tom. "Bioterrorism Defense Being Developed: Bay Area Companies Collaborate with Federal Agencies." *San Francisco Chronicle,* 25 September 2001.

Akst, Daniel. "It's Time for Terror-Proof Markets." *New York Times,* 7 October 2001.

Alexander, Dean C. & Yonah Alexander. "Monetizing Counterterror." *Washington Times,* 8 December 2002.

————. *Terrorism and Business: The Impact of September 11, 2001.* Ardsley, N.Y.: Transnational Publishers, 2002.

————. "Terrorism's Business Fallout." *Washington Times,* 28 May 2002.

Alexander, Keith. "Shuttles from National Lose Business to Train." *Washington Post,* 3 October 2001.

————. "The View from the Ground." *Washington Post,* 30 December 2001.

Alexander, Yonah & Robert A. Kilmarx, eds. *Business and the Middle East: Threats and Prospects.* New York: Pergamon Press, 1982.

————. *Political Terrorism and Business: The Threat and Response.* New York: Praeger, 1979.

Alexander, Yonah & Robert G. Picard, eds. *In the Camera's Eye: New Coverage of Terrorist Events.* Washington, D.C.: Brassey's (U.S.), 1991.

Altman, Daniel. "Wary Companies Are Staying in Muslim World." *New York Times,* 24 October 2002.

American Society for Industrial Security, Security Industry Buyers Guide. Alexandria, Va.: American Society for Industrial Security, 2003.

Ames, Ben. "DHS Asks Private Sector for Anti-Terror Technology." *Homeland Security Solutions,* June 2003, 1, 11.

————. "Neutron Scans and X-rays Reveal Bombs That Metal Detectors Miss." *Homeland Security Solutions,* June 2003, 1, 12.

————. "Technology Tightens Border Security." *Homeland Security Solutions,* June 2003, 13-17.

Andrews, Edmund. "More Signs of Downturn for Europe." *New York Times,* 15 November 2001.

Ante, Spencer et al. "High Tech Is Starting to Kick In." *Business Week,* 16 September 2002, 30-33.

"Association Works to Allay Economic Impact of Terrorist Attacks." National Restaurant Association, 4 October 2001.

"Attacks' Economic Effects Reverberate through Area." *Dallas Morning News,* 23 September 2001.

Belkin, Lisa. "Just Money." *New York Times,* 8 December 2002.

Berenson, Alex. "Feeling Vulnerable at Heart of Wall St." *New York Times,* 12 October 2001.

Berman, Dennis. "Disaster Gives New Life to Wireless Telecom Firms." *Wall Street Journal,* 3 October 2001.

Bernasek, Anna. "The Friction Economy." *Fortune,* 18 February 2002.

Berry, John. "Economy Shrinks for First Time Since 1993." *Washington Post,* 1 November 2001.

Berry, John & Steven Pearlstein. "Terror Feeds Recession Fear." *Washington Post,* 12 September 2001.

"Big Economies Near a Standstill, OECD Says." *AP,* 21 November 2001.

Block, Robert. "Shielding the Shield Makers." *Wall Street Journal,* 26 November 2003.

————. "U.S. Law Shields Company Data Tied to Security." *Wall Street Journal,* 18 February 2004.

Blustein, Paul. "Economy Showed Resilience after 9/11, but Costs Remain." *Washington Post,* 10 September 2002.

"Bombardier to Cut 3,800 Jobs." *Dallas Morning News,* 23 October 2001.

Bransten, Lisa. "Entrepreneurs Find Investors Are Venturing Less Capital." *Wall Street Journal,* 29 October 2001.

Brick, Michael & Floyd Norris. "Stocks Surge; Most Indexes Have Recouped September Loss." *New York Times,* 12 October 2001.

Broad, William. "Oh, What a Lovely War. If No One Dies." *New York Times,* 3 November 2002.

Brown, David. "Maker of Anthrax Vaccine to Reopen after Renovating Mich. Plant." *Washington Post,* 1 November 2001.

Brown, DeNeen. "Fallout from Terrorist Attacks Punishes Canadian Companies." *Washington Post,* 20 October 2001.

Brown, Stuart. "Stealth Rules." *Fortune,* 30 December 2002, 118-122.

Browning, E. S. "Blue Chips Decline as Investors React with Surprising Calm to U.S. Attacks." *Wall Street Journal,* 9 October 2001.

————. "Stocks Decline on Terror Report." *Wall Street Journal,* 12 March 2004.

———— "U.S. Stocks Sag on Latest Anthrax Worries." *Wall Street Journal,* 18 October 2001.

Calian, Sara. "New Accessory for Travelers: Terror Insurance." *Wall Street Journal,* 11 March 2003.

Carton, Barbara. "Apocalypse Now: Stocking Up to Survive the Worst." *Wall Street Journal,* 10 October 2001.

Cloud, David & Greg Jaffe. "U.S. Kills Al Qaeda Suspect in Yemen." *Wall Street Journal,* 5 November 2002.

Coolidge, Carrie. "Risky Business." *Forbes,* 15 October 2001.

"Combating Terrorism: Funding Data Reporting to Congress Should Be Improved." Government Accounting Office, November 2002, GAO-03-170.

Coy, Peter. "Betting on Terror: PR Disaster, Intriguing Idea." *Business Week*, 25 August 2003, 41.

Craig, Susanne. "SEC Examines Trading in Firms before Sept. 11." *Wall Street Journal*, 3 October 2001.

Crenshaw, Albert. "Businesses Face an Insurance Crunch." *Washington Post*, 11 October 2001.

Cushman, John. "Pentagon's Urgent Search for Speed." *New York Times*, 1 December 2002.

Davis, Joshua. "Battlefield Technology." *Wired*, June 2003, 95–104.

Davis, M. Thomas. "The Still Emerging Homeland Security Market." *Homeland Security Solutions*, June 2003, 22.

"Defense Stocks Await Spending Surge." www.moneycentral/msn.com, 2 October 2001.

"Dow Falls; Nasdaq Ekes Out a Gain." *Washington Post*, 19 October 2001.

Doyle, John. "DHS Wants Safety Act Applications Now Even Though Form Is Not Ready." *Homeland Security & Defense*, 17 September 2003, 3.

————. "Venture Capitalists See Opportunities for Investments in Homeland Security." *Homeland Security & Defense*, 14 January 2004, 1–2.

El Boghdady, Dina. "Safeguarding Data Gains New Urgency." *Washington Post*, 29 October 2001.

Emigh, Jacqueline. "The Promise and Pitfalls of Wireless." *Homeland Defense Journal*, July 2003, 22–25.

Essick, Kristi. "Venture Funds Renew Focus in Security, Mull Opportunities in a Climate of Fear." *Wall Street Journal*, 9 October 2001.

"European Stocks, Dollar Fall, Bonds Gain after Spain Bombings." *Bloomberg*, 11 March 2004.

Fernandez, Manny & Spencer S. Hsu. "Security Tightened for Tree Lighting." *Washington Post*, 17 November 2001.

"Firms Reviewing Mail-Handling Methods." *Dallas Morning News*, 15 October 2001.

Freedman, Michael & Daniel Kruger. "Collateral Damage." *Forbes*, 15 October 2001.

Fuerbringer, Jonathan. "Shares Hit New Lows for Year on Reports from Spain." *New York Times*, 16 March 2004.

Geyelin, Milo & Jess Bravin, Tobacco Lawyer Takes on Saudis in a Sept. 11 Suit, *Wall Street Journal*, 12 December 2002.

Gillis, Justin. "U.S. to Buy Anthrax Vaccine." *Washington Post*, 12 March 2004.

Golden, Daniel et al. "How Tyco Pushed ADT Dealers into Poor Areas to Boost Growth." *Wall Street Journal*, 15 November 2002.

Goo, Sara. "County Feels Impact of Decline in Travel Industry." *Washington Post*, 11 October 2001.

Gunn, Eric. "Laid Off and Joining a Crowd." *Washington Post*, 18 October 2001.

Guyon, Janet. "Brand America." *Fortune,* 27 October 2003, 179–182.

Hardin, Winn. "Thermal Imaging: A Hammer in the Counter-Terrorism Toolbox." *Homeland Security Solutions,* June 2003, 18–20.

Harwood, John. "Economic Anxiety Trumps War Talk." *Wall Street Journal,* 9 September 2002.

Hennessey, Raymond. "Military-Tied IPO Is Completed." *Wall Street Journal,* 13 November 2002.

Hensley, Scott. "Antibiotic Purchases Jump in New York." *Wall Street Journal,* 9 October 2001.

"Heros and Casualties." *Washington Business Journal,* March 21–27, 2002.

Hilsenrath, Jon. "Terror's Toll on the Economy." *Wall Street Journal,* 9 October 2001.

Hitt, Jack. "The Business of Fear." *Business 2.0,* June 2003, 106–122.

Homeland Security Directory. Washington, D.C.: McGraw-Hill, 2003.

"Hot Products." *Homeland Security Solutions,* June 2003, 21.

"Impact of Terrorist Attacks on the World Trade Center." Government Accounting Office, 29 May 2002, GAO-02-700R.

Ip, Greg. "Home Sales Dropped 11.7% in September." *Wall Street Journal,* 26 October 2001.

Johnson, Nicholas. "SafeNet to Buy California Company." *Washington Post,* 1 November 2002.

————. "Symantec to Buy Va.'s Riptech." *Washington Post,* 18 July 2002.

Jones, David. "Coping with the Threat of War." *New York Times,* 4 March 2003.

Kaihla, Paul. "Weapons of the Secret War." *Business 2.0,* November 2001.

Kelly, Kate. "Stocks Rally 196.58 Points on War News." *Wall Street Journal,* 14 November 2001.

Knight, Jerry. "Sorting Out Winners in War on Terrorism." *Washington Post,* 20 October 2001.

Kraus, Clifford. "Economic Pain Spreads from U.S. across Latin America." *New York Times,* 14 October 2001.

Lahart, Justin. "An Economic Pause for 9/11?" cnn.com, 26 August 2002.

Lauricella, Tom. "Some Military Investors Bear a Heavy 'Load.'" *Wall Street Journal,* 27 November 2002.

Leggett, Karby. "Conflict Grinds on Israeli Economy." *Wall Street Journal,* 3 May 2002.

Leonnig, Carol. "Iran Must Pay Family of Blast Victim, Court Says." *Washington Post,* 18 July 2003.

Lindsey, Brink. "The Trade Front: Combating Terrorism with Open Markets." Cato Institute, 5 August 2003.

Lohr, Greg. "Safe Enough." *Washington Business Journal,* 14–20 November 2003.

Lubove, Seth. "We See You, Saddam." *Forbes,* 6 January 2003, 102–108.

Lynch, Colum. "Deal Reached with Libya on Pan Am Bombing." *Washington Post,* 13 August 2002.

Machalaba, Daniel. "Amtrak's Acela Traffic Rises 35% As Airline Disruptions Add Riders." *Wall Street Journal,* 23 October 2001.

Mandel, Michael et al. "The Cost of Fighting Terrorism." *Business Week,* 16 September 2002, 26–28.

Mangalindan, Mylene & Michael Totty. "Slumping Tech Companies Go to Washington to Seek Sales." *Wall Street Journal,* 4 October 2002.

Marcial, Gene. "Napco Helps Keep the Homeland Safe." *Business Week,* 9 December 2002, 138.

————. "Siga Technologies Takes Aim at Smallpox." *Business Week,* 23 December 2002, 102.

"Market Indicators." *New York Times,* 18 September 2001.

"Market Indicators." *New York Times,* 16 November 2001.

Martha, Joseph & Sunil Subbakrishna. "When Just-in-Time Becomes Just-in-Case." *Wall Street Journal,* 23 October 2001.

McBride, Sarah. "Indonesia Ties Hurt Firms' Shares." *Wall Street Journal,* 17 October 2002.

McCarter, Mickey. "Pulsed Ultraviolet Light Kills Pathogens in Water." *Homeland Defense Journal,* July 2003, 16–17.

Merle, Renae. "Computer Sciences Plans to Acquire DynCorp." *Washington Post,* 14 December 2002.

————. "For U.S. Contractors, a Reminder." *Washington Post,* 14 May 2003.

————. "Military Business Boosts Defense Firms' Revenue." *Washington Post,* 17 October 2002.

————. "Northrop Grumman to Sell Two Business Units to L-3." *Washington Post,* 13 September 2002.

Milbank, Dana & Glenn Kessler. "Bush 'Deeply Concerned' about Possible Recession." *Washington Post,* 1 November 2001.

Mintz, John. "U.S. to Keep Key Data on Infrastructure Secret." *Washington Post,* 19 February 2004.

Morse, Dan. "Argenbright's New CEO Promises to Reshape Airport-Security Firm." *Wall Street Journal,* 12 November 2001.

Murphy, Verity. "Middle East and North Africa Mecca Cola Challenges U.S. Rivals." *BBC,* 9 January 2003.

Musgrove, Mike. "Fear, Mother of Invention." *Washington Post,* 25 October 2001.

"National Preparedness: Integrating New and Existing Technology and Information Sharing into an Effective Homeland Security Strategy." Government Accounting Office, 7 June 2002, GAO-02-811T.

Navarro, Peter & Aron Spencer. "September 11, 2001: Assessing the Costs of Terrorism." *Milken Institute Review,* 4th Quarter (2001).

Neely, Christopher. "The Federal Reserve's Response to the September 11 Attacks." Federal Reserve Bank of St. Louis, January 2002.

Neumeister, Larry. "Suit Claims Iraqis Knew of Plans." *AP,* 5 September 2002.

Noguchi, Yuki. "For Many without Guns, Attack Was a Call to Arm." *Washington Post,* 2 October 2001.

————. "Preparing for the Worst." *Washington Post,* 30 October 2001.

Norris, Floyd & Jonathan Fuerbringer. "Stocks Tumble Abroad; Exchanges in New York Never Opened for the Day." *New York Times,* 12 September 2001.

Oldenburg, Don. "Stocking Up in Hopes of Breathing Easier." *Washington Post,* 10 October 2001.

Orenstein, David. "How a Bomb Sniffer Works." *Business 2.0,* November 2001.

Oster, Christopher & Tom Hamburger. "Property Insurers Seek to Exclude Future Coverage against Terrorism." *Wall Street Journal,* 10 October 2001.

Oster, Christopher & Dean Starkman. "Cost of Terror Insurance Is Weighted." *Wall Street Journal,* 6 December 2002.

Pae, Peter. "Defense Buildup Is Expected to Be Gradual and Targeted." latimes.com, 9 October 2001.

Petersen, Andrea & Joseph Pereira. "Citizens Prepare Homes, Kids, Medicine Chests in Fear of New Attacks." *Wall Street Journal,* 9 October 2001.

Pollack, Andrew. "Company Says It Will Test a Safer Smallpox Vaccine." *New York Times,* 18 December 2002.

Radler, Melissa & Dan Izenberg. "U.S. Court Awards $183m. to Jerusalem Bombing Victim's Family." *Jerusalem Post,* 8 February 2002.

Reed, Fred. "Military to Deploy New Wave Weapons." *Washington Times,* 19 September 2002.

Richburg, Keith. "Libya to Pay $170 Million in Bombing of Airliner in '89." *Washington Post,* 10 January 2004.

Ruane, Michael. "Irradiation Explored As Answer to Anthrax." *Washington Post,* 23 October 2001.

Samuelson, Robert. "Figuring the Cost of War." *Washington Post,* 27 November 2002.

Schmidt, Susan. "Sept. 11 Families Join to Sue Saudis." *Washington Post,* 16 August 2002.

Schmitt, Richard. "Homeless, a Wall Street Law Firm Improvises." *Wall Street Journal,* 10 October 2001.

Schwartz, Nelson. "What Now for Investors?" *Fortune,* 1 October 2001.

"The September 11 Tragedy and the Response of the Financial Industry, Remarks by Chairman Alan Greenspan." Federal Reserve Board, 23 October 2001.

"Seven Families of Moment Café Victims Sue PA for NIS 135M." *Haaretz,* 9 March 2003.

Shah, Angela. "September 11 Attack Takes Big Toll on Small Businesses." *Dallas Morning News,* 3 September 2002.

Shanley, Agnes. "Chemical Defense on Main Street." *Homeland Defense Journal,* June 2003, 18–23.

Simon, Harvey. "Central DHS Procurement Office to Make Purchases for 14 Agencies." *Homeland Security & Defense,* 17 September 2003, 4.

————. "DHS Rushing Low-Cost Technologies to the Field and Searching for Breakthrough Products." *Homeland Security & Defense,* 17 September 2003, 1, 3.

————. "Radio Frequency Identification Gains Edge in Homeland Security." *Homeland Security & Defense,* 14 January 2004, 4.

————. "TSA Will Use Off-the-Shelf Technology in Testing EDS for Air Cargo Screening." *Homeland Security & Defense,* 14 January 2004, 1, 3.

Smith, Ray. "Battle Brews over Money-Laundering Rules." *Wall Street Journal,* 17 September 2003.

Spinner, Jackie. "Firms Warned on Terrorism Insurance." *Washington Post,* 18 January 2002.

————. "Insurers May Drop Coverage of Terrorism." *Washington Post,* 27 September 2001.

Squeo, Anne Marie. "Defense Industry Sees More Deals on the Horizon." *Wall Street Journal,* 25 September 2002.

————. "General Dynamics to Pay $1.1 Billion for GM Business." *Wall Street Journal,* 10 December 2002.

————. "Mergers Make It Tougher to Punish Federal Contractors." *Wall Street Journal,* 10 June 2003.

————. "Raytheon to Buy Solipsys, JPS Communications." *Wall Street Journal,* 23 December 2002.

————. "Stock Prices Gyrate on Defense Firms' Good, Bad News." *Wall Street Journal,* 18 October 2001.

Squeo, Anne Marie & J. Lynn Lunsford. "Boeing, Air Force Closer to Jet Deal." *Wall Street Journal,* 5 November 2002.

Starkman, Dean. "Foot Traffic in Malls Is Rebounding Close to Pre-Attack Levels." *Wall Street Journal,* 3 October 2001.

Starkman, Dean & Alex Frangos. "Judge Mulls Contempt Charge for Silverstein." *Wall Street Journal,* 17 March 2004.

Stewart, Thomas. "America's Secret Weapon." *Business 2.0,* December 2001, 58–68.

"Summary of Commentary on Current Economic Conditions by Federal Reserve District." *Federal Reserve Board,* 24 October 2001.

Talley, Karen. "Small Firms See Promise in Homeland Security." *Wall Street Journal,* 25 November 2002.

Tam, Pui-Wing. "Tech Companies Scramble to Fill Military Orders." *Wall Street Journal,* 24 March 2003.

"Technology vs. Terror: Special Report." *Popular Science,* September 2002.

"This Is Going to Leave a Huge Scar on All of Us." *Fortune,* 1 October 2001.

Timberg, Craig & Daniel LeDuc. "Md., Va. Warn Tax Revenue Shrinking." *Washington Post,* 16 October 2001.

Tomlinson, Richard. "Tower Struggle." *Fortune,* 29 September 2003, 44.

"Tough Times: How Long?" *Business Week,* 15 October 2001.

"Trading on Wall St. Comes to Standstill." *Washington Post,* 12 September 2001.

"U.S. Stock-Index Futures Drop; Madrid Bombs Spur Terror Concern." *Bloomberg,* 11 March 2004.

Vaida, Bara. "Businesses Band to Launch Homeland Security Association." *National Journal's Technology Daily,* 3 September 2002.

Wayne, Leslie. "Northrop to Buy TRW for $7.8 Billion." *New York Times,* 2 July 2002.

Weisman, Jonathan & Anitha Reddy. "Spending on Iraq Sets Off Gold Rush." *Washington Post,* 9 October 2003.

White, Ingrid. "Business and Industry: Now on the Front Line in the War against Terrorism." *New Hampshire Business Review,* July 2002.

Whitefield, Mimi & Beatrice Garcia. "High Security: Globalization and Technology Have Opened Up New Possibilities for Business—and Their Enemies." *Miami Herald,* 17 September 2001.

"With Any Luck, It Won't Work." *Fortune,* 30 December 2002.

Wong, Nicole. "Postal Delays Worrying Small Retailers." *Washington Post,* 20 October 2001.

Woo, Gordon. "Quantifying Insurance Terrorism Risk." (unpublished) 1 February 2002.

Woolley, Scott. "Spotting Evil." *Forbes,* 15 October 2001.

Zuckerman, Lawrence. "New Airline Board Is Given Wide Authority to Support the Industry." *New York Times,* 6 October 2001.

Web Sites

www.aviationnovw.com/awin (Aviation Week Intelligence Network).

www.businessroundtable.org (Business Roundtable).

www.ci-pinkerton.com (Pinkerton Consulting and Investigations).

www.contingencyplanning.com (Contingency Planning & Management).

www.csoonline.com (Resource for Security Executives, CSO Magazine).

www.dhs.gov (Department of Homeland Security).

www.homelanddefensejournal.com (Homeland Defense Journal).

www.house.gov/jec/ (House of Representative, Joint Economic Committee).

www.intersec.co.uk (Intersec Publishing).

www.isalliance.org (Internet Security Alliance).

www.krollworldwide.com (Kroll Inc.).

www.mcgraw-hillhomelandsecurity.com (McGraw-Hill Homeland Security).

www.9-11commission.gov (National Commission on Terrorist Attacks upon the United States).

www.nycp.org/impactstudy (September 11: Impact and Response, Partnership for New York City).

www.peerless-ins.com/business/terrorism/faqs.cfm (Peerless Insurance).

www.securitygateway.com (Security Industry News and Information, Security Industry Association).

www.securitymanagement.com/library/Counter_terror.html (Security Management).

www.securitymagazine.com (Security Magazine).

Index